JAMES BRYCE

(VISCOUNT BRYCE OF DECHMONT, O.M.)

VOLUME I

THE MACMILLAN COMPANY
NEW YORK · BOSTON · CHICAGO · DALLAS
ATLANTA · SAN FRANCISCO

MACMILLAN & CO., Limited
LONDON · BOMBAY · CALCUTTA
MELBOURNE

THE MACMILLAN CO. OF CANADA, Ltd.
TORONTO

James Bryce

1905

JAMES BRYCE

(VISCOUNT BRYCE OF DECHMONT, O.M.)

BY

H. A. L. FISHER

WARDEN OF NEW COLLEGE, OXFORD

VOLUME I

New York

THE MACMILLAN COMPANY

1927

All rights reserved

Norwood Press
J. S. Cushing Co. — Berwick & Smith Co.
Norwood, Mass., U.S.A.

PREFACE

THE story of a life so long, active and important as that of the subject of this biography might easily be made to extend over several volumes. I have not, however, attempted to follow Lord Bryce into all his activities. It has been my object to present a portrait of the man rather than a full catalogue of the events and transactions with which he was concerned, and but for the fact that this book contains a selection of letters, all that is here written might have been confined within the limits of a single not very bulky volume.

I am conscious that some criticism may be levelled against the proportions of this narrative. Lord Bryce's Parliamentary career has been dealt with somewhat cursorily, although it consumed a large measure of his intellectual energies during twenty-seven years of active manhood. So much, however, of a politician's effort is necessarily thrown into the common stock of his party, so much is good honest team work and so much again belongs rather to the political history of the times than to the sphere of biography, that I felt myself justified in exercising compression here. Again there has been no attempt to give a full and adequate account of Lord Bryce's most important publications, partly because these are familiar and partly from a fear that, were such an effort to be made, the reader's mind might be diverted

[v]

from the central interest of the book, which in a biography must always be the personality of the man. For reasons of a different order the important contribution which Lord Bryce made to the development of legal studies at Oxford during his tenure of the Regius Chair of Civil Law has not received its full meed of attention. Academic details are rather technical and the whole story of the renaissance of legal scholarship in the University of Sir William Blackstone is so remarkable as to deserve separate treatment.

So the main stress of the biography is laid, where, I imagine, Bryce would himself have wished that it should be laid, upon his connection with the United States, whose institutions he studied and described, for whose people he conceived a warm affection, and in whose co-operation with Britain and her dependencies in forwarding the great tasks of humanity he reposed his brightest hopes for the future. For this reason many of the letters printed in these volumes are chosen from his correspondence with American friends.

Apart from publications, which are accessible to all, such as the pages of Hansard and the files of the newspapers, the material on which this biography has been founded consists mainly of letters and diaries furnished me by the kindness of Lady Bryce and Miss Bryce. I have also through the courtesy of Sir Austen Chamberlain enjoyed access to papers in the Foreign Office relating to Lord Bryce's American Mission, and, through the good offices of my friend Professor Burr of Cornell University, have obtained transcripts of the letters to Goldwin Smith which are deposited in the Library at

Cornell. A large number of Bryce's friends, English and American, have kindly enabled me to see the letters in their possession, and if only a small selection of these is printed here, all have been read and weighed and have supplied their contribution to the narrative. Among the American friends of Lord Bryce to whom I am thus indebted I should wish to mention the names of Dr. Charles Eliot, Emeritus President, and of Dr. Lawrence Lowell, President of Harvard University, of Mr. Elihu Root, Mr. James Ford Rhodes, Dr. Nicolas Murray Butler, President of Columbia University, of Dr. Hadley, Emeritus Professor of Yale University, of Mr. R. Stannard Baker, who has been good enough to send me photostats of Lord Bryce's letters to President Wilson, of Mr. M. Storey, Mr. Seth Low, Mr. Villard, Mr. Holt, Mr. and Mrs. Bayard Henry, Mr. Chambliss, and Miss D. M. Raymond. To Mrs. Theodore Roosevelt I owe a debt of recognition for her kindness in allowing me to make use of the letters written to her husband which are deposited in the Library of Congress at Washington. I have also to acknowledge similar help from Lord Bryce's English and Irish friends, notably from the Archbishop of Canterbury, the Marquis of Lansdowne, Lord Fitzmaurice, Sir George Trevelyan, Sir Horace Plunkett, and Professor J. H. Morgan.

A second source of information has consisted in the impressions and recollections kindly supplied me by friends and associates, as well as in my own personal memories. Dr. Edwards of Glasgow, Sir William Boyd Dawkins, The Provost of Oriel College, Earl Buxton, Viscount Gladstone, Viscount Chelmsford, Sir Frederic

Preface

Kenyon, the late Sir Adolphus Ward, Mr. Douglas Fresh-field, Sir Michael Sadler, Bishop Talbot, Mr. W. R. Davies, C. B. (Lord Bryce's Private Secretary in Ireland), Mr. George Young (his First Secretary at Washington), Dr. R. L. Poole, the President of Trinity College, Oxford, as well as many of the American friends, whose names are cited above, have either in writing or in conversation made contributions. First and foremost, however, my acknowledgments are due to Lady Bryce, without whose unstinted confidence and ever ready help and counsel this book would not have been and could not have been written.

H. F.

CONTENTS

VOLUME ONE

LIST OF ILLUSTRATIONS

JAMES BRYCE

(VISCOUNT BRYCE OF DECHMONT, O.M.)

VOLUME I

JAMES BRYCE

CHAPTER I

'Ηδέα πάντα κέλευθα λάχεν βίος

Pleasant are the paths of life.

JULIANUS ÆGYPTIUS

IN the middle of the Seventeenth Century there lived in Cambuslang, Lanarkshire, one Robert Bryce (the name is possibly a corruption of Bruce) whose son Archibald settled at Dechmont Hill, Lanarkshire, as a small laird owning his own land; and there died about 1738 leaving, among other children, a youngest son John. Of this John we know that he lived at Airdrie not far from Glasgow, that he was an Elder of the established Church, and that he married Robina, daughter of James Allan of Airdrie, a wool miller of a family once affluent but impoverished in the religious wars of the Seventeenth Century. The issue of this union was James, the grandfather of the subject of this memoir.

If little is known of these early Bryces, it is probably because they were not remarkable; but with Robina Allan's entry into the family we notice a change. Her son, her grandsons, and her great-grandsons are clearly members of a family of unusual strength and tenacity.

The origin of genius or exceptional talent is one of the

mysteries of life. We cannot tell how or why it arises, how long it will be sustained or at what intervals it will manifest itself, but that some stocks are more continuously effective than others is one of the commonplaces of observation. Now Robina Allan brought a strain of Covenanting blood into the Bryce family. Two of her ancestors had fought at the battle of Bothwell Bridge, immortalised in one of the finest of the Waverley Novels, and it was with a sentiment of pride that the James Bryce of this volume would recall the Westland Whig forbears who had taken a hand in that famous quarrel a century and a half before his birth.

There is no stock in the world more passionate for right or more obstinate in scruple, more tenacious in purpose or more independent in judgment, less pliant to the stress of outward convenience or more harshly indifferent to the calls of indolence, luxury, and self-indulgence than that of the Scottish Covenanter. To the eye of posterity the scruples of the Covenanters may seem overdrawn, their distinctions fantastic, their intolerance odious or grotesque. But, even in an age which has long outgrown the creeds for which they lived and were prepared to die, it is no bad preparation for the strenuous life to have a good drop of Covenanting blood in the veins.

Of this resolute hard-bitten spirit, as it may be tempered and refined by a larger culture, there can be no better embodiment than the Rev. James Bryce, the son of "Elder" John and the grandfather of the statesman who is commemorated in this volume. His longevity, for he died in his ninetieth year, his independence of spirit, his utter contempt for worldly advantage when it seemed to conflict with theological or political principle, his bold defiance of authority and indomitable energy make of him a remarkable figure in the annals of the Presbyterian Church. Certainly it was vouchsafed to him to receive a full measure of that "copious outpouring of the spirit of secession" for which the little schismatic community of anti-burghers to which he belonged so quaintly offered prayers to their Maker. We hear of him first as quite a young minister at Wick in Caithness, being suspended for latitudinarianism by the synod of his Church, for he, an anti-burgher, had actually preached in a burgher Church (he had been pastor at Pulteney Towers, Wick); next, as being driven by the intolerance of his native land to cross St. George's Channel and to settle in Northern Ireland, where again he found himself in revolt for, alone among his anti-burgher brethren, he refused to accept the conditions attached to the distribution among the Presbyterian clergy of an addition to that royal bounty or Regium Donum by which it was hoped to conciliate religious feeling in Northern Ireland to the passage of the Union. "Christ is my King," he exclaimed. On no account would he take Lord Castlereagh's bounty, accompanied as it was by a system of classification under which some ministers would receive more than others, and by the requirement of an oath of allegiance before two magistrates, and what seemed most humiliating of all, the approval of the Lord Lieutenant before a penny of the State stipend could be paid.

Threats, unpopularity, excommunication, could not move him. Though he was minister of one of the poorest congregations of the synod (Killaig, in the parish of

Aghadoey in the County of Antrim) and a married man with a family of eleven, he faced obloquy and poverty with a stout heart, supported first by his own little Antiburgher congregation, then finding seven like-minded congregations and organising them into a miniature Church, "the Associate Presbytery of Scotland," with himself high pontiff and daring even to ordain a minister. In his wife Catherine Annan of Auchtermuchty he discovered a woman of like constancy to himself, who was prepared to see her children go without many comforts rather than touch the accursed gold. An accomplished woman she is acknowledged to have been, for she taught Greek and Latin to her children and to the village lads, and contributed articles to the magazines.

From this poor home among the flats of Antrim, where Greek was the only luxury, there issued in course of time a remarkable brood of sons. Reuben John became Head of the Belfast Academy, then one of the foremost boys' schools in Northern Ireland, as well as Minister of a Presbyterian Church in the City; Robert grew up to be a well-known physician in Belfast, James became a distinguished geologist and mathematical master in Glasgow, William became a homeopathic physician of repute in Edinburgh, while Archibald Hamilton, the youngest of the seven sons, lived to rule over the Edinburgh Collegiate School. Never have resolution and independence been more amply justified by their fruits.

The two most eminent members of this large family were Reuben John the eldest and James the third son. Reuben John, "Uncle John" as he will be called in some letters hereafter to be printed, was a man of exceptional force of mind and character and a leader in the educational and religious life in Northern Ireland. His quality can perhaps be best assessed by the admirable sketch of a plan for a system of education in Northern Ireland, (1828) in which he argues that no good system of education for the upper classes as distinct from the rest of the people can exist, and that all endeavours to improve education must utterly fail unless teachers are enabled to study education as a moral art founded on the philosophy of the human mind. "We want," he wrote, "to create a race of schoolmasters," and as one means to this end he advocated the establishment of Chairs of Education in every University. In this and other matters educational, "Uncle John" was well ahead of his time.

James also was an educator, whose memory as a brilliant teacher of mathematics and geography is still gratefully cherished in the minds of his few surviving Glasgow pupils. He was born at Killaig in 1806 and was educated first by his father and elder brother at home and afterwards at the University of Glasgow, which provided for all the male members of the Bryce family that strong intellectual diet of solid subjects and rigorous drill with no concessions to individual taste and temperament which was characteristic of Scottish education in those Spartan days. Here the young Ulster Scot after achieving high distinction in classical studies graduated in 1828. Ambitious of a legal career but too poor to realise his ambition James Bryce the Second threw himself with the energy of his race into the business of schoolmastering. A man of his vigour of mind and body could not fail to impress his class, and "Paddy Bryce," as the boys called him with reference to his Irish birth-place, was able to keep discipline with little help from cane or taw. In one important particular he was an educational pioneer, for at a time when there was no regular provision for scientific teaching in the Scottish High Schools he not only steadily advocated the claims of natural history and natural science to be included among the subjects of school study, but took every opportunity of acting on his own precepts, by giving voluntary instruction in the new learning. Especially was he interested in Geology, writing many important papers embodying the results of his geological researches in Ireland, Scotland, and Northern England, and among these contributing the first full explanation and rationale of the structure of the Giants' Causeway near his father's old home. He was also the author of a Treatise on Algebra, an introduction to Mathematical Astronomy and Geography, a cyclopædia of Geography and a work on the Geology and Antiquities of Arran and other islands on the Clyde, researches which not only indicate a range of mental enterprise unusual in a mathematical master but were in this case associated with an eager love of natural beauty in all its manifold forms. More particularly did he love the glens of Antrim, among which he had spent his boyhood. Here he learnt Irish from the Glen folk and thither after he had removed to Glasgow he would come for at least one long visit in the year to refresh mind and body with the wild beauties of his Irish home.

It may readily be imagined how stimulating was the society of a father, so vigorous, eager, and observant, so full of outdoor interests and scientific curiosity, to the mind of an intelligent boy. From his earliest years James Bryce the Third was encouraged to take an interest in geography, botany, and geology, subjects frequently discussed at home and receiving fresh and delightful illustrations on every country walk and holiday ramble.

The geologist-mathematician died in action. On July 11, 1877 when he was already past seventy years of age but still in the full enjoyment of his mental and physical powers, he was examining a remarkable mass of eruptive granite at Inverfarigaig on the shores of Loch Ness. Some loose stones disturbed by the strokes of his hammer caused the blocks above to fall upon his head and killed him instantaneously. An inscription still marks the place where he died.

To judge by his portrait James Bryce the Second must have been a fine figure of a man; dark, keen-eyed, aquiline, with a spacious brow and a mingled air of force and refinement in every line of his face. His wife, Margaret Young, the eldest daughter of Mr. James Young, a leading Belfast merchant, I remember as an impressive lady on a sofa; tall and slim with brilliant dark eyes, a clear note of Ulster in her incisive voice and a power of trenchant and vivacious conversation on the serious issues of the day which was truly astonishing in an octogenarian. As a girl she had been a voracious reader, and having a mind of unusual force and clearness and free access to her father's library had acquired at an early age a wide knowledge of literature; but she was too much the Irishwoman to be precious or pedantic and her learning seemed to be of little account in comparison with the fun and liveliness and quick gifts of repartee which were hers by right of the Celtic temperament. Soon after her marriage her health became uncertain and what appeared to be an affection of the heart made her more or less an invalid for the remainder of her days, but illness made no change in the essentials of her strong and impressive character. She remained an attractive and dominating figure, drawing on a wealth of spiritual resources and living a full and eager life in her quiet room.

Ulster Scots are proverbially a tough race, but surely few even among the stalwart families of Ulster can claim to eclipse the Bryce record for longevity. The subject of this biography died with his zest for life still unsatisfied and insatiable at eighty-three. His mother lived to within three weeks of ninety. His father showed every sign of a long career when he was killed at a little over seventy in what appeared to be the bloom of robust manhood. His uncle Reuben John failed to reach ninety by three months. His uncle William, botanist, physician, and golfer, died at ninety-three, his uncle Archibald at eighty. His aunt Catherine lived to be ninety, his grandfather, the Minister of Killaig, was active at ninety and preached two sermons on the Sunday before he died. Of his maternal uncles one (The Right Honourable Robert Young of Belfast) lived to be ninety-four, another to be over eighty, while a maternal aunt (Mrs. Lyle) "Aunt Elizabeth" died at eighty-six. A brood of men and women more hale and vigorous it would be difficult to find.

Longevity and torturing scruples go ill together. A hearty belief in the tenets of the United Presbyterian Church was combined in the Bryce family with that enlivening zeal for knowledge which is an honourable mark of the Scottish character. On questions of Presbyterian orthodoxy Uncle John, the Head of the Family, was naturally the arbiter. What does Uncle John think? We shall see that Uncle John's opinions are regarded by his nephew as "a little overstrained" when the thorny subject of chapel attendance or the signature of the Articles comes up for consideration at Oxford; but they were always important. Nor is it a matter for surprise that Dr. James Bryce, the scientific expert of the family, should have taken the field against the dangerous Darwinian theory of evolution.

A deep simple old-world piety quickened by lively intellectual interests and accompanied by a manly enjoyment in physical exercise was an atmosphere characteristic of the household and conducive to length of days.

James Bryce was born on the 10th May, 1838, in Arthur St., Belfast, and spent the first eight years of his life there and in a country house belonging to his maternal grandfather Mr. James Young on the shores of Belfast Lough. It was here that the boy, who was practically an only child during those early years, for Reuben, the second son, died at the age of three and John Annan was not born till 1843, conceived an early passion for the sea which lasted through his life. Having no brothers or sisters near to him in age,[1] James was brought up among older people and being by nature precocious and thoughtful, though full of physical energy, was able at a very early age to derive advantage from his constant association with older minds of high cultivation and varied intellectual and scientific curiosity. An interest in constitutional

[1] The younger members of the family were John Annan, b. 1843, Mary and Katharine.

history was soon developed. There is a story of the boy
of eight insisting on sitting next his Uncle John during
a long drive in an Irish car, in order that he might question him on the British Constitution. Uncle John was the
first of a long line of patients of every race and tongue
who were in due course called on to pay their tribute to
the same vast and eager curiosity.

In 1846 Mr. Bryce received a call to the High School
at Glasgow, but though the Bryces were henceforth settled
in Scotland the family still kept up a close connection
with Ulster and spent many holidays there. Ulster of
course was the predominant interest. "Of the rest of
Ireland we knew or heard very little after the failure
of the rebellion of 1848." But the long glens of Antrim
and the fine rock-bound coast of Northern Ireland were
happy holiday ground, and apart from these open-air
associations the Bryces were helped by their numerous
Irish friends and relations to follow with interest the
course of feeling and affairs in the Northern Province.

Childish memories are among the most precious things
in life. Bryce's childhood, solitary though it may have
been in some respects, was full of romantic enjoyment.
The Bible, bringing with it the sentiment of the East
and of high antiquity, and creating, as he said afterwards,
a feeling of awe and mystery by the word "wilderness"
alone, the Arabian Nights, the books of old travellers
in the Andes, such as Humboldt's *Aspects of Nature*,
filled his mind with imaginative musings on distant
places and far-off times. "Ever since as a boy I had read
of a great inland sea lying between the two ranges of the
Cordilleras almost as high above the ocean as is the top

of the Jungfrau, I had wondered as to what the scenery of such mountains and such a sea might be like and had searched books and questioned travellers without getting from them what I sought." [1] When he was twelve years old, long before he had crossed the English Channel, he knew most of the peaks of the Bernese Oberland and the Pennines from pictures and descriptions, and could have given the height of many of them. Nor was his imagination quickened only by the thoughts which came from books. In the scenery, the traditions and the folk lore of the wild glens of Antrim, there was much to arouse the curiosity and the emotions of an intelligent boy. The peasants in the glens knew well that a water spirit under the form of a bull infested the river in which he fished and warned him against it. Nature worship, older and more elemental than Christianity, was about his childish ways and found an answering echo in his heart.

[1] Speech to the Alpine Club on the last occasion he took the chair. (1901.)

CHAPTER II

GLASGOW COLLEGE

Glasgow has a larger share in romance and romantic tradition than most people recognise; though they have the salmon and the ring in the City Arms to remind them. There is an imaginative, a spiritual City of Glasgow to be found in the books of different romancers and historians; it is not all vanity.

W. P. Ker.

SCHOOL must have come to Bryce with less of a shock than it does to most boys, for after his family had removed to Glasgow, he naturally attended the High School where his father was a master, living at home and walking in to town for his classes during the term.[1] In those days games had not begun to exercise their tyranny, the leisure moments of a schoolboy were still imperfectly organised, and it was possible for a country-bred lad attending a day school in Glasgow to gratify the taste for sport, scenery, and natural history which he had formed in the spacious freedom of childhood. Bryce took part in such school games as were going but his real diversions were not found in the school yard, but rather in holiday rambles among the hills and glens of Western Scotland, in fishing and botanising and geologising and in talks with his father over astronomy at night. The class work presented

[1] The Bryces lived for some time in a house in Lansdowne Crescent but afterwards moved into the country, to a house at Blantyre.

[12]

so few difficulties that more than a year before he could enter college, he felt that he had got all the benefit which it was possible for the High School to give him. It was probably for this reason that when he had reached the age of fourteen his parents sent him to live for a time with his uncle, Dr. Bryce, at Belfast. Here he attended classes at the academy and learnt from his erudite relative, who was enthusiastic for Irish antiquities, the elements of the Erse language.

His boyhood, however, though full of sunshine was not without clouds. In after life he would say that when he was about fifteen he suffered from great fits of depression, and we may conjecture that while in part his melancholia may have been due to physical causes, it was also not a little the consequence of precocious development. His mind, while still growing and unformed was attempting to grapple with the deeper problems and mysteries of life.

At the age of sixteen (1854) Bryce passed on from school to the Glasgow University, where he spent three years — an episode in his life happily illuminated by a charming autobiographical fragment which has hitherto escaped publication.

GLASGOW COLLEGE (1854–57)

As my grandfather, and my father and two uncles had all been at Glasgow University and we then lived in Glasgow, it was natural that I should go there. The first year I took the Senior Latin Class and the Middle Greek Class (Provectiores). The Professor of Latin was William Ramsay, a man then of about sixty. He was an admirable teacher, stimulating and vivacious, a complete master

[13]

of his subject and the author of one of the best Classical textbooks extant, "Manual of Roman Antiquities,"
which contained an extraordinary wealth of information,
accurate for that day, of everything connected with the
public and private life of the Romans. It was a real
pleasure to be taught by him. The Class met twice a day ;
the morning lecture was catechetical, while in the later
lecture he read and expounded an author. That year it
was Catullus, and he made one know and understand and
appreciate everything in the poems that were in the
printed text he had prepared, from which some few poems
were necessarily omitted. At the end of the course I
knew nearly the whole of Catullus by heart. He used to
ask those who were willing to translate certain of the
poems into English verse. I did a good many of these —
indeed I think all that were proposed — often with the
help of my mother, and they had a considerable success.
He criticised all that were sent in, sometimes in an amusing way. My principal competitor in the class was Donald Crawford, who came from the Edinburgh Academy
and went, after two years, to Oxford on a Snell Exhibition to Balliol. He entered the Scotch Bar and was afterwards member of the House of Commons for North East
Lanarkshire. He became Sheriff of Aberdeen and Kincar-
dine in 1895 and held that office for a good many years.
He was a very able high-minded man of wide culture, but
unfortunately not a fluent speaker and rather deficient in
the energy which pushes a man at the Bar, where he also
suffered from having independent means. We became
warm friends in later life, and I spent some days with
him at a house he had taken near Habbe's How in the

Pentland Hills in August 1918, just before the illness of which he died a few months later.

The Greek Professor was Edmund Lushington who had married Tennyson's sister, and is referred to as her bridegroom in the little poem Tennyson wrote on the occasion of her wedding. He had been a contemporary of Tennyson's at Cambridge where he was Senior Classic. He was more learned and a scholar of finer quality than Ramsay, but not so stimulating a teacher. He kept equally good order in his class, inspiring a deferential respect which was felt by even the roughest kind of student. We never talked of "undergraduates" at Glasgow.

After he retired from the chair he was elected Lord Rector, the only instance I can remember of a Glasgow Professor receiving that honour. He spent his later life in his country house near Maidstone where my sister and I used, when we lived in London, to go down to spend week-ends with him in the delightful quiet of a recluse life. There was no one in the house except his three elderly sisters and his daughter, and sometimes old Edmund Venables of the Parliamentary Bar who used to write the political articles in the "Saturday Review" and belonged to that type of Londoner which called itself Liberal and was Conservative, disliked sentiment, and detested Gladstone. In private I always found him pleasant, and he was singularly handsome, a well-known figure in the semi-legal semi-literary circles of that day. Lushington, like all his family, was a Whig, but he shared the dislike of the Whigs for Gladstone; and although he said very little I could see that he was grieved that I was a Home Ruler and had taken office in Mr. Gladstone's

Ministry of 1886. In his last years he had taken to the study of Egyptian hieroglyphics which his powerful mind easily mastered, and he produced some interesting translations of Egyptian texts. He remains in my memory as a perfect example of the finished scholar who led the philosophic life, seeming to desire nothing beyond what he had, and finding his happiness in the enjoyment of intellectual pleasures.

The professor of Logic, the Rev. Robert Buchanan, whom the students called "Logic Bob," was a pure Scotchman and a highly efficient teacher in a different kind of way. He had been educated for the Ministry, but either never got, or did not seek, a parish. He had delivered the same course of lectures for very many years, and manuscript notes of those lectures taken by students of former generations were purchasable; but most of us took our notes for ourselves, knowing that this was the best way of getting them into our minds. He lectured for two hours, the first of which was occupied by the reading of the lecture, the second by his examining the class upon the subject of the lecture of the preceding day. This he did with admirable skill and apparently with as much freshness as he had been doing it for the preceding twenty or thirty years. He kept the whole class of sixty or seventy students interested, and almost excited, the whole time, making us think and clearing up any points that might have been misunderstood in the previous lecture. He carried on the tradition and methods and ideas of old Dr. Thomas Reid, who had taught in Glasgow eighty years before — the founder of the so-called Scottish School. Neither Kant nor Hegel, nor Fichte, nor Schelling, were ever mentioned, though sometimes we heard of Descartes and Malebranche, and I think Condillac; and his examples of argument and devices in rhetoric were drawn from eighteenth century writers, among whom I remember Warburton as being several times referred to. His lectures would be thought little of to-day, but in their simple treatment of the fundamentals of psychology and logic they were highly appreciated by the students and very profitable. The old gentleman was a bachelor and led a solitary life. He was believed, and I think truly, to have written a drama with Sir William Wallace for its hero, and there were students who professed to have seen it, but I could not learn that, if printed, any copies were for sale. The only reference the lectures made to any current philosophy was in a passage which he had lately inserted among the leaves yellow with age and which dealt with the quantification of the predicate — an innovation invented by Sir William Hamilton who was then Professor at Edinburgh, and who, though far more learned and far more eminent in the sphere of philosophy, was by all accounts by no means so good a teacher as Buchanan.

My second year's classes were Senior Greek and Mathematics. The Senior Greek was extremely interesting because it gave us a better opportunity of appreciating Lushington's scholarship. He took us through the Agamemnon, translating it himself and commenting as he went along, the comments almost entirely on the language, but now and then helping us to appreciate the poetry. He encouraged us to translate some of the choruses into English verse and this again was an excellent training. He

also gave us English pieces to turn into Homeric hexameters. This is the only kind of classical verse composition I ever enjoyed or attained any facility in, perhaps
because Homer appealed to me more than any of the
ancient poets had yet done, and I could remember the
verses better. A great many passages naturally clung to
one's memory, but some I set myself to learn and learnt
very easily. I think it was in one day that I got by heart
the whole of the eighth book of the Iliad, which struck me
as particularly splendid in its majestic roll. I also began
to learn by heart the narrative of his wanderings which
Odysseus gives in the ninth, tenth, eleventh, and twelfth
Books of the Odyssey, and got as far as to the end of
the eleventh Book. I do not think I ever finished the
twelfth. I remember a good deal of it to this day, and
how delightful it all is.

The other class of the second year was that of Mathematics, under Professor Hugh Blackburn. He was a
Scot and I think a brother of the lawyer Lord Blackburn,
a high Cambridge Wrangler and an excellent mathemati-
cian, but a poor teacher. Perhaps anyone of a marked
mathematical talent might have profited by his lectures,
but having only a mediocre capacity for the subject I
learnt very little and found little pleasure in the class.
He did not succeed, partly because he failed to awaken
the interest of the class, even in keeping order. There
was always noise and talking going on. I do not remember to have myself seen, but was told that on days when
snow was falling, students would sometimes bring in
snowballs, and launch them at the blackboard so that the
melting snow obliterated the mathematical figures or

calculations drawn on the board. Blackburn's wife was a talented artist. Her drawings of animals especially were quite famous, and she outshone her rather tame and pliant husband.

It was a sign of unsatisfactory teaching when the class prizes went wrong. The prizes were awarded by the votes of the students — a plan which seemed absurd to those who did not see it in operation. In point of fact, however, it worked well whenever the Professor gave good catechetical teaching which gave the student called up for examination a chance of showing his quality. If there were five or six prizes to be given, the first, second and third, and probably the fourth, were pretty sure to go to the best men in the right order; the lowest prizes not so certain because the differences in excellence were less marked. The Professors themselves praised the system and would on no account have changed it. But in a class like Blackburn's it was only the first two prizes which could be counted on to go to the right men. Between the rest the students had no sufficient means of deciding, and they might vote for men whose names they knew as having done well in other classes though not specially well in Mathematics. This happened in my own case, for I was voted a prize in the Mathematical class which I certainly did not deserve.

Competition was very keen for the class prizes. There was a great deal of ambition and rivalry among the students. On the third or fourth day after the opening of a Session they would begin to talk to one another as to who would win the class prizes, and when towards the middle of the Session a few horses had drawn to the front there was keen speculation about the highest place. There was, however, very little private canvassing for votes. A competitor would have damaged himself by such tactics. The students had a high sense of their duty to vote for the best man. There were, however, a few prizes given by the Professors for essays on prescribed subjects, and there were two prizes, one in Latin and the other in Greek — Gold Medals given under a special Foundation. Each candidate gave in a long list of Latin books and Greek books which he "professed" ("hos libros profiteor"), and the Professors sitting in conclave chose passages in which to test him. I tried for both of these, but the Latin Medal, though a very close thing, went to Donald Crawford. The next year my turn came to "profess" Greek Books and this Medal came to me, my competitor being another Edinburgh Academy man named Grant. This Greek prize gave great pleasure to my father, for he had won it himself about 1820.

One of the most interesting features of the Scotch Universities is the election of a Lord Rector, which is made by the votes of the Professors and the students taken together — which in practice means the students as being incomparably more numerous. They vote by "Nations," an interesting survival from mediæval usage. Glasgow University was founded by Pope Nicholas V. on the model of Bologna; "cum privilegiis Bononiensibus," so I suppose the "Nations" come from that source. In Glasgow there are four in which a student is registered according to his place of birth — Glottiani (*i.e.* Clydesdale), Rothsaiana (called from Rothsay the capital of the South West Highlands, and including Ireland, whence in those days many students came), Transforthana (*i.e.* East Scotland North of the Forth), and Londoniana (*i.e.* Lothian, South East Scotland and England). In those days the Rector was elected for two years. Sometimes a leading politician was put forward, sometimes a man eminent in letters or science. In 1853 the Liberals brought forward Carlyle and the Tories Disraeli. Many students calling themselves Liberals knew too little about Carlyle to be keen on him, but were strongly opposed to Disraeli, and their choice fell on the Duke of Argyll, who had already made a figure by his brilliant oratory and was President of the British Association, whose next meeting was to be in Glasgow. I was one of these and had my first experience in public speaking on this occasion. He was carried by a considerable majority. The liveliest part of the campaign consisted in the squibs, some of them very witty, directed against Disraeli. In the following Rectorial Election Bulwer Lytton was chosen, but as a literary man rather than as a politician. I remember his Address as a brilliant piece of rhetoric. I think it seems a pity that now-a-days Rectorial Elections are always fought on political lines, so that the men of Letters and Science only are "out of it," and a pity that there are permanent Liberal and Conservative organisations, leading students to range themselves definitely on one side or the other in politics at a very early age. In my time a Committee was got up "pro hac vice" for the Election only, but I do not think there was a permanent Liberal Association.

The thing most deficient in the University (though this I did not realise until I saw the College system at Oxford) lay in the absence of personal social touch between the students and the Professors, and in the want of opportunities for social intercourse among the students themselves. Except on the very rare occasions when a Professor asked two or three promising students to dinner, the teacher never met the taught save in the class-room. The students lived some of them at home with their parents, some in lodgings here and there in the great city, and had no means of coming together and cultivating friendship. Those who had a vacant hour between one class and another used to wander together in groups over a great open grassy space adjacent to the College and belonging to it.

Here I remember not a few long arguments over the freedom of the will and other metaphysical topics to which the Scottish mind was prone. But there were no societies till in my third year a little group established what was to have been something between a Debating Society and a Mutual Improvement Essay Society. How it fared thereafter I never heard. Neither were there any Athletic Societies or Clubs, or any Athletic Sports whatever. Sometimes a group would gather on the green and kick backwards and forwards a football, but I never could make out that a regular game was being played. The students whose homes were in Glasgow played rounders in the suburbs, where they lived. Cricket had then hardly been heard of in Scotland. But the students from a distance had no amusements, and most of them were far too poor to be able to afford any. Some among them earned money enough during the summer to pay their living and their fees during the Session in the winter which

lasted only five and a half months. I remember one
stalwart fellow who was one of the best men in the Logic
class following the trade of a blacksmith during most of
the year.

Needless to say this was no social disparagement.
Indeed the men who supported themselves in this way
were all the more respected. Some of the ablest men
came from Wales with scholarships or bursaries provided
by a Foundation for sending Nonconformists to be educated in Scotland. The endowments had been provided
at the time when not even undergraduates were admitted
to Oxford and Cambridge unless they signed the Thirty-
Nine Articles. I recall two or three of these men, brilliant in the class and as speakers at Rectorial contests,
and expected for some of them a distinguished future,
but could never ascertain what became of them after
leaving Glasgow. The natural thing would have been
for them to enter the Nonconformist Ministry. One
of them was named Abercromby — a man of great metaphysical talent. I think he must have died young, or
else he would have been heard of in after life.

It seems strange that it should be so hard to know what
became of College acquaintances. I kept up correspondence with four or five for some years, and with two or
three even longer; but Scotchmen have a way of scat-
tering themselves over the world, and traces get lost.
One of those whom I knew best, Peter Sinclair Menzies,
went to Australia and became eminent as a Presbyterian
Minister at Melbourne. He had real eloquence and was
greatly respected and admired there, but he died comparatively young. Of those who remained in Scotland

there was John Nichol, whom I knew afterwards at Oxford and ultimately became Professor of English Literature in Glasgow itself. There were two McLeods, Norman and Johnny, cousins, if I remember right, of Dr. Norman McLeod who was then Minister of the Barony parish — a tall, handsome Highland man, well known in literary as well as ecclesiastical circles and a prime favourite with Queen Victoria. Johnny McLeod, who was already a Divinity student two or three years my senior, was a brilliant creature, an eloquent speaker, an excellent writer. He became Minister first at Dunse and afterwards at Govan, and incurred some trouble in his later years by adopting fixed forms of prayer and tendencies which would have been called in English partly High Church and partly Broad. Besides these there was George M. Grant whom I knew better, a Nova Scotian Highlander who spoke Gaelic and had the Gaelic gift of ready speech and a genial manner. He returned to Canada and became head of the University at Queenstown, Ontario. He acquired a great influence in Canada and well deserved it. Wherever he was, he was a force for good, an Imperialist of the best kind who valued British power only as it was exerted for justice. We renewed our acquaintance after many years about 1898; it was always a pleasure to exchange ideas with him.

In spite of the deficient opportunities for intellectual intercourse the atmosphere of College life was highly stimulating, more so than I found that of Oxford afterwards. The class work kept us on the "qui vive" and nearly the whole class wanted to learn and enjoyed learn-

ing. Whenever we had a chance we talked about our
work, discussing the questions that came up, an incessant sharpening of wits upon one another's whetstones.
We spoke very little about theology and not much about
politics, and though we cared about classics the ambition
of most of us would have been to be metaphysicians.
That seemed the highest kind of mental exertion. There
were omissions in the curriculum. History was not taught
at all; there was no professor. Neither was English
Literature, nor any branch of Natural History, except
Botany which was taken only by a few medical students.
We were most of us young — I entered at fifteen and was
by no means the youngest in many of my classes. Some
were much older — bearded men of from twenty to thirty
— but there was little difference between young and old.
In the competition for prizes neither age nor youth told.
All alike were eager in the pursuit of knowledge, those
who had come from parish schools of low degree and the
sons of wealthy merchants who had got all that the best
schools of Edinburgh and Glasgow could give. We knew
little of one another's private lives. Some frequented
taverns, but I never remember to have seen anyone the
worse for liquor, though every third or fourth building
in the High Street was a public house. The medicals
were the roughest and led the least orderly lives, but in
the Art Classes most of us were younger and nearer to the
innocence of boyhood. I do not remember to have heard
a single coarse expression, seldom even an oath, from my
class companions. There was no better way of understanding the Scotch spirit as it has been ever since the
middle of the 16th century than to be a student of Glas-

gow College in those days. These days, sixty-five years later, may be very different.

During the Session I had to rise at 6.30 every morning and walk three miles to college to attend a class at 8 A.M., and three miles back at 9 A.M. for a second breakfast; and in again at 11 o'clock for a class at 12, and home again in the afternoon; twelve miles to and fro. "*Sic fortis Etruria crevit.*"

THE LONG SUMMERS

The Sessions of the Scotch Universities began in those days in October and ended about the 20th April. There were about ten days holiday at Christmas and New Year, and there were the two Fast Days in October and April, but all the rest of the winter we worked steadily. All the summer we had to ourselves — that is, those who did not have to work for their living. To me the summers were the one great delight of boyhood and youth, for we spent them at the seaside or in the Scottish Highlands where I swam, and boated, and fished, and climbed mountains, often alone, to my heart's content. The first of these summer outings that I recall was spent at Oban in 1848, where I remember reading for the first time Macpherson's "Ossian" and George Buchanan's History of Scotland, with the mythical Kings from Fergus I. who founded the Kingdom of the Scots at Dunstaffnage — only three miles from Oban on Loch Etive — in the year 300 and odd B.C. down to Kenneth McAlpine who joined Scots and Picts and is something of a historic character.

Next year we spent at Cushendall on the coast of County Antrim — a delightful summer, for I had four months here and was for the first time taken by my Father on his geological excursions, and ascended my first mountain, Trostan, the highest in Ulster, the view from which, looking across the broad valley of the Bann to the far-off blue mountains of Donegal I remember as if it was yesterday. My father could speak some Irish and used to talk a little with the peasants in the glens, nearly all Roman Catholics. They were considered quite a distinct race by the Presbyterians of the lower country, but they got on perfectly well together. À propos of religion, it was at this time first that I attended services of the Church of England, for there was no Presbyterian Church within ten miles, and greatly were we puzzled to find our way up and down the Episcopalian Prayer Book. The services were not inspiriting, but the sermons rather shorter than the Presbyterian. I remember here first hearing the Irish pipes. There was a fine old piper who wandered with his family and gave a concert in the Inn, and explained the superiority of the Irish pipes to the Scotch, and also assured us that the pipes was really the true national instrument of Ireland, and (despite Tom Moore), not the harp. Cushendall is a singularly picturesque and beautiful valley, three glens converging to its little bay with a bright strand excellent for bathing and guarded by rocks off which we fished with long rods. Two miles to the north on the edge of a bold cliff above the sea are the ruins of a very ancient church in which are buried some of the MacDonnells who fought along with Alastair MacDonnell (Milton's Colkitto), in the wars of Scotland, when Montrose was fighting the Covenanters. No place I saw in my childhood touched imagination so much by its

[27]

hoar antiquity and the sadness of its solitude — the waves murmuring on the rocks below. It seemed a place where a man might feel that he would lie at rest.

It was this summer also that I first saw what still seems to me the most grand and solemn ocean view in our islands — that from the top of the majestic Fair Head — looking out on the right hand to Ailsa and the mountains of Arran, and north to Isla and Jura, and close by over Rathlin, and far away to the west the long line of Inishowen on the coast of Donegal. This is the spot where you realise the unity of the Scottish race on both sides of the Channel, filling all the country that is now the counties of Bute and Argyll as far north as Mull, or perhaps further; and inland as far as the sources of the Tay and its tributaries. The stormy sea with its strong currents between Cantire and Antrim is the Sea of Moyle, the scene of one of the most touching ancient Irish legends — the three daughters of the Sea God Lir who were turned into wild swans. When I bathed at Tor Point, some miles south of the Fair Head, the tide sweep was so strong that the country folk bade me not to swim more than a few yards from the shore. I have seen a vessel under full sail with a good wind behind her unable to make way ahead when the tide turned against her. It is one of the most romantic spots in all Ireland.

The summer of 1850 included a short visit to the Lake Country where my Uncle William was then living at Kendal. We ascended Helvellyn for the first time and were delighted with Windermere, and Grasmere, and Rydal, and the view from the top of Scouts Scar to the west of Kendal. The beauties of the Lake Country made a profound impression on me, and Wordworth's house was pointed out where he had died that year. It was the first thing that brought into my consciousness the great poet who has been so much to me ever since. If I remember right we spent the autumn of this year at Dunoon, and I went up every day by steamboat from there to Glasgow to school, a journey of more than two hours, and back the same evening. Perched on the lee side of the paddle-box I learnt my lessons for next day, and had no work to do in the evening. It sounds a long time to spend in going to and fro to school, but to be four or five hours every day with the sea air blowing round one was a fine thing for a growing boy. Every now and then the September fogs in the Firth and on the river made the steamer late in reaching Glasgow and one missed some school — a matter of envy to the other boys who lived in Glasgow.

The summer of 1851 was spent at Arrochar, where the love of mountain climbing, which had become a passion with me since Cushendall, had ample opportunity for indulging itself. There are several mountains close back which approach or exceed 3,000 ft. There were also burns and lochs full of little trout, and I have often spent a long summer's day walking five or six miles over the hills to these remote spots, with a piece of bread in my pocket, fishing all day long in solitude and not returning till dark. There is nothing more delightful than following up or down its course a Highland burn. Whether one caught the trout or not made little difference. It was the wild pastures and birch thickets and rocks, and the stream itself with its ripples and its sunny pools, and now and then a waterfall tumbling into a deep black lynn, that made the enjoyment.

In 1851 my father took Annan and myself to London to see the great Exhibition. This Exhibition was an event the importance of which people find it hard to realise to-day. It made a profound impression on the world, being the first thing of the kind ever attempted, and drawing samples of raw materials as well as manufactured goods from every part of the world. The fact that the building was of glass, towering over high elms in Hyde Park, gave it a kind of romance. It certainly was a far more beautiful thing of the kind than has ever been seen since. Even now, after seventy years, its brilliance comes up like a picture before me, the gleam of the light from above through the glass, the gay and quickly moving crowds below, the hum which in the vast space never rose to a din, the plash of the water as it rose and fell into the basin of the fountain entirely made of glass. This fountain, which was about the centre, was the accepted rendez-vous for all who meant to meet one another in the Exhibition. One learnt in strolling about the stalls a great deal about distant countries which gave an unwonted stimulus to curiosity.

We spent nearly a fortnight in London, lodging somewhere in the angle between Oxford Street, east of Oxford Circus, and Langham Place. I forget the street, but remember that my favourite amusement was to go out in the morning before breakfast, lose myself in unknown streets and then find my way back to the lodgings. London was very different from what it is now, especially along the river between Westminster Bridge and London

Bridge, where, in the Charing Cross region there was a ricketty old structure called Hungerford Bridge and a great number of quaint old houses (long since removed) backing on the river, for if I remember right there was no continuous street along the north bank where the Embankment runs now. We were taken to see the House of Commons which was then meeting in a temporary building — the new Houses being then under construction. We got seats in the gallery — one of them given by Mr. Disraeli, and the other by Richard Cobden, both of whom happened to be known to the relative who took us there. In those days, however, many years before dynamite had been invented, anyone strolling in the Lobby might ask any member for a stranger's Order, and count upon getting one. I little thought that twenty seven years of my life would be passed in that place, but my experience is that one never anticipates. We saw the usual sights of which the British Museum, and the Coronation Chair in Westminster Abbey, were to me the most interesting — the latter, perhaps, because I had seen Dunstaffnage whence the Lia Fail came, according to tradition.

The summer of 1852 was spent at Newcastle on the coast of County Down, then a very small place, but now a town much resorted to by golfers. It lies at the foot of Slieve Donard, the highest of the Mourne Mountains, and my father took me with him on his geological excursions up and among the bold peaks of that range. There was good bathing and good sea fishing, so it was altogether an enjoyable time. My uncle John was also staying there in a house near us, and he had brought down a young Irish scholar who afterwards became Professor of Gaelic in Queen's College, Galway. His name was Crow. My uncle was taking lessons from him in Gaelic and asked me to join him, which I did, and made enough progress in the language to have enabled me, (if I had kept it up) to read it with the help of a dictionary. Unluckily, I dropped it, and when I went back to the study of it in 1906, found that I had forgotten almost everything.

In 1853 we went for the first time to Arran, and so fell in love with it as to spend two or three succeeding summers there — the last in 1856. It is altogether the most delightful island in its varied beauty that the British seas contain. My Father enjoyed it especially because its geological features were so interesting; and I enjoyed it specially because my Uncle William Bryce, who was then studying medicine in Edinburgh, had taught me the elements of botany and set me to collecting plants and forming a herbarium. He had me to stay with him for some days in the May of (I think) 1853, though perhaps 1854, and insisted on my accompanying him on botanical rambles in the country round Edinburgh. I remember being a little reluctant the first day, but by the end of it he had got me interested, and on the remaining days I was as keen as he could wish. Few people realise what an enormous difference to the life of a boy or a girl may be made by the implanting of a taste at the right moment, and by persevering even if the first seed sown does not seem to be taking root. My uncle took me out a second, a third and a fourth day on short excursions, and by the last day the seed had taken root so deeply that the taste has remained with me ever since and constituted one of the chief pleasures of my life. It fell in happily with the passion for mountain climbing and exploring every new region where one happened to be, and from that time on I never saw a mountain or a wood, or a common, or a river bank without searching for uncommon plants; and even on railway journeys I tried to catch (when the speed was not too great) the plants that grew along the line. Without those four days I should never have taken to botany, never have formed the habit of closely observing nature, and should have lost half the pleasure of foreign travel.

It was fortunate that the summer of 1853 was spent in the Isle of Arran where we took a house at Invercloy, and I ranged the mountains all over the island — sometimes alone, but more frequently accompanying my father on his geological excursions. Continued in subsequent summers they led him ultimately to write a book upon the geology of the island, in which he described the general aspects of its scenery, and I added to this book a chapter containing a list of the less common herbaceous plants, trees, shrubs, and ferns, based partly on Dr. Landsborough's list, but adding a good many species and localities which my father and I had noted.

This was my first excursion into the fields of literature. These summers were the most enjoyable of all my youth, with constant open air life, long walks, and frequent climbs, bathing, and fishing, rowing or sailing round the picturesque coast. Arran had very few visitors then and there was no hotel at Invercloy. The accommodation everywhere was of the simplest. There were hardly any vehicles to hire, and when people wanted to have a long excursion with a picnic they took a cart which carried the elder ladies and the provisions and the children, while

[33]

the boys and girls walked. This took the whole day, but when the day was fine it never was too long. The last of these Arran summers was 1856, and we occupied a house at Glen Sherag. Not far from us were living a Glasgow family whom we knew slightly — that of Dr. David Brown, a Free Church Minister in Glasgow. His elder son was slightly known to me, having been at Glasgow College where he was my senior by a year. He had just gone to Oxford and obtained by competition a scholarship at Queen's. This interested me, for it was like a glimpse into an unknown land. He was an interesting young man of marked intellectual tastes and capacity. Never before had I or any of my intimates thought of going to an English University. It was not in our tradition. For all of us Glasgow University had been enough, and England seemed almost like a foreign country. However, the novelty of the idea fascinated me and roused a sort of spirit of adventure — absurd as it seems now to call such a thing an adventure. But in those days Scotland was far further from England than it is now, and I doubt if anyone in our circle knew the name of any Oxford luminary except Dr. Pusey, and his was not a name to attract. With Cambridge it was rather different, because my father knew personally some of the leading scientific men there, and we had all heard of the greatness of Trinity College and the fame of Whewell, its Master, whose Essay on the Plurality of Worlds had been widely read in religious circles in Scotland. I asked Alexander Brown a good deal about Oxford, and he promised to get information for me if I wanted it. He won a high place in the Indian Civil Service Examination (I think in the first

[34]

year they were held), and went out to India in or about 1860. From there he wrote to me several times, interested in the country and enjoying the prospect of work there; but after some months he contracted an illness which carried him off before the age of twenty-four. Had he lived, he would have risen high and done fine work.

CHAPTER III

OXFORD

The saints take pleasure in her stones.
The very dust to them is dear.

FRANCIS ROUS

IT was not altogether without misgiving that the young
Scottish Presbyterian contemplated the Oxford career
to which ambition and early intellectual success clearly
designed him. Oxford had, indeed, been aroused from
her dogmatic torpor first by the galaxy of brilliant and
devout spirits who in the forties had brought about that
revival of religious feeling and historic sentiment which
goes by the name of the Oxford Movement, and then by a
quickened sense of educational responsibility finding an
expression in the Executive Commission of 1854 which
abolished close Fellowships and in the establishment of
organised teaching in Natural Science. A scholarship at
Balliol or a Fellowship at Oriel were regarded as the
blue ribands of intellectual success in the open field of
ability. Mark Pattison was in learned retreat at Lincoln, Jowett was beginning to establish his unique ascend-
ency over young minds in Balliol, but though there was
plenty of intellectual ferment in the Oxford of the late
fifties and early sixties, the atmosphere of the place was
still profoundly Anglican. In theory, if not in strictest
practice, the University was still what Archbishop Laud

James Bryce as an Undergraduate

designed it to be, a training ground for the sons of the Established Church. If here and there a dissenter received an education in her Colleges, it was as it were on sufferance, since subscription to the Thirty-nine Articles was a condition precedent to the M.A. degree. As her bells rang their music into the air, as her organs pealed from the ancient chapels, as her doctors and masters thronged to St. Mary's to listen to the University sermon on Sunday morning, in these and a hundred other ways Oxford proclaimed herself to be not only the intellectual champion of the Established Church but the heiress of the Middle Ages, a miraculous survival from a distant past. A young Scottish Presbyterian with a strict father and a still stricter uncle, each of whom he held in warm affection and regard, might well feel qualms as he passed into this enchanting but alien region of humane learning and doctrinal peril.

A difficulty met the boy at the threshold of his career. In May 1857, when he was just nineteen, Bryce went up to Oxford to stand for a scholarship at Trinity, a college then consisting of twelve fellows and twelve scholars with some sixty commoners in residence and ruled over by Dr. Wilson, a rigid Conservative steeped in the recondite antiquities of his little society.

Here he was at once confronted with the awkward announcement that the scholars of Trinity were not only expected to attend Chapel but also to sign the Thirty-nine Articles. Attendance at Chapel, being part of the ordinary College routine, did not appear to Bryce to be objectionable, but rather than sign the Articles, which he would have regarded as treason to the faith of his ancestors, he would forego the scholarship and indeed the prospect of an Oxford career. For some days the dispute continued between the obscure Scottish student and the College dons, but Bryce, who was privately urged to stand firm by some of the younger fellows desirous of seeing the Tests removed, was unshakeable and in the end carried his point. Later on when the time came for taking the M. A. degree the tests still stood in his way. He became a B. A., then a D. C. L., but never an M. A. It is not surprising that some years after when the battle of the Tests was engaged Bryce was one of those who fought hardest for the liberation of his University from these ancient fetters on religious and intellectual freedom.

The letters written to his father and mother during the struggle with the Trinity Test are so characteristic that some extracts may be printed here.

June 1st, 1857.

I think it likely that if asked to sign at Trinity, I shall be told it is merely a form, but to me that would not make it less wrong to do it. From the moment I heard of it, I determined not for a thousand times the honour and the money to do it. Yet surely we are eccentric, for I feel certain there is no one else in Oxford or Cambridge, and very, very few in Scotland who feel as we do on this point.

By far the best thing in every way would be for me to get a Snell-Exhibition, they are equal to a scholarship of an inferior college, for them you need sign nothing, nor take any sacraments; they give you £150 a year for 5 years, and are in Balliol College, which is by far the best college in Oxford for tutors' reputation and liberal and improving society. In fact I do not know but what this last would be the greatest benefit of all.

Oxford

This being the first day of examination I went in at 9 o'clock, got a paper to turn into Latin Verse, and was getting on with it first rate when the old President of Trinity College entered the room. He called up all in turn, and pointing to the Killeague Certificate, enquired if I was a member of the Church of England, showing me a paper containing a declaration of conformity and adherence to her articles and liturgy. I at once answered that I was a Scotch Presbyterian, and the old man, who seemed rather a kindly sort of person, said that to sign this was necessary for those who wished to enter, but that he would not wish me to do it unless I fully agreed. I enquired if I could be elected without signing it, he answered "No," but said I might go on with the Examination, though he would only tell me in general terms where I should have stood in rank. I said that I should have no objection to attend Chapel (this is *not* a religious thing at all and I might safely attend it after refusing this), but that I was afraid I could hardly sign these, certainly not this way. I put the thing in the easiest way, hoping that he would allow me to compete like the rest, in which case I should probably have got a scholarship, the *kudos* therefrom resulting, and a chance of holding it without being forced to sign, or at all events, could have resigned it with dignity. Of course I never for a moment dreamt of signing even the Articles much less the Popish Liturgy. But as he gave no hope that I could be elected without signing, I determined to drop the Exam. at once, as useless trouble, and as I should seem defeated, whatever the result might really be.

. . . .

With regard to Chapel my own conscience says that it is no harm to attend it on weekdays; especially as I have shown that I will not conform, and as it is a college institution *not* a religious act — but if you disapprove of it I shall be ready to resign anything whatsoever, though I think it would be quite idle to do so, after having already refused to become a member or conform.

[39]

Under any circumstances it is considered necessary to attend it, and everyone does so, not more for a scholar than a commoner. I should not make any barter by doing so. On this point Uncle John's views, from whom I had a letter this morning, seem to me overstrained.

June 5th, 1857.

I may say that so far from making any concession or bating a shadow of principle by going into this College, I shall on the contrary win a triumph in being allowed to go in without signing this test, which they have hitherto by a private statute imposed on all commoners as much as scholars — and shall probably by getting in under exemption do much to break up this obnoxious statute altogether, for what use to keep it up when it has been broken? Whether they will permit it to be broken at all I still much doubt, but if they do, it will be a victory gained in the cause of liberty and dissent, and help to open up this College, so it will be a positive good. As for Chapel, no one thinks about it as having any business with religion, it is a matter of course — a part of College routine. No one compromises himself by attending in any way. It exists in every College in Oxford — Balliol of course — though the Principal is wrong in saying there are tests there — an attempt was made to set them up, but defeated. As for "religious instruction by a high-church functionary" — there is no such thing — for of course no one would call lectures on the Greek Testament high church religious instruction. And I do not know even whether they are considered compulsory, but I should certainly of my own accord be eager to attend them. You see, I am sure, what a false position we should be placed in by objecting to Chapel. The tutor said everything in the most liberal manner, said he would not think of forcing the sacraments on any account, said he and his fellows would try to bend the President, and would probably never have thought of Chapel — for as I tell you, it is in a different category, had not I mentioned it. If I withdraw now for fear of Chapel, I act the part not of a conscientious but of a wrongheaded person. I get no

[40]

kudos, not even the chance of refusing, but on the contrary, astonishment and contempt, not undeserved, I lose the opportunity of breaking down the old barriers of the College — and to crown all I either get the Snell — and go to Chapel — or get the Queen's Scholarship — and go to Chapel — or am beaten for both — go home — and subside into merited obscurity in the Ethic class.

Were there a shadow of principle in the case I feel certain that you would find me determined — as I think I have already sufficiently proved — but here conscience plainly tells me it is my duty to go in, if I can, and thereby do good to the cause of dissent and of conscience herself. If you do not now see it as I do, I need write no more. If I go in now — I go in utterly unfettered by test or bond of any kind, only doing ordinary College business like eating my dinner — and if reflection shall lead anyone, which it cannot, to think that wrong — I can retire with the reputation of ability — if not of wisdom.

June 7th, 1857.

This morning I received a summons to Mr. Pinder's rooms at twelve, and Mr. Meyrick, the Proctor and a Fellow of Trinity, seeing me coming out from hearing the University sermon invited me to his rooms at one.

Pinder talked over the thing, expressed himself in a most friendly and liberal way, said he admired my honest and conscientious course of conduct all through — said how very good and indeed brilliant some of my papers were, lamented the monarchical constitution of the College which put so much power into the hands of the President, whom he designated as honest, but terribly prejudiced and old school. He gave me clearly to understand that I should have been quite certain even of a high place among the five if it had not been for this — declared he would do all he could — advised me to let the President know that it was not the doctrine of the Articles but the meaning of the thing that I especially objected to, and took me to the President. The latter received me kindly, and asked me

about the thing. I told him how it stood, that you and Uncle
John had consented to Chapel, but that I could take no test,
though on the whole I would agree well enough with the doctrine. I showed how I had reason to feel particularly strongly
on the subject on account of Uncle John and Pater, and that
especially since I had refused at first it would be dishonourable
to do it now. He said the scholars took a certain part in the
chapel services, but did not state whether he would exempt me
or not, which I thought it best not inquire, for if he had said it
was necessary I might have felt doubtful precisely what to say
without deliberation. He then talked with me nearly an hour
on various topics and I left, he saying it would be decided tomorrow. What that decision may be of course no one can guess
— it will depend partly upon what support he finds among the
fellows.

June 8th, 1857

This morning I went to Queen's to stand for the scholarship.
After I had worked an hour the Vice-President of Trinity,
Haddan, the man I had seen before, came in and wanted to know
what I would do, deputed by the conclave then sitting. I consented to read the Bible in Chapel, knowing that Uncle John
would approve, also to say Grace after dinner in my turn. He
then asked me to promise general conformity while I was a
scholar though he explained that it was nothing more than this.
But this I entirely refused, though greatly tempted, for he said
the communion would be excepted, but I prayed for strength,
and was enabled to refuse. He then went away, and I thought I
had lost all my chance. But half an hour afterwards a messenger
came in and told me I had been elected scholar at the head of the
whole five out of the twenty seven competitors. I then went
to Trinity and was admitted, the President understanding I was
to comply with the regulations in attending Chapel &c., but not
taking the Sacrament, and he expressly said that if you or Uncle
John objected I might resign at once. However, I have pledged
myself to nothing whatever, but Chapel and grace, which Uncle

John and you approved. I am thankful I have not been led into anything wrong, anything unworthy of Pater, yourself and Uncle John.

So that awful Scotch fellow who outwrote everybody[1] was elected to a scholarship at Trinity at the head of the list.

June 12th, 1857.

I reserve details regarding the whole affair at Oxford. The place is very different from, and much more liberal and improving than, what I had expected.

But the aspect of the affair that pleases me best was that expressed by the Revd. Lewis Campbell, a Fellow of Queen's, and an old Snell man, when he called it "the triumph of liberalism in Oxford." They will of course never venture to put this test in Trinity again when it has once been broken through, and the affair has been a good deal talked of in Oxford, and produced, I hope, rather a good effect altogether."

The Oxford of that day was free of many of the unsightly accretions which have since gathered round the magic circle of its ancient Colleges. To imagine Oxford as it was in the early sixties we must first think away the populous and comfortable suburbs which now spread an envelope of commonness round the grey heart of the ancient city. We must think away the obtruding noises of car and tram and bus. We must imagine open fields north of St. Giles and an Iffley Road undefaced by villa residences, a new Taylorian Museum not yet confronted by the gaunt pretensions of the Randolph, and an air of old-world piety, persisting even in the names of the principal inns of the city, the Mitre, the Angel, and the Star. As for the lesser hostelries, there was plenty of history in

[1] So George Ramsay (later Professor of Latin at Glasgow University) described him to his brother.

[43]

the very signs, still happily preserved of the Roebuck, the Cape of Good Hope, and, until the late War, of the King of Prussia; but though the railway had come to Oxford, breaking down its earlier seclusion, the life of the University was still very much centred upon itself. The married dons were few; the old order of celibate fellows still constituted the majority of the teaching body, and many a young graduate had seen in Dr. Routh, not long dead, a strange link with a distant past, for the venerable President of Magdalen wore a wig and was thirty years of age in the year of Dr. Johnson's death.

At that time the University consisted of no more than twelve hundred undergraduates, all living within the College walls and many preparing themselves by a judicious admixture of sport and study for the pleasant ease of a country parsonage. Neither football nor hockey had yet been introduced, but rowing and cricket were eagerly pursued and since the proportion of undergraduates drawn from the land-holding class was greater than it now is, the streets of Oxford would resound during the hunting season with the cheerful clatter of hacks and hunters carrying lively young men into the country for a scamper over the grass fields of the South Oxfordshire and the Bicester or the favourite stone walls of the Heythrop Hunt.

The distinction between scholars and commoners was perhaps more clearly marked than it is now, for in general the scholars had their own table in Hall and were apt to keep to themselves so that every College tended to divide itself into two groups, one a small company of serious students, the other a much larger body of young men who came up to the University chiefly for social reasons and were far more concerned with riding, rowing, and cricket than with the intellectual athletics of the place. In Trinity the cleft was deep, the scholars being regarded as a particularly steady and serious group of young men while the commoners were light-hearted and fond of sport. Bryce was a Trinity scholar and in addition a member of the intellectual Balliol set. For this reason, though his reputation for knowledge and ability was widely spread through the University, he had not a very large or diversified circle of acquaintance in the undergraduate world.

Once installed in Trinity, a college which he continued to hold in great affection, Bryce soon made his mark as an undergraduate of singular force and width of knowledge. It is true that he took little part in the athletic sports of his contemporaries, which at that time occupied a far smaller share of attention than is now the case. Indeed he was always of opinion that the over-development of athletics at school, by leading boys to neglect natural history and the cultivation of their powers of observation out of doors had inflicted a real injury on education.

He was not then athletic in the conventional meaning of that term; but he had all the best qualities of the athletic temperament and a native vigour of mind and body which could not fail to impress his coevals.

At this time he was of fresh complexion with very thick dark brown hair falling low over the forehead; the eyes beautiful and deep-set of the real Celtic blue, the expression when at rest often grave and stern, but full of mobility and animation in conversation. In stature he was of medium height, in frame strong and wiry with well-knit muscles and of great physical activity. Thus although he took no part in games, he rowed on the river, exercised in the gymnasium, drilled as a volunteer when volunteering became the fashion, was a good swimmer and an indefatigable bather and walked all over the surrounding country. In the vacations climbing, sailing, and fishing were added to the category of outdoor amusements which were none the less heartily enjoyed because they were usually accompanied by a strong spice of scientific curiosity about tides and currents, flora and fauna, the geological formation of rocks, and the behaviour of glaciers.

A shower of academic honours descended on him. In view of his excellent classical training in Glasgow it was inevitable that he should obtain a First Class in Classical Moderations and no matter for surprise that he should also succeed in winning the Gaisford Prize for Greek Prose with an Essay on the Plague of London. What is remarkable is that in one and the same year 1861 he should have been "distinctly the best" of the two First Classes in Greats and publicly complimented by the examiners, "a very signal and unusual honour," that he should have won the Gaisford Greek Verse Prize with a graceful Theocritean exercise on the May Queen ("did it in haste in the Isle of Wight while busy with Greats") been placed in the First Class in the School of Law and Modern History and that a few days afterwards he should have gained the Vinerian Scholarship in Law. For the last of these ordeals he was unable to make any special preparation. "History Viva was on Monday. The Vinerian Examination occupied

Wednesday and Thursday. Of course I had no opportunity of making any preparation for it." And these successes are the more remarkable when we consider that over and above the sum of knowledge which they represent the scholar of Trinity was widely informed in more than one branch of Natural Science.[1]

These academic trophies were not secured without hard work. We read in his letters home of a working day of ten hours in preparation for Greats and of trouble from headaches; but hard worker though he was there was nothing of the uncompanionable recluse about Bryce. He made friends easily and had a genius for keeping his friendships alive. Indeed, in after life he would often say that one of the principal advantages of Oxford was not the lectures, still less the examinations, but the opportunity which the University afforded to young men of making life-long friendships.

Albert Dicey, three years his senior and for a short period his tutor, was a close friend never at any time divided from him even during the sharpest political controversies of later life.[2] Other friends and contemporaries were Henry Nettleship, Kenelm Digby, T. H. Green, Arthur Butler, T. H. Holland, George Brodrick, Aeneas Mackay, and slightly junior in University standing Courtenay Ilbert, and Walter Pater. Among his seniors Jowett, E. A. Freeman, Goldwin Smith, Edwin Palmer, Mark Pattison, and Matthew Arnold stood towards him in varying degrees of friendly

[1] Bryce attended, for instance, Sir Benjamin Brodie's lectures in Chemistry while reading for his degree.

[2] Dicey was elected Fellow of Trinity in 1860, Robinson Ellis, the famous Latinist in 1858.

intimacy. But indeed it would be tedious to note the well-known Oxford men with whom Bryce was then or afterwards on terms of easy and cordial companionship. The harder task would be to enumerate the men of ability who were repelled by him or to whom he was not always the best and simplest of good fellows.

At that time the great orator of the Oxford Union was Albert Dicey. Bryce was less conspicuous and, indeed, only seems to have spoken twice but nevertheless became in succession Librarian and President (1862). He also became a member in November 1857 of a small undergraduate Essay Society which by reason of the brilliant achievement of its members has attained some fame in the annals of Oxford. The original members of the Old Mortality Society founded by John Nichol of Balliol were Albert Venn Dicey, John Nichol, Algernon S. Grenfell, Algernon C. Swinburne, George Rankine Luke, all of Balliol, and George Birkbeck Hill of Lincoln.[1] The Society

[1] Subsequent additions were:

1857	Broughton R.,	Balliol.	1861	Latham, F. A. B.,	New College.
	Wright, R. S.,	Balliol.		Lee-Warner, J.,	Trinity.
	Bryce, J.,	Trinity.		Robinson, A.,	University.
1858	Green, T. H.,	Balliol.		Shadwell, C. L.,	Christ Church.
	Holland, T. E.,	Magdalen.		Boyle, E. C.,	Trinity.
	Brown, A.,	Queen's.		Berkley, W.,	Brasenose.
1859	Mackay, A. E.,	University.		Giffard, H. A.,	Corpus.
1860	Hook, J. W.,	Queen's.		Magrath, R. R.,	Oriel.
	Essex, W.,	St. Johns.	1862	Thompson, H. L.,	Christ Church.
	Nettleship, H.,	Corpus.		Bywater, J.,	Queen's.
	Paine, J. F.,	Magdalen.		Pater, W.,	Queen's.
				Browne, H.,	Jesus.
				Clive, R. R.,	Balliol.
				Wordsworth, J.,	New College.
				Brooke, S. R.,	Corpus.
				Wallace, W.,	Balliol.
				Cassel, E.,	Balliol.

met on Saturday evenings in the rooms of its members, and the President for the evening read either select passages in English prose or an original essay, after which a discussion would be opened. The subjects chosen by Bryce were indicative of four principal interests which remained with him to the end: History, scenery, Greek letters, and education. They were Gibbons' account of the origin of Monasticism and Asceticism, Ruskin's views on the appreciation of Landscape in Greek poetry and National Education, "with illustrative reference to the educational condition of Scotland and Ireland." At the Union it is interesting to observe that he spoke (Feb. 6, 1862) in opposition to a motion "That while the recognition of the Southern States will probably be ere long inevitable, the time for such recognition has not yet arrived." It was his first public appearance on an American question.

During Bryce's undergraduate days a great revival of historical studies was in progress. The Regius Chair of Modern History was held by Goldwin Smith, the most brilliant of historical publicists, who lectured in the Hall of University College, and undergraduates flocked to the Sheldonian to enjoy the dazzling eloquence of Arthur Stanley who until he was promoted to the deanery of Westminster in 1863 held the Chair of Ecclesiastical History. Bryce sat at the feet of both professors and was soon admitted to the circle of their friends. In a charming but discriminating tribute to Dean Stanley he records the impression made upon his mind by Stanley's historical qualities, "his sense of the unity of history; of the permanently valuable truths which history has to teach, his poet's eye for human character, his admirable pictures of historical scenes" as well as the impersonal delivery which made his teaching and preaching memorable to those who heard it. A bust of Stanley became a treasured possession and was a favourite ornament of his study in later life.

The year which witnessed Bryce's birth was also the natal year of John Morley and George Trevelyan, each destined to win high distinction in the connected fields of Liberal politics and humane letters. Trevelyan went up to Cambridge, and only after taking his degree was adopted "into the joyous and intimate circle" of his Oxford contemporaries and at a time "when Oxford thought and hope were the brightest mediums that perhaps ever existed." Morley was Bryce's contemporary at Oxford but he was a poor man, living a retired life in a small College, and though it would seem that he made Bryce's acquaintance as an undergraduate, it was only under the stress of political association in later life, that the two men became intimate with one another. To the young Cambridge observer Bryce appeared to tower above the brilliant group of Oxford Bachelors of Arts who were then employing the keen edge of their vigorous intellects on the problems of life and mind. "When I think," writes Sir George Trevelyan, "of what sort of men his set were — R. S. Wright, William Sidgwick, Lyulph Stanley and that he stood out above them all it was a measure of what he was, and of the promise he then gave."

Two events, one in the scientific, and one in the political sphere created a great stir among the intellectual undergraduates of Bryce's generation. The first of these was the appearance of Darwin's "Origin of Species," which

long afterwards Bryce described to an American audience
as one of the most exciting intellectual influences of his
young manhood. No less exhilarating and perturbing,
though in quite a different category, were the nationalist
movements against the Austrian Empire. Here was
everything calculated to appeal to the ardent and forward-
reaching mind, romance, adventure, Liberalism, golden
aspirations for the future mingled with historic memories
of a distant past. To learn Italian from Aurelio Saffi, the
poetic exile, became part of the ritual of cultured Liberalism in Oxford and an initiation into the spirit of the
Risorgimento. Bryce went further in his Italian enthusiasm and was only deterred from joining Garibaldi as a
volunteer by learning from his tutor that military service
in a foreign country would be regarded as incompatible
with a Trinity scholarship. Nor were his interests confined to Italy. As a boy he had heard Kossuth speak in
Scotland and long afterwards in the autumn of 1889 when
he happened to be passing through Turin, he sought out
the veteran liberator of Hungary and expressed to him the
sympathy of a faithful admirer.

The Easter holiday before Greats was spent at Freshwater in the Isle of Wight with a small reading party, and
here Bryce had the good fortune to make the acquaintance
of Tennyson. The letter to his mother describing his
visit to Farringford gives a good impression of his descriptive powers as an undergraduate.

Cliffe Hall, Freshwater, Isle of Wight,
April 10th, 1861.
"I wish I could afford to sit down and give you a detailed
description of Tennyson's appearance, conversation and sur-

roundings — but with such time as I can spare that is impossible, so I must be contented to notice a few points only, and reserve the rest for chatting over when I see you. You may suppose how astonished I was at finding the invitation waiting me, not a little alarmed, too, at the idea of appearing alone before him, Mrs. Tennyson and Jowett all at once; so I dressed in Boyle's black suit, which, strange as it may seem, fitted me all right, and started off at 8 P.M. on Monday in no slight trepidation. Going in Jowett and Mrs. T. were at tea in the drawing room, and he introduced me to her. She was dressed in white, with a loose scarf, almost like a veil, thrown round her shoulders, was rather tall, pale, with a delicate refined air, a slow and deliberate way of speaking, — smiling gracefully — and in a subdued tone. She seemed not strong, and though she might certainly have been once a beauty could not be called so now. The white dress gave a very strange effect. She and Jowett seemed great friends; we talked about the island, she asking how long we had been here, and mentioning that she had heard of my being here from Franklin Lushington — our Lushington's brother, who seemed to have been with them. In about half an hour's time the door opened and Tennyson came up to the table and shook hands, then went round to the tea tray which Mrs. Tennyson left, seated himself and drank tea out of a larger cup, using both cream and sugar, fashion nothwithstanding. (Are not these details in the best American penny-a-liner style? If they are Jenkinsesque they at least show how sharply I felt obliged to use my eyes.) The Laureate is generally much like his pictures, tall and erect, with a coat buttoned tight on his breast, long, though not very thick, black hair, black beard and mustache, a fine high symmetrical round head, not very long or massive, but graceful, commanding, well-set, nose somewhat aquiline, contour of the face bold and striking. He is extremely short sighted and wears spectacles, seldom opening his eyes fully. He has little colour, cheeks rather sunken and dark; altogether he looked more withered than one would have expected, though perfectly vigorous. He first began talking about some dispute about a road he has got to make, and a disputed right of way at the little watering place of Freshwater Gate just below his house, where he bought some ground because houses were being built on it which intercepted his superb view along the south coast of the island as far as St. Catherine's Down at its S. extremity, near Ventnor. He went on in a sort of grumbling growl about these things for a while, talking all about money, per cent, lawyers, and so on, — Mrs. Tennyson trying to turn him off by giving different pieces of news which he half in fun rejected. "News, I hate news!" "Major So and so is come to the fort," said she, "I have had enough of Colonels and Majors," etc. etc. etc. At last after some talk with Jowett he came round to other subjects, talked a little about Edmund Lushington and Glasgow, asked some questions about Glasgow College, and what it cost to live there, and compared it to Oxford; began to talk about Scotland, denounced Wallace on the strength of a book he had just read defending Edward I., and which he made me take the loan of, and ran on in an exaggerating amusing way, half abusing Scotland for being discontented, half exalting the cuteness and success of the lowland Scotch everywhere — directing all this against me. Jowett and I laughed incessantly, occasionally attempting a little defence, and he ran on in this way, still in a kind of interruptedly growling tone, seldom bringing out his voice fully, always with great force of emphasis and expression.

Then he said something about America, said he had been offered £3000 and his expenses paid to go over and read there; denounced the slaveholders and thought the North would be all the better for the separation, imitated the Yankee twang very amusingly. Then he spoke of Mr. Sumner, and from a speech of his in which he had quoted Robert Pollok, passed to speak of Pollok — whom he denied to be a poet, though he and Jowett agreed in putting him far above Tupper, of whom he spoke scornfully rather, and Robert Montgomery. He then described Robert Montgomery or "Bab" as he called him. It appeared he had never read Macaulay's article. He made me repeat to him five or six times two of the most glaring lines which Macaulay cuts up there, and commented on them very amusingly. After this various topics were touched on; he praised Pope's Homer, censured Matthew Arnold's translations of Homer into English hexameters, maintaining that Homer ought to be and could be rendered into English blank verse line for line. He spoke of the sea at the Isle of Wight as petty and wretched, described the Great Atlantic waves at Valentia Island and the sea in Cornwall, and so on; talked about transplanting trees and described how a machine might be made to raise the largest tree by steam, imitating grotesquely the noise it would make in lifting the roots, till we all burst out laughing.

I came away about 10.40 P.M., of course immensely delighted at such a piece of good fortune, and grateful beyond measure to you and Papa for having procured it for me. Boyle will probably have a chance of seeing Tennyson again as he knows Bradley well, but I was greatly vexed that Mackay did not also see the lion of the place. Tomorrow I suppose that I shall have to make a call, but he is not himself likely to see visitors, so probably it will amount to leaving a card."

Having obtained his degree Bryce stayed up in Oxford for a time, taking pupils and reading widely in law and history. His primary ambition was to win a Fellowship, but where? At Lincoln a Fellow would be required to sign the Thirty-nine Articles. At Balliol, "a society more pleasant than most," the test was not imposed but then no Fellowship would be available for a year. At Queen's a Fellow was not necessarily required to proceed to the M. A. degree. Then there was Oriel, where a Fellowship was not only worth £280 or so but retained much of its former glamour and would moreover be offered to competition in April 1862. "Oriel is not a pleasant College to reside at — its head is specially disagreeable and would doubtless vote against me on the score of the Articles. However he is always outvoted anyway and probably could do me very little harm afterwards." Eventually, however, largely it would appear through the good offices of S. W. Wayte, a Fellow of Trinity, Oriel was decided on. A Fellowship here would be compatible either with an academic career in Oxford or with legal work in London, alternatives between which it would appear that his mind for a time hovered, always inclining, when the matter was seriously reflected on, to the more active career.

Oxford,
March 23rd, 1862.

I have often felt a sort of wish to stay here instead of going up to London, but it has always remained vague. There is a great deal of useful work to be done here and great need of someone with ideas on educational subjects to devote himself to it; especially the field of University Reform wants Labourers. Thus I have often thought that it would perhaps be more in the way of duty to stay here than to pursue a phantom of ambition; which I feel to be unsubstantial — at the bar or elsewhere in active life. Two main reasons however have always deterred me, the one that not being a member of the Church of England, and feeling little sympathy with some of her manifestations — one's opportunities of usefulness would be greatly marred; it would be — at least for me — difficult to do tutorial work as well as if I was on common ground in this respect with one's pupils. Though no doubt — as Nettleship has often urged to me — the community of feeling which many, I fear most tutors have — is on these grounds, slender — so little interest do they show at all; so that even thus one might be more useful than most are now. But next — I feel sure that one's vigour for Oxford work would probably be greatly impaired after forty — if one lived so long, while one's interest in the work — especially in teaching passmen, would probably languish long before that

— and after that there is no other field of life open to one. Most men here indeed then resort, if they have not before resorted, either to a school mastership — in which profession no one can rise very high without becoming an English clergyman — or to the Church itself; in the first instance they take a parish somewhere. This of course is a course I could never adopt — and thus I cannot see what there would be open to me at that age, except some precarious subsistence by literature or the very slender chance of a Scotch situation.

I go into all this now, because several people have suggested to me to go in at Ch. Ch. to fill Luke's place — which from the possible candidates I ought certainly to have a fair prospect of getting. Now if I had meant or did mean to stay up here, no duty could call so loudly as that to strive — wretchedly indeed — to carry on the work he began there — to try to keep up the memory of so noble an example. But having previously decided not to stay here — I have answered that I could not do so. It is about this that I want your opinion — do you not think that on the whole I am right in declining such a post? . . .

Meanwhile pending the Fellowship examination at Oriel he was taking his first pupils.

I send enclosed, he writes to his father on April 1st, the first fruits of my spear and my bow, which the four captives of this term have rendered up to me. As the first money I have ever made by my own toil, I want you to take it; either to go to the Continent with or do what else you think best. But indeed it is not mine at all, for not only that I can draw the bow in any way is owing to you who fitted my hands to it; and both I and all I may ever have are and ought to and I hope, if I be guided aright always will be, yours and not mine.

The Oriel Fellowship was a formidable ordeal in more ways than one. The competition attracted the ablest men in the University but over and above the competition there was the menacing shadow of a religious test. A Fellow of Oriel could, so averred Provost Hawkins, a very stout defender of all the orthodoxies, be ejected from the College who did not take the sacraments — a condition, which, if insisted on, would have been fatal to Bryce. But in Wayte Bryce had a friend at court, and any reluctance which the old Provost may have felt to the admission of a Presbyterian was by Wayte's good offices smoothed away before the end of the examination. On the morning of April 25th, the glad news was brought to him of his election to the Fellowship.[1] His answer to the paternal congratulations is worth printing.

Oxford,
May 15th, 1862

You may understand how much pleasure your letter of Saturday last gave me, and though these anniversaries are more sobering than joyous, and though your letter was far beyond anything I have deserved, surely nothing has a right to give me such true and deep pleasure as to have been the means of giving happiness to you and Mamma, and, of showing some result from the so constant care and cultivation you gave my mind when most boys have none at all.

The fellows of Oriel in residence are not at all a remarkable set of men — the fame of the body rests much more on its non-residents — and more I think on previous ones than on the present generation. As far as influences go — religious or political or social — I am likely to be far less in the way of any influence of any kind than at Trinity and in the society of one's friends generally.

Then followed a period of college teaching.

I have begun now to give a lecture in the college to seven men who come thrice a week and seem pleasant fellows. In one

[1] Lyulph Stanley, afterwards Lord Sheffield, came second.

[57]

way it is more agreeable than individual coaching, as you can ask questions of one man after another and so relieve yourself for a moment. There is too a certain sense of dignity about it, though this I fear wears off before long. To be an oracle for an hour to any seven of one's fellow creatures has something flattering about it. The most dolorous point about Oxford to any one who should live long here would be, I think, the absence of motion and progress. Not that life is dull, it is much more animated and varied, though of course by small incidents, than almost anywhere else, but there seems to be a constant cycle of events always repeating themselves, little sensation of growth or improvement either in the individual mind or the institution as a whole. However it is celestial compared to what London will be.

The absence of "motion" and "progress" of which Bryce complained in Oxford was compensated in his case by regular doses of motion and progress during the vacations. Thus in 1860 he went on a reading party with three English and two Scottish friends to Glengariff and Killarney, finding the country in "a wretched state of poverty and general backwardness but pretty quiet," and "all ideas of insurrection gone underground or to America." Then there was walking and fishing in the hilly regions of Scotland and Wales, a tour in Switzerland, and finally in the summer of 1863 an excursion to Heidelberg where Bryce had resolved to pass a semester studying law under Von Vangerow and perfecting himself in the knowledge of the German language. Here Bryce's party, which consisted of Henry Nettleship, Aeneas Mackay, and himself, fell in with two other Oxford reading parties, one led by Albert Dicey and the other by T. H. Green. It may be readily imagined how pleasantly the summer must have run on for this brilliant group of young Oxford men gathered together by the rushing waters of the Neckar in one of the loveliest of German towns at a time when all German things were held in high honour in England and when every young Englishman with intellectual ambitions made it part of his duty to learn at first hand from the country of Goethe and Schiller, of Kant and Hegel, of Waitz and Dahlmann and Döllinger.

For Bryce this semester at Heidelberg led to the formation not only of many personal friendships among Germans but also to a genuine affection and admiration for the great qualities of the German people which remained unimpaired until the shock of the Great War. More particularly did he admire the work of the eminent professors under whom he studied and from whom he obtained a far wider conspectus of the field of jurisprudence than was open to young Englishmen who were proposing to embrace a legal career. Of his own character and prospects at this period of his life his friend Dicey has left the following shrewd estimate.

"Bryce is the life of our party. The real strength of his character lies, I think, in the happy combination of various qualities, each of which may be found separately as fully developed in other persons. Most successful at the University, he does not seem to possess extraordinary, so much as admirably balanced, talents. His papers, of which I have seen many, were not perhaps strikingly original, but they were always good and clear, and what was required for the occasion. He has, I fancy, great capacity for development. His most agreeable, and I truly believe his most valuable quality is his childlike "life" and go. His kindness and friendship is beyond praise. He stirs us all up, rushes about like a shepherd's dog, collects his friends, makes us meet, leads us into plans and adventures, and keeps everything going. His life will, I predict, be one of great and deserved success. Most of the Oxford men of ability are deficient in spirits. Bryce, who has talents and spirits, will go much further than many of his contemporaries, even though as able as himself. No one could do otherwise than rejoice should my prediction be verified. His success has never for a moment puffed him up. He has a rare amount of honesty as shown by his conduct at Oriel, and perhaps an even rarer affectionateness and kindliness of disposition. A person must be jaundiced who can grudge him good fortune. *Sit felix.*[1]

[1] A. V. Dicey by R. S. Rait.

CHAPTER IV

THE HOLY ROMAN EMPIRE

Una est sola respublica totius populi Christiani, ergo de nec-
essitate erit et unus solus princeps et rex illius reipublicæ.

ENGLEBERT: *De Ortu, Progressu et
Fine Imperii Romani.*

BAR AND OXFORD

1862–5

THE admirable balance of faculties which Dicey had noticed in his young companion at Heidelberg was in itself prohibitive of a cloistered life among books. Bryce was a man of a temperament far too active and stirring to be content with a College existence even in Oxford where the horizons were opening out and a fresh air of scientific curiosity was already disturbing the old and traditional routine of studies. Perfect health, high spirits, untiring energy, a love of travel and adventure combined with a keen interest in liberal causes to indicate an active career. The Fellowship at Oriel, aided by the emoluments to be derived from teaching, examining, and writing for the papers, made it possible for him to enter for the bar, then as now the easiest avenue into political life for a young man of scanty means and high ambition. The bar however was an instrument rather than an end. Though in course of time Bryce obtained a respectable

[61]

junior practice and was engaged in some important commercial cases, his was not the nature out of which great practising barristers are made. His interests were too wide, his curiosity too spacious, his habit of mind too historical to be compatible with the formation of that kind of judgment, slow, sure, schooled in subtle minutiæ and saturated with the atmosphere of the Courts which is essential to the higher forms of success in the legal profession.

"Here at least," he writes from London, "Oxford training seems to clog me as much as it helps. It is all very well to talk of high education and very true in its way. But the man with an attorney's intellect is the man for the Bar of England while the law remains as it is."

Bryce began to eat dinners in Lincoln's Inn in the spring of 1862, and on being called to the bar in 1867 worked in the Chambers of John Holker, soon to become in succession a Q. C., leader of the Northern Circuit, Attorney General and a Judge of the Supreme Court. Of Holker, a stalwart specimen of Lancashire shrewdness and solidity, Bryce always held the highest opinion, and it was probably through the influence of his master in the law that Bryce joined the Northern Circuit. The first brief came in 1868 and was soon followed by others, but it may be suspected that the visits to Spain and Portugal which arose out of his practice were of more interest to him than the precedents upon which his clients relied to win their case. It is difficult to play many rôles to perfection at the same time, and in Bryce the traveller, jurist and historian were always more prominent than the practising lawyer.

The Holy Roman Empire

At the opening of 1864 the young Scot, sensitive, somewhat reserved, feeling himself as it were in the capital of a foreign country in spite of all his Oxford friendships, was established in London, "the best place in the world," as he explained, "for anyone to learn his own insignificance." At first one week was very much like another.

"Streaming down Oxford Street, about 11 every morning to the Inn; then books, very dreary books it must be said, most of them interminable records of minute facts through which it is not easy to trace the course of a consistent and clarifying principle till 1.30; then lunch often in some man's company and dropping about a little, then more books till 5.30; then dinner in the hall of Lincoln's Inn, disagreeable in this that one rises from table to walk two miles through narrow dirty streets homewards."

A brilliant young Oxford man with a Fellowship behind him does not easily rust in London and Bryce soon found his way into the intellectual world of the capital. He attended Dean Stanley's Saturday evenings at Westminster where he met George Grote and the great Whewell and other stars in the intellectual and social firmament, and noted the distant and detached manners of the fine ladies when confronted with insignificant youths who could not possibly form part of their permanent world.

In his letters there is no trace of bitterness, only a little amusement, the amusement of a naturalist collecting a quaint specimen of a certain novelty. London, he explains, enables him to understand for the first time Thackeray's Newcomes.

It must have been at this period of his life that Bryce first met Robert Reid of Balliol who afterwards became

Lord Loreburn. The two young men were staying for a week-end at Trinity with their common friend R. W. Raper. As the party drew to its close each of the guests separately confided to Raper his opinion of the other. "I like your friend Reid," said Bryce, "but he won't go far, he is much too narrow." "Bryce is a good fellow," said Reid, "but I don't expect a great career for him, he is far too versatile." Neither narrowness nor versatility proved to be the serious obstacles which were anticipated.

Meanwhile the young law student had suddenly leapt into fame as the author of a contribution to historical literature which, on its first appearance was proclaimed as a masterpiece and has won an enduring place as a text-book on the subject of which it treats. *The Holy Roman Empire* was the winning essay in the competition for the Arnold Prize in 1862 and was first published "greatly changed and enlarged" in 1864, so much changed that it was said of it by Freeman, "Mr. Bryce's book has been written since it gained the historical prize at Oxford."

The thin volume of a hundred and seventy-six pages has been progressively expanded in subsequent editions. New chapters have been added, old chapters have been broken up and enlarged, suggestions from learned friends at home and abroad have been received and deftly woven into the text: but all this subsequent elaboration, while it has opened out new vistas into the past and contributed copiously to the illustration of the imperial idea through the ages has not altered the essential message of the *editio princeps*, which was to exhibit what the mediæval conception of the Empire really was, and "the strange

but very human process by which religion and ethical
sentiment came to attach itself to an institution which
was associated in the mind of antiquity with the idea of
material power and military conquest."

In a review of the book Freeman described it as the first
complete and connected view of the Mediæval Empire
which had ever been given to English readers. He alluded
to the depth of thought, the thoroughness of research,
the familiarity with a whole learning of a very recondite
kind which stood revealed in every page of the volume.
"Mr. Bryce's essay," he continued, "may seem ephemeral
in form, but it is not ephemeral in substance. He has in
truth by a single youthful effort placed himself on a level
with men who have given their lives to historical study."

Enthusiastic and generous as is this estimate, no student
of history will regard it as overdrawn. For a young man
of twenty-six the book is a wonderful feat of learning and
intellectual force. Original in the sense in which that
adjective may denote the discovery of historical truths
previously undiscerned the book was not. The "vulgar
creed" as Freeman termed it, that the Roman Empire
had come to an end in 476 A.D. had already been dispelled
by Palgrave and Finlay for English readers, while Döllinger with immense learning had brought out in two admirable addresses the true significance of the coronation of
Charles the Great.[1] Nor was the book entirely free from

[1] Döllinger's two addresses (Das Kaiserthum Karls des Grossen und seiner
Nachfolger) were delivered before the Royal Bavarian Academy in 1862 and
published in the *Munchner Historisches Jahrbuch* in 1865. Later editions of the
Holy Roman Empire bear numerous traces of indebtedness to these masterly
papers which have been well rendered into English by Miss Warre (*Döllinger's
Historical Addresses* 1894).

slips. The *Privilegium Austriacum*, for instance (forged
by an Austrian Archduke in the fourteenth century), was
quoted as a genuine document of Frederick I. Such
blemishes, however, do not seriously detract from the
value of the *Holy Roman Empire*. In essentials the
picture is true. Even if the writer had galloped through
the great collections, his quick eye had noted the significant facts. Moreover the essay differed from previous
treatises on the subject in two particulars. It was comprehensive and it was a work of art.

The *chiaroscuro* of the book, the skill with which the
salient facts and epochs were made to stand out was, as
Charles Kingsley observed, greatly to be admired. For
the first time the idea of the Empire, as an active agency
in the lives of generations of men, was made thoroughly
intelligible to the general public through the imagination
of a glowing mind served but not controlled by historical
learning. For many students in many lands the book has
been a lamp irradiating the central course of mediæval
history. And when one considers how early Bryce was in
the field and how little had been done (outside the work
of Von Savigny) to explain the political and social theories
of the Middle Ages, his achievement is the more remarkable. It may be added that two of the finest chapters in
the later editions, the seventh on the Theory of the
Mediæval Empire and the fifteenth on the Empire as an
International Power are to be found in the *Editio Princeps*.[1]

What is specially remarkable as a sign of historical
power is the gift of sound generalisation based upon a

[1] For some observations in the preceding paragraphs I am indebted to my
friend Dr. Ernest Barker, Principal of King's College, London, who has allowed
me to draw upon his rich store of mediæval learning.

wide study of facts. Such a gift was made abundantly evident in the work of the young Oxford graduate. Here is one example:

"The Middle Ages were essentially unpolitical. Ideas as familiar to the commonwealths of antiquity as to ourselves, ideas of the common good as the object of the State, of the rights of the people, of the merits of different forms of government, were to them, though sometimes carried out in fact, in their speculative form unknown, perhaps incomprehensible. Feudalism was the one great institution to which those times gave birth, and feudalism was a social and legal system, only indirectly and by consequence a political one. Yet the human mind, so far from being idle, was in certain directions never more active; nor was it possible for it to remain without general conceptions regarding the relations of men to each other in this world. Such conceptions were neither made an expression of the actual present condition of things nor drawn from an induction of the past; they were partly inherited from the system that had preceded, partly evolved from the principles of that metaphysical theology which was ripening into scholasticism. Now the two great ideas which expiring antiquity bequeathed to the ages which followed were those of a World Monarchy and a World Religion."

The historical grasp exhibited in such a passage as this is truly amazing when we remember the age of the author and the large share of his mental activities which had been consumed by the literary study of the classical authors and in the gratification of his bent for natural science. It is not however only to its power of generalisation, or its lucidity of arrangement or its wealth of ideas that the *Holy Roman Empire* owes its wide circle of readers. Goethe once said that the value of history consists in the enthusiasm which it excites, and the *Holy*

Roman Empire is charged with the romantic sentiment which excites enthusiasm. Of this, the eloquent account of the impression left on the German mind by the career of Barbarossa may be taken as an example:

"To the south-west of the green plain that girdles the rock of Saltzburg, the gigantic mass of the Untersberg frowns over the road which winds up a long defile to the glen and lake of Berchtesgaden. There, far up among its limestone crags, in a spot scarcely accessible to human foot, the peasants of the valley point out to the traveller the black mouth of a cavern, and tell him that within Barbarossa lies amid his knights in an enchanted sleep, waiting the hour when the ravens shall cease to hover round the peak and the pear tree blossom in the Valley, to descend with the Crusaders and bring back to Germany the Golden age of peace and strength and unity. Often in the evil days that followed the fall of Frederick's house, often when tyranny seemed unendurable and anarchy endless, men thought on that cavern, and sighed for the day when the long sleep of the just Emperor should be broken, and his shield should be hung aloft once more in the camp's midst, a sign of help to the poor and oppressed."

A passage like this could not have been written by a man who was out of sympathy with the German spirit. Now the first edition of the Arnold Essay was published while it could be truthfully said of the Germans that they were "a peaceful people — submissive to paternal government, and given to the quiet enjoyment of art, music, and meditation, for if the Holy Roman Empire had brought political weakness there was," so argued the historian, "a bright side to German disunion."

"To the variety which so many small governments have produced may be partly attributed the breadth of development in German thought and literature, by virtue of which it transcends the French hardly less than the Greek surpassed the Roman. Paris no doubt is great, but a country may lose as well as gain by the predominance of a single city; and Germany need not mourn that she above many modern states has not and never has had a capital."

Six years after these words were first published the old Germany of the poets and dreamers which Bryce admired passed away. The quiet enjoyments of art, music, and meditation were replaced by Prussian ideals of blood and iron. The grandiose ostentation of Berlin overshadowed the tranquil beauties of Weimar; and it is difficult to believe that had the *Holy Roman Empire* been written after Sédan, it would not have lost some of the affectionate glow with which it is warmed. In another respect also the *Holy Roman Empire* bears clear traces of the particular point of time at which it was given to the world. The merits of the old Empire had recently been the subject of a brisk discussion among several German professors of history, the spokesmen of the Austrian or Roman Catholic party claiming for the Hapsburg Monarch the honour of being the legitimate representative of the mediæval Empire, while North Germans like Von Sybel represented the Empire as the source from which all the political evils of Germany flowed.[1]

Bryce, like his friend Freeman, was violently opposed to the Austrian Empire as an unnatural tyranny, based upon the oppression of non-German races. "The Ger-

---

[1] R. Pauli, whose acquaintance Bryce had made in the Tyrol in 1863 in a letter acknowledging a copy of the first edition of the *Holy Roman Empire* (Nov. 30, 1864) describes it as a "very fair and very intellectual review of a very intricate and *rather repulsive* subject."

mans," he writes, "are welcome to appeal to the old Empire to prove that they were once a united people. Nor is there any harm in their comparing the politics of the twelfth century with those of the nineteenth, though to argue from one to the other means to betray a want of historical judgement. But the one thing which is wholly absurd is to make Francis Joseph of Austria the successor of Frederick of Hohenstauffen and justify the most sordid and ungenial of modern despotisms by the example of the mirror of mediæval chivalry, the noblest creation of mediæval thought."

If Bryce had been a musician he might have been disposed to assign more merit to Austria than a contemplation of the political map of South-Eastern Europe suggested. But the history of the musical art was one of the few topics as to which he was uninformed. He used, indeed, to tell a story against himself of how being engaged as a young man upon the inspection of a girl's school, he found, to his consternation that he was expected by the Headmistress to pass judgment upon the piano-playing of the highest form. To confess that he had no technical knowledge of music would never have done. It was necessary to show a bold front. "Take the foot smartly from the pedal," said the examiner, shooting his arrow at a venture, with what results upon the execution of the docile class history does not record.

This, however, is a digression. The *Holy Roman Empire* must be judged not by the few slips and shortcomings inevitable in a work of large design but by the power with which it illumines one of the central truths of history. So judged it has stood and will continue to stand

[70]

the test of time and to pass from one end to the other of the republic of letters.[1]

[1] An amusing instance of its reputation abroad is given by Lady Bryce. ' On one occasion many years ago in the Alps we were crossing from the Tosa Falls on the Italian slope over a glacier to descend into the Rhone Valley. Halting for a short rest on the moraine after crossing the glacier we met a party of Swiss professors, who were going over to Tosa Falls, and it was proposed by the guides themselves that they should exchange parties and so enable each guide to return to his own village that day. After arranging this with the Swiss party my husband had a little talk with them, and found they were friends of Professor Borgeaud of Lausanne, who was an old friend of his, and he asked them to convey his remembrances when next they should meet him. "With pleasure," they said, "And what name shall we give to Professor Borgeaud?" "Oh, Mr. Bryce," said my husband, whereupon the Professors all took off their hats exclaiming "Holy Roman Empire," and salaamed in the most impressive manner. The scene, in the midst of the lonely pass, with the rocks and ice and snow all around us, remains clearly before me now as I saw it then, a quarter of a century ago.'

CHAPTER V

AN ITALIAN INTERLUDE

Soleva Roma, che il buon mondo feo,
Due Soli aver, che l'una e l'altra strada
Facean vedere, e del mondo e di Deo.
L'un l'altro ha spento; ed è giunta la spada
Col pastorale.

DANTE Purg. XVI. 1. 73

Rome, that the world so well bestowed
Two suns was wont to guard that showed
Both paths that should be trod
To the world and to God

Now are these twain no more, for one
The other's shining hath undone:
And in one hand combined
The sword and crook are joined.

C. L. SHADWELL.

To the student of world history the winter which followed the publication of this remarkable treatise is mainly to be remembered as witnessing the concluding stages of the American Civil War. Of that great drama the young Oxford historian was no indifferent observer. In common with most of his Liberal contemporaries at the University Bryce sided with the North, holding with John Bright, who in this issue spoke the mind of the great mass of the British nation, that as between Freedom and Slavery there was only one possible choice. Though he was not yet a professed student of American affairs, the contrasted modes in which the great American duel reflected itself in the mirror of British opinion made a lasting impression upon him. He saw that, in the main, public opinion in his own country followed the lines of social cleavage, that the few were on the side of the South, which he felt to be wrong, and the many on the side of the North, which he knew to be right; and the moral which he drew from this American example was that in broad matters of human sentiment the popular instinct is generally to be preferred to the conclusions of the cultivated and comfortable minority.

America, however, in those days before the cable, was very far away. To the admirer of Garibaldi and the Historian of the *Holy Roman Empire*, there were sources of interest nearer and more absorbing than Sherman's march through Georgia or Grant's great struggle with Lee in the Virginian Wilderness. There was Italy with its young Kingdom, its mediæval Papacy, its affluence of immortal memories of ancient Rome. For the moment there was a specious lull in the Italian contest; but it was settled that the capital should be moved from Turin, and the world suspected that even if King Victor Emmanuel might halt in Florence, he would find his way to Rome in the end. How could the Papacy, soon to be denuded of its French Janissaries, make head against the rising tide of Italian Nationalism? The Roman question was on the lips of all, and the chief preoccupation of those who were concerned to defend or attack the Temporal Power of the Pope.

In the winter of 1864 Bryce went with Courtenay Ilbert and Charles Robartes to Italy. They saw Rome and

Naples and the famous monastery of Monte Cassino and Florence, and it is perhaps unnecessary to add that Bryce climbed Mount Soracte. The evening before the ascent was spent by the historian of the *Holy Roman Empire* in a prison cell. Through some misunderstanding Robartes had been left behind in Rome, and finding that Bryce had already started he telegraphed to the station-master at the little station whence the walk was to be begun, "*Fermate il Inglese colla barba rossa.*"[1] The Italian officials promptly acted on these instructions. The red-bearded Englishman, suspected of the most heinous crimes, was despite all his protests committed to prison where he remained until overtaken by his English friend on the following day.

In a series of vivacious letters addressed to his family circle Bryce records his Italian impressions and incidentally supplies a vivid picture of Rome during the declining years of the Papal State. The fact most surprising to the student of his life is the avowal that he had ever entertained the thought that he might conceivably go over to the Catholic Communion. It would appear, however, that with him as with Luther a visit to the Papal Capital proved to be a decisive and effectual deterrent. He was shocked by what he saw, and though he remained throughout life a great student of Dante and had been fully emancipated by his historical studies from the narrow kind of anti-Roman prejudice, he was never afterwards drawn nearer to the Roman Communion. Rather he stood at the point at which religions meet, seeing some good in all forms of Christianity, but himself increasingly

[1] Stop the Englishman with the red beard.

impatient of dogmatic fetters and exasperated by the suspicion of dogmatic tests.

Rome is a wonderful place, but Murray shall tell you about it. There are three lines (slightly altered) from Clough's "Amours de Voyage," which I feel mightily inclined to apply just now, professing my own inability to give you not only any description, but not even a sort of notion of the place. Nor can so much as an impression of it be given.

For it has not made any definite impression on me at all, only a vague sense of something strange and incomprehensible, something which I don't understand and which is perfectly unlike all I had expected, something which confuses one's notions of time and history and national differences altogether. At Florence everything was bright, cheerful, picturesque, clear, and vivid, everything was harmonious, the old buildings carried me back in a moment to the Middle Ages. The new ones and the aspect of men spoke of the "Risorgimento" and Victor Emmanuel; one saw, as if watching the angel who descends the ladder of Jacob's vision, the beginning, the middle and the end, or present, of Florence, each in its place and all in clear and beautiful relation. But here it is, to me at least, mere confusion. The dirty public-house of to-day leans on the Corinthian column of a temple which Augustus built; the altar which some Consul dedicated to Juno is a shrine of the Immaculate Virgin; a pair of wings are clapped upon the shoulder instead of the feet of Mercury and he is worshipped as St. Michael the Archangel. In course of time all this will perhaps clear itself away, and we may begin to understand Rome; meantime it is all a dissolving point of view to me.

Scarcely a relic of the Middle Ages is to be seen, though one recognises the spots famous in history then, even the great basilica of Constantine in which so many emperors were crowned, which alone connected the old world of the city with the new, is gone without a trace, and in its stead we see a gigantic Renaissance temple, built in the decline even of the Papacy itself, and recalling only the materialism and the tastelessness of modern Italy. The Rome of Hildebrand and Innocent — of Arnold and Rienzi is vanished as — nay far more completely — than the Rome of Cicero and Virgil, of Sulla and Cæsar. As to that temple itself, disappointing as the first view is — for it really looks lower than St. Paul's —, it is nevertheless a wonderful building, finer, or at least grander, than I had at all expected. Cologne Cathedral and the Florentine Duomo are far more beautiful and far more religious; nevertheless St. Peter's is very wonderful and even sublime in its way, and is no inapt emblem of both the greatness and the faults of modern Catholicism.

I thought leaving England very possibly I might turn Catholic here — having always thought of late years that there was a great deal to be said on their side of the question, but St. Peter's to-day has not at all tended to urge me in that direction, rather indeed away from it; the influences of Rome lead one rather towards the religion of Cicero than towards that of Antonelli. The worship of modern Italy, so far as one can judge from the outside, is paganism, and a paganism unredeemed by the virtues of the ancients, a paganism which is superstitious without faith, and sceptical without philosophy. That an Anglican however should be made a Catholic by coming to Rome one can well understand, seeing indeed that no man can logically be an Anglican at all, but must either trust himself far more boldly to the conclusions of human reason, as Protestantism in its genuine forms does, or else fling himself with eyes tight shut, into the bosom of an infallible church. Indeed the wonder is that more Anglicans don't take the latter alternative. Speaking generally, one would say that Rome, if it influenced men's religion at all, would make of the strong sceptics, and Catholics only of the weak.

It was a tedious night journey, yet we were repaid, for on awaking from a short and uneasy slumber at 6.30 A.M., we found ourselves just descending the great Cimian range, looking South over the boundless plain to the distant sea and the scarcely visible outlines of Alban hills, and East to the long ranges of the Umbrian Apennines, with their bold offsets breaking down into the dark valley of the Tiber and the far off snowy summits of their central chain rising clear and sharp against the faintly reddish blue of an Italian dawn. Below, starting up from the Campagna at our feet, was the ridgy peak of Soracte, in height and shape another Slemish. Thence on for some ten or twelve miles, till we were fairly into the plain that surrounds Rome, the views were magnificent; and it was not without interest to remember as we strained our eyes for a glimpse of some tower or dome of the great city that from the same slope each successive host of invaders had scanned from afar with hungry eyes their prey.

They call the Campagna a plain, and so it seems looked down upon from the encircling hills, but it is a plain not like that of Berlin or of Lombardy, but in the sense of Salisbury Plain or the Plateau of Langres. Ridges traverse it every way, along the top of which runs the road, deep irregular hollows open suddenly upon you, often with a deadly swamp at the bottom, here and there a circular basin seems to announce some old volcano. One such we passed through, which Murray declared to be a crater, but all the rocks I could see were tertiary. The country is perfectly lovely; houses there must be, for now and then a tattered peasant met us driving a brown and half-starved donkey; cultivated fields appear here and there, but there was no other sign of life or industry over those fertile lands on which Rome and Veii had so often striven, and which must then have swarmed with a warlike and laborious population. The country is not brown, as they describe it, nor ugly, nor even black and bare, its dells are wooded and green, and a bushy ilex stands up every now and then upon the ridges, but it is desolate and melancholy, as if cursed by the blood with which every yard of it is stained, and you are at the gates of Rome before anything suggests the presence of a capital.

For the beauty of the distant landscape I was nowise prepared, having always thought the mountains so far from Rome as not to be objects in her view. In reality they seem, in that clear air, as near as Ben Voirlich does to Stirling; Soracte, Lucretilis, the Alban group, with the higher Volscian ranges of Southern Latium peering over these; then, further, but still conspicuous, the high flat topped and snow besprinkled line of the Umbrian and Sabine Apennines on the N. E. while straight eastwards beyond the valley of the Anio two or three sharp snowy peaks are seen which must lie round Lake Fucinus, and may be satellites of the great Monte Corno himself. It need not be said how a single glance at the panorama cleared up one's notions of early Roman history, and I can't help thinking that even Arnold who had a thoroughly geographical eye and understood its value for history more than others, has hardly made the most of these natural features in his account of the rise of the city and her wars with the surrounding races.

Rome,
December 8th, 1884.

To-day was one of the grand festivals of the Catholic Church, of which I may as well tell you while it is fresh in my remembrance, since in their way these pageants are among the regular sights of Rome, and to many men and most women, the most attractive of them.

Just ten years ago the present Pope summoned a vast array of cardinals, archbishops, bishops, doctors, and other clergy from all the world, and by their consent and his authority as the voice of the Holy Ghost pronounced the dogma of the Immaculate Conception of the Virgin Mary, that is, declared that she was born perfectly sinless, free from all the taint of human corruption inherited by all other human beings from Adam. By this the already popular worship of the Virgin was still further promoted and glorified, till now it may be said that neither God nor Christ, but only Mary is worshipped in Italy. This feast therefore is celebrated here with no small pomp and devotion. At $10\frac{1}{2}$ A.M., High Mass is performed by the Pope himself in the Sistine Chapel, the private chapel of the Vatican, a magnificent room, of plain Greek architecture, but adorned with the most superb frescoes, among which those by Michael Angelo on the roof and his great Last Judgment on the east end wall are especially splendid as works of art. Hither we repaired at 9.45 in evening dress, and found a crowd, chiefly of ladies, all in black with black veils (those coming in any other vesture were turned back) already thronging the door. Once in we waited patiently standing behind a high boarding covered with cloth which fenced off the upper two thirds of the Chapel for the great personages. At last they came, first cardinals one by one, each with a cape of snowy fur, a gown and sweeping train of a bright pink — almost scarlet, and a small scarlet skull-cap of cloth, each followed by an attendant robed in violet (that being the colour proper to Advent), each as he entered kneeling before the altar and then walking, or rather waddling to his high seat along the walls, where the attendant placed him, rolled up his train behind him, and sat down at his feet. Among the scarlet herd there rose conspicuous the tall, lithe form, firm head, and evil crafty face of Antonelli, the man most hated of all in Italy. When they were seated to the number of twenty-three, a long procession of priests in red and chamberlains in black and other priests with towering candles, and more priests still in robes of dazzling white, embroidered with gold, and crozier bearers and mitre bearers, ushered in an old man, tallish, stout, and hale, with a venerable head and a cheery hearty face, who paced slowly to a great throne on the right of the altar, while the choir broke out into peals of voluptuous song. This was the Head of the Church, the successor of so many saints and monsters of iniquity; of Peter and Hildebrand, of Sixtus V and Alexander VI. He himself was in long and gorgeous embroidered robes of white and gold, with a light violet skull-cap, visible when his mitre was removed and as you may fancy, the whole company of richly caparisoned figures flitting to and fro with candles, utensils, censers, from which incense rose in fragrant clouds, and all the paraphernalia which the ceremonial invention of eighteen centuries has been able to accumulate, was wonderfully seductive to those whose religious feelings depend on their senses and impressive enough to any person of imagination at all. The English Romanizers have plenty of work before them, if they mean to rival their great model.

As to the rites that followed, they were too long and too intricate to be described here, and few of them had for me anything but an antiquarian interest; they were curious from their being peculiar to Rome and from their vast antiquity, but otherwise matter for laughter as much as for reverence. Each cardinal advanced to the throne of the Holy Father, and kissed his hand; then the Pope himself performed Mass — all from his throne, save once he descended to a little golden altar placed in front of the high altar, knelt there, having his skull cap lifted by an attendant, behind him kneeling two by two a long line of dignitaries, while at the same moment all else in the chapel, some of the Protestants behind excepted, fell on their knees, and only here and there a stolid Englishman fixed his opera glass in his eye and glared steadily at the scene. At 12 it was all over, and the gorgeous flamingoes paced slowly out and scattered themselves down the magnificent staircases, and out into that great piazza of St. Peter's Church. You have seen so many photographs. One wonders how long this pageantry will last; there are still people who believe in it, one must suppose, but an intelligent man in the train the other day told us what everything confirms. That no educated man in Italy any longer believes in anything at all. What will it all end in?

> 52, Via Frattina,
> Rome,
> December 27th, 1864.

After all, what distinguishes Rome from all other places in the world is the tremendous consciousness of the Past with which it presses upon one. Elsewhere we know indeed that much has been done and suffered by the generations that have gone before us, but it is removed far from our present sight, it is not realised, it is like our consciousness of a dream when it is past. But here it is always before one, and returns in every street and building, every name and word and custom, for the greatness of the city has lasted ever since history begins, and has wound itself up with everything else; modern European society; with politics, religion, art, law, poetry. However let the Past be never so vivid, the present is after all that which comes home to men and most constantly occupies their thoughts. So, interesting as are the ruins and the statues, the pictures and the churches of the first Christian centuries, it is after all upon modern Catholicism that one's mind is most often turned. So far as I have seen yet both the exterior of the system in its churches and ceremonies, and in its inner workings upon the character and social condition of the people, and the individual Catholics — the converts from Protestantism especially — whom one meets, there is nothing to make it attractive to any but the weakest minds. Indeed it is quite the other way, and one rather understands how important a "moment" in Luther's life must have been that journey to Rome which showed him the inner corruption of that which seemed from afar so fair. Everything in Rome and the papal provinces generally witnesses to the debasing and enslaving character of ecclesiastical rule. The city is horribly dirty and ill-drained; there are no manufactures, agriculture languishes, the police are powerless except for the annoyance of travellers, the people detest their government. Everything wears the guise of religion, but it is a religion which has little or nothing to do with morality and is rejected in a very modified sense by all the more intelligent.

Sunday last was Christmas Day, and then in St. Peter's, the grandest of all modern churches, we saw the grandest of all Catholic ceremonies, high mass celebrated by the Pope himself. As a spectacle nothing could be more perfect, the building, the gorgeous robes, superbly various, the rites, the music, the incense rising in odorous clouds, all was the result of the most perfect taste and skill exerted for many centuries in choosing from and embellishing the ancient customs of the church, and all equally fitted to impress the senses. But it was very little more than a spectacle. The choir sang splendidly, but the people did not join; they all, save here and there a German or English Protestant knelt when the Host was elevated by the Pope, but there was no rational and intelligent participation in the worship; plenty indeed of devotional feeling, but a devotion which is rather of the senses than the intellect, and seems to have little or no influence on their conduct. However, they are externally, and really, sincerely devout here in a way to which our country affords no parallel; and they do carry out their theory of an externally beautiful religion very finely and gracefully. Beside the ceremonies here, how poor, meagre, and frigid does the English Church appear, with her faint and hesitating attempts in the same direction. But the great slur upon Catholicism here is the temporal power, and the evils it has caused. If the Pope and cardinals would give up this gaudy ostentation of being secular princes, and devote themselves more to religion and less to screwing money out of their wretched subjects and the credulity of the rest of Europe, they might really make a great thing of it, and there need be little to prevent our people from fraternising completely with them.

Indeed some are already very liberal, though they dare not avow it. Dining on Christmas Day with a Catholic lady here, a convert from Protestantism, I met a priest, professor of eloquence in the University of Rome, with whom I fell into a conversation in Latin. Having ascertained that I was not a Catholic, he bent over behind an Italian girl who sat between us, and said in a low emphatic voice, "There are many things believed among us which we who are educated don't believe. And I myself think that if anyone believes the chief doctrines of the Gospel, it does not matter in what church he is, salvation is alike to all. We here are fettered and forbidden to think for ourselves, you are happily free." This man had himself been in S. Angelo, for Antonelli makes short work of those whom he suspects. This party was a pleasant one altogether; as giving me some notion of Italian manners. Among the guests was a certain Monsignor, highly connected, and a probable cardinal. While we were waiting for tea, he was induced to sing, and gave

us accordingly what seemed to be a love song, for the word
"amore" recurred constantly. And after this, which all ap-
plauded, he began to mimic the Pope's Sistine Chapel choir to the
great amusement of the rest. The lady with whom we dined
was herself an interesting personage. Though a convert she is a
very liberal Catholic; the famous Father Passaglia was her
chaplain and intimate friend, and when Antonelli sent to arrest
him, she confronted the officers, I know not whether of the police
or of the Inquisition, refused to admit them, and kept search at
bay till he had escaped. We were introduced to her by two very
pleasant and kindly Scotch ladies here, to whom Archibald
Smith, whose cousins they are, introduced me, and at whose
house I have been several times. Indeed altogether one has been
at no loss for society in Rome, we have gone to no large parties,
except a great musical one on Christmas Eve at the American
Vice-Consul's, where Palestrina was well given, but we have
frequently been out to tea or making visits in the evening, and
have met many pleasant people, mostly of course English, but
English of the quasi artistic type, more interesting than the
average Tyburnian merchant, round whose mahogany one sometimes spends a melancholy hour.

One night I went to a Yankee's house, a Federal of course, and
was amused at the difference of the girls one saw there from the
English; so much more freedom in their manners; the accent
and air not quite so good and correct, but the absence of prim-
ness a very agreeable relief. They were busy making up dolls
and other presents to hang on a Xmas tree. For here too in
Rome, the most trivial of modern customs have full play, and
foreign society goes on with its parties and visits and its drives
on the Pincian, and all its petty cares and gossips and interests,
just as if all the grandeur of the ancient city was not lying
buried under their feet. Indeed they reck little of it; and know
as little as they care. I heard the other day of a lady who had
been here fifteen years without seeing the Apollo Belvedere.
Another said to a friend of mine, who told her he was to be in
Rome only a month, "And pray what do you expect to see of

society here in that time?" Such is life! The same here as everywhere else. And such it is in danger of becoming to us, for as Juvenal said that in his time the Syrian Orontes had flowed into the Tiber, so now have the Isis and Cherwell of Oxford. We can't turn into a church, or descend to the subterranean chamber of a ruin without finding some university acquaintance poking about. They — and indeed the mass of English travellers seem to come knowing mighty little about ancient Rome, except what Horace and Livy tell them, and nothing at all about Rome mediæval. Indeed most of them seem to see sights for no purpose but that of verifying their Murray, which they do with praiseworthy perseverance in front of a crowd of kneeling worshippers in a church or perched on the steps of some ruined temple.

As to the language, it is by no means so easy to speak as one fancies at first, or as the ease of reading might make apparent. Nothing can surpass its sweetness and grace, especially of course in the mouths of the women. They are not however so frequently beautiful as you may expect, strikingly beautiful faces perhaps no commoner than in England; yet a greater number of pretty and interesting ones; fine dark eyes and eyebrows, with a mobile expression which gives brightness to the whole countenance. The manners of all are full of softness and courtesy, but not a word they say can be trusted.

Perhaps our most enjoyable day was last Saturday. At 7.30 Ilbert, Robartes and I set off for Frascati by train, hired there horses and a guide (it is fourteen miles from Rome), rode up to the ruins of ancient Tusculum, thence over an undulating country, rich and beautiful even in midwinter, to the top of the Alban Mount, where the great temple of Jupiter, the common sanctuary of the Latin League, looked down upon their thirty towns, with Rome gleaming in the distance, and the great blue sea stretched out along the West horizon. Right at your feet lie the two lakes of Alban and Nemi, each in its deep, wooded, volcanic hollow; the steep shores dotted here and there by some white convent embowered among the chestnut groves. Altogether it would be hard to find any view in which are so combined the

An Italian Interlude

most exquisite picturesque beauty and the keenest historical interest. I could make a long story by describing the adventures of our twenty five mile ride, but reserve this and much else I hope for evening chats in Welbeck Street. Meantime I hope you are enjoying your vacation, wherever you are, and wish you the happiest of New Years. I don't quite know when I may be back, so much here is interesting, but in all probability before the end of January.

Though the year will be old enough before this reaches you, it is new now, and I wish you all many happy returns of it. With you it is probably a bright frosty day, and Annan has gone down to the Clyde to skate on the Monday that is, which no doubt will replace New Year's Day itself with you. Here it is wet still, warm, and they say unhealthy; the Tiber is high, the Sabine mountains are draped with heavy clouds; everything is like an English April, if Rome can be said to be like anything English at all. For, certainly, it has a character unlike not only our own but any and every other capital in Europe, just because it remains still the capital not of a nation but of Christendom. Nowhere else has one the same feeling of cosmopolitanism. You cannot be jostled in a crowd without hearing five or six languages around you; it is always a question whether to ask your way in French, German, English, or Italian; you may even then be answered in Spanish or Polish; so too here there are four or five national societies moving in minor orbits of their own around the great central society of which the Holy Father is the sun. Of several of these I have seen something, and it has been pleasant, even at the sacrifice of precious evenings, to pass from English to Germans and thence to Italians.

The regular British society here is as completely insular as it can be made, differing from that of Belgravia only in the semi-ecclesiastical character which the presence of many perverts with the cardinals and monsignors whom they worship throws over it. It is just as starchy and formal, as reverential of titles, as devoid of wit or intellect as Mayfair itself. Anyone who living a winter in Rome desired to steep himself in the feeling of the old city, ancient or mediæval, would do well to eschew it altogether, even loneliness would be more profitable if little more pleasant. American society follows next; in former years both gay and numerous, but now, owing to the war and the paper money, greatly shrunken, and scarcely able to maintain itself alone. Besides Story, I have had an introduction to a certain Mr. Burrows here, an intelligent and pleasant northerner, who expects the speedy submission of the South and abolition of slavery. The highest Italian society is supposed to be very exclusive, cultivated, and somewhat languid, cut off as the secular nobility are from all political action, and liable to be banished without trial on even a suspicion of liberalism. The most liberal and accomplished is also the head of the most ancient of the great houses of Rome, Michael Angelo Caetani, Duke of Sermoneta, whose family traces itself back to the ninth century. Boniface VIII belonged to it. Stanley gave me an introduction to him. I have been there two or three times — once dining, and found him and his wife very pleasant, though as he speaks little English and talks Italian so fast and in a sort of tone so mumbling that I find it hard to follow him, my conversation has been chiefly with his wife, who is English. To Rossi of Catacomb celebrity I have also had an introduction; which has availed to enable me and two friends to join one of his parties to the Catacombs. Running across all these different social formations cutting them like a whin dyke, is the artist society, English, Italian, German, American, separated into groups according to their language, yet having much in common, and forming a link to unite the rest.

To this class belong almost all the Germans living in Rome — except of course the ecclesiastics — and excepting also a few archeologists and historical students who live here hunting up inscriptions, collecting and figuring Etruscan vases, discussing in endless German schrifts and blatts the question whether a half buried column belonged to a temple of Mars, Ultor or the Baths of Lucius and Caius Cæsar, grubbing for months together in old archives for an exhaustive biography of some thirteenth century pope. Wherever the hard, thankless, thorough and most necessary work of the scientific world is to be done, there one finds a German doing it. Of one of their most considerable people here I have made the acquaintance. Gregorovius, author of a history of Rome in the Middle Ages, which has already reached its fifth out of probably ten or twelve volumes. At the German Artists' Club, to which however I have been only twice or thrice altogether, I have met also one or two artists, pleasant fellows with their teutonic roughness and simplicity. One not rough, however, had a very pleasant musical evening last Thursday at which some Beethoven was well given. A daughter of Chambers of Edinburgh was there, who has married a German much older than she seems to be.

You remember how Clough's hero expresses his disappointment with Rome. That is not the word for the feeling of the place; though it is meaner, dirtier, more prosaic, more wholly modern than any traveller expects. It is not disappointing, for it is real, and expresses in its form and dress all its character and history. But it is perfectly unlike what fancy had pictured it. The ruins are not below one's ideas of them, for they point to a splendour and wealth and grandeur of conception and execution in the times of the later republic, and empire, such as no modern city makes the feeblest approach to. But all is so changed that one gives up in despair the notion of reconstructing the ancient city, and contrary to all my expectations, that which has most interested me, has seemed most suggestive and capable of giving really definite and valuable results, has been the monuments of primitive Christianity; the old churches with their singular mosaics, the catacombs with their paintings, the sarcophagi with their emblematic devices. Especially interesting was the visit to the Catacombs with Rossi, who knows and explains them better than anyone else, having devoted his life to their exploration. There is, indeed, less positively to be seen than one expects, for the barbarians who broke in and ransacked them in the sixth and seventh centuries for treasure and the ornaments of the dead have removed most of the bones, while the piety or cupidity of the Popes of the last two centuries has carried off the rest, some to enrich the reliquaries of the churches of Rome, others to be sold to the faithful of Spain and France. Still the wall paintings are left, showing more vividly than anything else could do the religious notions of the first Christians, and showing certainly as it seems to me how very soon after the Apostolic Age that change in doctrine and worship which Protestants call corruption, began, how much in fact of what we style Romanism grew up as soon as the first spiritual impulse, the first direct conception of the new life as revealed by Christ, had begun to wax fainter. And then besides this, one sees here the very chapels in which the immediate successors, perhaps the disciples of the Apostles, performed their still simple, though even then sacrificial service; the very graves, narrow shelves hewn out of the crumbling rock, in which their bodies were laid. Conceive an endless series of narrow irregular galleries, opening into each other and branching off every way, running for miles below the ground, with rarely an air hole admitting some faint ray from above, bordered everywhere on both sides by these innumerable graves, and then think of the nightly meetings and the funerals by stealth and the flight of the clergy hither when a new edict of persecution was issued by the Emperor, and some trembling messenger finding his way down at night to the fugitives telling of the martyrs who had that day fallen in the amphitheatre under the claws of the wild beasts.

And then returning to the upper air we drive back through the solitudes of the old city, a waste of shapeless brickwork with here and there a half ruined convent whose monks have fled from the malaria, and see towering over the houseroofs of the newer town, the great dome of St. Peter's, to which a sunbeam clings when all below is dark, and we think passing under the silent Palatine how strange the reverse of fortune that has made the successor of the persecuted bishops the sovereign of Rome and half the Christian world, and left the palaces of the persecuting emperors to be like Babylon, a dwelling of bats and owls, the memory of whose builders and whose dwellers is for ever lost.

An Italian Interlude

Not less curious is it to reflect that the same will be said five centuries hence of these gorgeous Popes themselves, by men who will wonder whence their power over the soul arose. Rome now is not one city but two, a pagan city on one side the Capitol, a Christian one on the other; and if she is won by Italy and made a capital once more a third may arise as unlike these two as they are to each other. The power gained and the energy of purpose to construct it are wanting now, that is plain enough, but the Italians are sanguine of a great career, and seem in everything to be shaking off the long torpor in which foreign tyranny and priestly intrigue has bound them.

52, via Frattina,
Rome,
January 11th, 1865.

My time in Rome is nearly over now, yet it seems as if I was only beginning to get that sort of familiarity with the external part which is needed before one can enter into the spirit of a place. I have examined more or less carefully some sixty or seventy churches, that is to say have carefully gone round them, verifying my Murray, as is the wont of the English tourist, have admired the "Sebastiano del Piombo at the third altar on the right" and anathematised the "Carlo Muretta at the fourth on the left of the entrance," and strained my eyes and twisted my neck in the effort to make something of the frescoes on the cupola. Then we have gone prowling about the ruins, admiring more and more the magnificent solidity with which the gigantic arches of brickwork were built, and abhorring the equally barbarous vandalism which burnt the columns of these temples for lime, which stripped the roofs of their gorgeous bronze and the walls of their glittering marbles. We have been, of course, both interested and instructed in these pursuits; yet they are somewhat unsatisfying, for the life of old Rome has gone out of this dead shapeless brickwork, and the life of new Rome which has effloresced in the varnish and gilding of the Renaissance churches with their statues all drapery and their paintings all washed out

[89]

sentiment is not a noble phenomenon at all, and very little worth studying.

It is really in two things that the interest of Rome lies, the statues, paintings, inscriptions, and so forth, which survive as real records of the society and manners, not less than of the thoughts and religion of a people infinitely removed from ourselves; and then secondly, the scenery and local character of the city and the country about it, not only because they are beautiful in themselves, but because it is round them that the associations of all the history from first to last cluster. In this respect the excursion to Tivoli a few days ago was very interesting. We left at 7.20 A.M. in three carriages, twelve men in all, and drove all the way to the foot of the Sabine hills over the lovely Campagna. It is not a plain, that is, not a piece of flat land like Lombardy or Bavaria or the Bog of Allan, but an undulating country, intersected by narrow deep watercourses with miniature cliffs of crumbling tufa, covered with green grass, no trees, no houses, no arable land, only roving herds of oxen and here and there a rude mediæval tower with some tumbledown farm buildings nestling around it. The soil is of that crumbling loamy black earth which looks exuberantly fertile, but malaria and misgovernment have made it a desert. At last, when the sun has grown almost unpleasantly strong, we creep up under the glittering limestone mountains; dawdle for an hour about Hadrian's Villa at their foot, a mass of ruins, theatres, porticoes, halls, arbours, libraries, and what not, two or three miles in circuit, a wonderful monument of boundless resources and the restless fancies of a capricious despot; then mount a steep hill through thick woods of olive to the rocky height of Tivoli. Tivoli is not fashionable as of yore, when, as you remember, the greatest compliment that could be paid Catullus was to call his town Tiburtine and not Sabine — it was in one of these odes you translated for me ten years ago; for the Roman nobles go to Frascati or Albano now, but it is beautiful in its decline as ever, and the graceful ruins of Vesta's temple still look down from its craggy shelf over the foaming Anio. The hill on which the town stands is all of limestone — travertine indeed — and honey-combed with grottoes, from which fountains burst forth, so that the whole slope is alive with tiny cascades dancing in the sunlight, while an exquisite waving iris hangs over the great pool into which the Anio makes its leap of some two hundred feet. The one great charm which the scenery of these countries has, compared with our own, is the combination of beauties their climate permits. Our mountains are as rugged, but their tops are bare and herbless; here towers and temples crown the peaks, while olives and chestnuts spread their green over the slopes. If one had had time it would have been delightful to penetrate the hills away up to the frontier of Italy (Naples that was) and see the snowy Marsic hills themselves in Lake Fucinus. But we must turn back to the measureless level that lay beneath, veiled by a sunny haze out of which rose alone the dome of St. Peter's; the first of all Rome's buildings which the approaching traveller sees, the last he loses. Since that day I have not had any great expedition, and the details of sightseeing are fitter for a journal than a letter.

The Etruscan museum took our fancy greatly, and made me regret more than ever not having been able to stop at Clusium and explore the tombs. You could not believe without seeing the exquisite grace and delicate workmanship of the jewellery of this strange people, such that the modern Italians are obliged to copy from these models which they cannot rival, while the rest of Europe hardly attempts to make their ornaments really beautiful at all. One feels here how poor and uncultivated the taste of our people especially is, compared with that of these southern nations. The French may be a little better than the English, but they are much more behind the Italians.

One morning — Epiphany day — we went to the Greek Church, and found the music more agreeable than that which is common in the churches here. It is more severe and plain, something between a chant and a hymn, with none of the violent floridity of the papal choirs, though no doubt they are technically far superior. The service was not unlike the Roman, and quite as much a matter of mere priestly ceremonial; a great deal of it went on behind a screen, from which the high priest issued at last with a plate of consecrated bread, which the spectators crowded up to take from his hands and carry home as a sort of talisman. The same evening a curious fair takes place in the streets round the Pantheon; booths holding nothing but toys are set up in the streets, and the whole native population pours out with its children to make Twelfth Night presents to them of these dolls and dragons and soldiers and miniature houses, musical instruments, whips, and all else in which children delight in Scotland as well as in Rome. These are supposed to be brought to the child by a certain Beffanoe (a corruption of Epiphany), an old woman, half saint, half fairy, very benevolent, but sure to mark her displeasure at naughty children by bringing them nothing. It is something like the American Santa Claus. The scene what with the crowd, the lights, the shouts of the children, and the blowing of the penny trumpets is indescribable.

Naples, January 17th,
Monte Casino, January 15th & 16th /65.

Think of the time when the Franks had just entered Gaul and the Saxons held only the S. E. part of England, when there were no Danes in Ireland and probably no Scots in Scotland, when Justinian was compiling the Pandects, when no prophet had yet arisen in Arabia, and think of all that has happened since then if you wish to have an idea of the antiquity of this great monastery, founded by S. Benedict himself, the source and pattern of all others in the West. Here in Italy one is weighed upon by the notion of time. The Past is so long and so eventful that it becomes perpetual; it is the Present, for it is more real, and we live in an eternal everchangeful Now. If you have a Milman by you, and read his account of St. Benedict's life, you will be interested even by the set narrative; how much more if you were here now under this roof among a body more ancient than any other in Europe, for its existence has been unbroken, its object and rules always the same. Therefore it is the oldest thing in Italy.

This morning I left Rome by the train at ten twenty with Boyle and another friend; (they (the engineers) have had to cut away a good piece of the agger of Servius Tullius to make additional sidings — as good an instance of Roman contrasts as you can have), and by twelve we were beyond Velletri in a country entirely new to me; and of which I never found any geographical description give any idea. The line from Rome first crosses the Campagna to near Albano as you will see by the map, skirts the Alban group of hills on their W. side, where they break down in little glens and bosky undulations to the Latian plain. Then turning round by Velletri it holds close along their S. slope; you see on your right the great level of the Pontine marshes stretching down to Circeii and Anxur; bordered on the S. W. side by the sea, on the other by a splendid mountain range which beginning from near a place called Valmontone runs right through Latium and away into Campania. It is really a spur of the Appenines, one of those numerous longitudinal ranges by which the whole configuration of this side of Italy is governed, and which causes all her rivers to run parallel with them at right angles to the central chain. Leaving the Alban hills at Valmontone, the railway runs right down a long straight valley, sometimes widening into a plain between this Volscian Range (as we may call it), and the even higher mass of the Aequian and Hernican Appenines on the E., following the course of the Sacco and Liris as far as San Germano, where I am now. What is curious about the matter is that the Volscian range, though evidently geologically and physically a part of the Appenine system, whereas the Alban group is altogether volcanic, isolated and unconnected, is nevertheless geographically almost independent of the Appenine chain. Between Velletri and Segni, the railway crosses the summit level, and does so with no great ascent, while just south of it the limestone mountains rise boldly some four or five thousand feet above the sea. It is not till the train has got some distance down the Sacco Valley that you feel the connection of the ranges on either side, composed of similar rocks and almost meeting above the narrow gorge of the river. Just at the head of the valley, where it is not a valley but a sort of plateau, stretching back to the Roman Campagna between Tivoli and Frascati, there is a tract so like the North of Ireland I could have thought myself between Ballymoney and Kilrea. The ground is undulating, breaking off constantly into little scars, pointed by quasi basaltic columns, the rocks have the same colour, the grass the same vivid green, the land is as desolate, the occasional farm houses as wretched. Lower down the Sacco, by Anagnia and Aquino the aspect of the scenery is very different. Grand mountains, gleaming white with lime-stone below and streaks of snow above rise on either side, a rich valley teeming with oil and wine; sharp projecting peaks rise off the lower spurs of these hills, each the citadel of some ancient city, whose modern representative hangs upon the slope below, deep glens open up eastward and bring the eye back among the thirsty summits that tower over the Lake Fucino and shelter the brigands of the Abruzzi. Everywhere here as in Etruria, the same phrase recurs, "tot congesta manu praeruptis oppida saxis."

At San Germano I left the train, which carried the other two men on to Naples, and climbed with a black carpet bag the long steep-rock paved path that winds from the town up to this mountain pinnacle. The hill is one mass of bare glittering lime-stone, among whose crevices a sharp grass and some evergreen shrubs shoot forth, and if hard enough to climb now what must it have been in S. Benedict's days and the even ruder times that followed. A Padre has just told me a pretty legend about him. When he built his cell on the hill-top his sister S. Scholastica followed him and dwelt in a sort of convent or hermitage at the mountain foot. They were wont to meet often at night to talk of spiritual things; and once when after such an interview Benedict set out to climb homewards, his sister begged him to stay and talk on till morning. He refused, since a self-imposed rule forced him to spend every night in his cell; and when she could not persuade him, she told him that if he would not stay, she must; prayed earnestly, and brought up over the serene sky heavy rain and lightning, so that he could not but remain. Next day at their usual meeting hour she appeared to him in the form of a dove and flew away to heaven. Benedict and his brethren descending found her body, and bore it up to the monastery, where he now lies buried beside her. The whole poetry, as well as the whole intellect of those ages, seems to have found its sphere in religion or the church.

Reaching the monastery, I was cordially received by the Padre Tosti, to whom I had brought a letter from Stanley, dined alone with him in their vast vaulted refectory by the light of a solitary lamp, had a most interesting conversation on the prosperity of Italy and Catholicism, and am now just going into my inner cell to jump into a bed which looks a good deal more comfortable than any S. Benedict would have permitted or enjoyed. However Monte Casino is, to use an Oxford analogy, the All Souls of monasteries; only men of independent means are admitted brethren, and these seem to devote themselves to literature and education (a large seminary is attached to the convent) rather than to anything savouring of asceticism. They still maintain their traditional reputation in literature — it was here more than elsewhere in the W. that the classical manuscripts were chiefly preserved and copied during the dark ages; their library is exceedingly rich in manuscripts, their archives the oldest and most complete in Europe. This is what one is told; I have not yet seen any. And if one can judge from Padre Tosti himself, the men are worthy of the spot; he is learned, judicious, and liberal; and indeed, like the whole place, represents Catholicism under the most engaging aspect I have yet seen it wear. 'Tis a pity that men have agreed that monasticism is unfit for the nineteenth century, for there was something winning and soothing about it; and stripped of the supposed inward austerity and the undoubted outward dirt with which one sees it most commonly associated, a man might lead a worse life now. However, it *is* past, so there is no more to be said.

Of the buildings and arrangement I have seen little yet. The two cells I have got as sitting and bedroom are plain white-washed chambers; white curtains on the windows, a writing table and chest of drawers, no looking-glass, perhaps because it would encourage carnal vanities, a portrait of San Benedetto on the wall; by the bedside a crucifix, with, also, a Madonna behind it. The catacombs sufficiently prove that the primitive Christians made a great deal more of the Virgin than Protestant prejudice will allow; still S. Benedict would hardly have put her where she hangs now. However, after all the chief use of appealing to the primitive church is to prove that we can't appeal; they and their circumstances were so unlike us and ours that their practice and modes of statement need no wise bind us. But they ought to make us at any rate more charitable.

The room is in the second or third storey from the base of the wall, the steep hillside goes down unbroken to the flat of San Germano, whose castle, founded centuries after this monastery, has been now for centuries in ruins. The night is grey and dark, still there is light enough to trace the slopes of the huge peaks opposite, by whose outline, on some murky night like this, Benedict would guide his course, as he scrambled down over the rocks and shrubs to meet Scholastica below.

Jan. 16: Next morning the good father, who seems to be Abbot and looks and speaks his part, takes me into the church, modern comparatively, for earthquakes, storms and mortal enemies have destroyed Monte Casino time after time, and there is now but one vestige of S. Benedict's building, shows me the gorgeously decorated interior, rich with rare marbles and Floren-tine mosaic, and brings the organist to let me hear their organ, one of the best in Italy. It gets so dark, about 10 A.M. that we can scarcely see, and a tremendous rain storm whirls about the roofs and moans through the long dark corridors. At last we venture out on the terrace, the sky is serene, the valleys of the Cacco and Garigliano below are bathed in sunlight; right above rises a gigantic peak, covered from head to foot with dazzling snow; far up in the East the eye strives vainly to discern mountain from white clouds among the wild peaks of the Abruzzi, the land whence descended the all but unconquerable Samnites. Few places even in this country of lavish beauty combine the splendours of nature with the interest of history and religion as does this.

Then we descend into the Archivio, the richest in its way in the world, and the librarian shows manuscripts, exhibiting every form of character from the fifth century down to the sixteenth; while among the collection of charters and donations to the monastery are many of the 8th, 9th, 10th, centuries, bulls of Leo IX and Innocent Third, and one of Alexander II to which the name of Hildebrand, archdeacon of the Roman Church is subscribed. The writing, the phrases, the quaint old waxen seals, carry one back into the dark ages, while the portly Abbot seated in a chair with three or four monks grouped round him, looks as his predecessors may have looked when news came that Alexander's consecrated banner had won for William of Normandy the crown of England. I doubt, however, if the Abbot of that day was as tolerant and gentle as the excellent Tosti, who is now writing cards of salutation for Gladstone, whom he knew at Naples, and Stanley; and with whom last night and to-day I have long discussions on the relations of Catholicism and Protestantism and their hopes for the future. He is quite dispassionate, but a strong Catholic, though apparently willing to abandon the temporal power; has written many books on the history of the church, and talks with great animation and power of figurative language.

At 1 P.M. I leave, descend the hill, and have time before starting by train to see the theatres at San Germano below. You cannot conceive what an idea of Roman or rather ancient Italian energy and culture the ruins scattered over Italy give. Here is Casinum, not more important in Italy than Preston, or Greenock might be among ourselves, and it has two superb theatres, one for the drama, the other for the beasts and gladiators, able to hold some three thousand people or more, built so firmly that its shell stands now, and once, if one may judge from fragments, faced with a rare foreign marble — the "giallo antico."

Locanda delle Crocelle,
Naples,
January 20th, 1865.

Florence — to indulge in one of those generalisations which are the necessary relief of a mind and memory overloaded by endless particulars, Florence is mediæval, Rome is of all times. Naples either of none or merely modern. As a city, it has less character and individuality than any — out of England — which I have seen. Not that you could mistake it for any other; for its position, its climate, the faces and dress of its inhabitants, even its buildings, such as they are, are all peculiar; that is to say, such as you don't see elsewhere. Nevertheless there is nothing to impress you; none of that undefinable character which the other great cities of Italy show themselves by at once, and by which one remembers each just as clearly as you do some striking personality. On the whole my impression is best conveyed by saying that Naples is something between what Cork is and what I fancy Cairo may be: there is all the laziness and squalor, all the sprightliness and fun of an Irish town, together with an oriental look about the houses, the sea, the swarthy faces of the people. As to the glorious climate and colours, that is all faith, for since we came it has rained and blown without intermission so that even to see the ordinary sights has been no easy work. In the town isself there is but one thing to see, the Museum, an inexhaustible mine of ancient curiosities, statues, fine, though of course not to be compared to those of the Vatican; exquisite bronze and terra cotta ornaments and implements, mostly from Pompeii; a superb series of vases, bowls, and so forth, from Cumæ and other South Italian cities; a fair picture gallery, and a collection of fresco paintings brought from the house walls at Pompeii; of the greatest interest both from their own beauty and as our only specimens of this branch of ancient art.

An Italian Interlude

Of the buildings there is little to tell; partly because the building stone is a crumbling tufa, which lasts only a few hundred years, partly because Naples has not, like the Italian cities of the North, a grand republican period in the Middle Ages — and indeed — speaking generally, has no history at all; most of all perhaps because the bigoted and tasteless Spaniards have been more powerful here than anywhere else in Italy, and did their best during their long rule to deface or destroy all the best works which a purer age had bequeathed. Only two or three Gothic churches remain, and even those ruined by so-called restorations. In this vast city, so long the capital of a monarchy, there is not one to be named in the same breath with the Cathedral of Pisa or the Dom of Strassburg. There are several castles; two or three huge red-stuccoed palaces, and a great many handsome modern villas in the new town; but nothing to carry one back into the past, nothing to remain in one's memory, nothing that expresses an idea, religious or political. Take away the colour and the size, and a London Square is little more uninteresting. However, the place is prosperous; it covers a space three or four times as great as modern Rome, and swarms with a densely packed population greater than that of any city in Britain except London. How the people live is a marvel, for one sees no manufactures. The trade is not very large; there are no public works or fisheries of consequence. To be sure life is easy in a mild climate, where one needs no fire, little clothing, and only some macaroni for food; and these lively dirty wretches seem to find the world a pleasant place enough, for they lounge and laugh all day long; do a little ecstatic image worship in their incense reeking church, and then cheat you with all the courtesy in life afterwards. Picturesque too they are, the women chiefly, with their rich brown faces, heavy black hair, liquid eyes and scarlet handkerchiefs draped round the head; not as a rule pretty; the faces are too low for that. But full of grace and that sort of natural charm which our women want. Everywhere in the poorest quarters, where the narrowest lanes are choked with dirt and smells indescribable almost bar advance,

I have seen groups which might have been painted as they stood; mothers with babies, girls dancing under an archway while someone beats a tambourine, men conversing with gesticulations enough for all the theatres in England.

Baiae is a lovely little bay; its encircling hills low, but the view southwards to Posilippo, and the mountains beyond, Vesuvius, the Salernite ranges and Capri quite enchanting. Very little remains to mark the spot where all the luxury and dissipation of the Roman Empire centred. However, here at least one need not complain of the want of memorials of antiquity, for in Pompeii it is revealed far more fully and plainly than anyone who has not seen it can believe. No matter how much one expects, the reality is sure to surpass anticipation. It would be endless to describe what you have read about and seen photographs of over and over again. But the things one does see and the impression they give is not what books and travellers' reports lead you to expect. You see very little that gives one the notion of sudden destruction, hardly any bones or traces of them; none of the things people dropped in the flight; no money bags of a delay-ful Lot's wife clasped in skeleton fingers; no domestic utensils or articles of furniture; these all, together with the charred fruit and bread, the ornaments and clothes have been removed to the Museum in Naples, and there only remains the streets and walls of the houses, and the rows of broken columns which show where temples stood. Yet in these how much; in these far more really and vividly than in the half vulgar half sensational interest which attaches to the personal relics of the people suddenly overwhelmed, is the life and feeling of those times brought back to us, for in these frescoed walls, this profusion of graceful statues, the whole simple yet tasteful and artistic ordering of daily life we seem to catch some breaths of that pure fresh air which the many changes and corruptions of the world have soiled and thickened. Of course I don't mean moral purity; of that those Pompeians had as little as can well be fancied, but a sort of simplicity, a power of eliciting beauty from plain things in a natural way, of which the Italians have retained more than most other European nations, yet only a part of what their ancestors enjoyed.

Of the profusion and elegance of the wall paintings (they are not strictly frescoes), it is hard not to speak in exaggerated terms. They are generally roughly done, and being all from the Greek mythology, there is no great variety in their subjects. But they are so full of ease and grace, and show often so much power of composition that one is forced to conclude the average of skill in painting among the Romans to have been very high. For of course all at a third rate provincial town like Pompeii, a place which might be the Ayr or Portobello of the Romans, as Baiae was their Brighton, must have been executed by ordinary workmen, and merely copied from the great works of previous artists. If then the ordinary copies are so good, what shall we say of the originals. The general idea one gets is that the ancients must have lived altogether in an artistic atmosphere quite different from anything modern times can show; unless Italy in the time of Lorenzo and Leo X may be thought to supply a parallel. And the strangest part is that this should have been quite uncreative, for certainly there were in none of the arts, any more than in poetry really great and original geniuses after the generation of Augustus. Looking at these houses, one can't but think a great many hints remain to be gathered from them for the design and ornamentation of our own; indeed I have been wishing often enough to have £20,000 to spend on a house and grounds now, it would be so pleasant trying to reproduce some of these effects. The excavations are still carried on briskly — hitherto only one third part of the whole town has been laid bare — and we stood by while the workman's spade dislodged the crumbling soil from the walls, and beautiful heads, coloured as vividly as the one that hangs in your drawing room, started to life from their unsightly shroud.

No one can read these eager, unstudied letters without seeing the great power which large effects of scenery and the wider forms of historical association combined to

[101]

exert on the writer's mind. In comparison with the attractions of history and landscape the gift of minute social observation, such for instance as is exhibited in Prosper Merrimée's brilliant *La Rome Contemporaine*, is less obviously apparent. To the historian of the Holy Roman Empire, bringing to Italy all the enthusiasm generated by his wide knowledge and recent researches, the past was more living than the present, and the present chiefly significant as throwing a backward light upon the past. Yet to this rule there was one exception. Brought into contact for the first time with the visual glories of Papal Rome, and contemplating its sumptuous apparatus of ordered rite and ceremony, Bryce felt bound to give an account to himself and to his Presbyterian relatives, of his disposition towards this strange and famous religion. As we have seen, the predominant emotion was one of repulsion. The taste, the beauty, the sense of external order characteristic of Roman religion did not compensate for the superstitions, or the levities which Bryce found everywhere prevalent among the Catholic populace of Rome. The grandson of the Manse felt no temptation to abjure the faith of his Presbyterian forbears. As he entered Italy, so he returned to his home in London, immune to the seductions of Catholic worship, yet alive to the great part which the Roman Church had played in human history, and conscious of its many and conspicuous services to the consolation and support of mankind.

CHAPTER VI

THE SCHOOLS COMMISSION

It is to keep a man awake, to keep him alive to his own soul
and its fixed design of righteousness, that the better part of
moral and religious education is directed; not only that of words
and doctors, but the sharp ferule of calamity under which we
are all God's scholars till we die.

R. L. Stevenson.

In 1865, while he was combining Oxford work with the
study of the law in Sir John Holker's chambers, Bryce
received an appointment which opened out many
new avenues of interest. A Royal Commission had been
set up under the chairmanship of Lord Taunton to report
on all schools in England and Wales (with the exception
of the nine ancient and important foundations which
had been previously examined) excluded from the operation of the Parliamentary grant. It was therefore an
enquiry covering a very wide range and inviting decision
upon a large number of educational issues. It raised the
whole question of the adequacy of the provision for
secondary education and the education of girls, of the
comparative value of private and public schools, of the
ideal size of schools, use and abuse of educational endowments, of curricula, of teaching efficiency, of material
equipment, of the training of teachers, of the fee-paying
as opposed to the free system, as well as of the geographi-

cal distribution of schools, endowed, proprietary and private. In order the better to carry out their investigations the Commissioners selected typical districts in England and Wales and within each district appointed an Assistant Commissioner to inspect the endowed, proprietary, and private schools for boys and girls, to test the attainments of the scholars and to obtain as complete a view as possible of the demand for education in the district and of the extent to which that demand was supplied. Bryce was appointed Assistant Commissioner for Lancashire and Birkenhead as well as for the counties of Salop (excluding Shrewsbury) Worcester, Monmouth (excluding the town of Monmouth), Brecon, Radnor, Carmarthen, Pembroke, Cardigan, Merioneth, Carnarvon, and Anglesea. For the next two years the labours of the Commission occupied a great share of his time and energies.

The work was thoroughly congenial. It gratified the two master passions of travel and enquiry, was associated with the promotion of a great social cause which he had much at heart and was the means of introducing him to the life of the industrial north and the more serious section of Lancashire society. It was through the educational journeys connected with this Commission that Bryce became friends with Henry Roscoe and the remarkable circle of men connected with the foundation of Owen's College, Manchester, where he held for a short time the Chair of Jurisprudence. It was these journeys of inspection which taught him for the first time something of the stuff of which Lancashire was made, and filled his mind with the importance of the new movement for developing Universities in the great industrial centres of the country. The growth of the Civic Universities, now one of the most hopeful features in our social and industrial life, owes not a little to the interest which was aroused during the pursuit of this educational mission and to the advocacy which flowered from its seed.

Bryce's reports on individual schools are models of the way in which such work should be accomplished, clear, precise, and practical, placing each school in its proper national and social setting with more of life and colour and with a more frequent recourse to generalities than are usually found in official documents. Here are two characteristic excursions:

"It is the glory of Hawkshead school to have been the school of Wordsworth. In his time boys from all the dales for many miles round, up and down the lake country used to flock to it, lodging in the houses of the villagers or with the neighbouring farmers. Now the gentry and professional men send their sons to the boarding schools of the south, the yeoman sends his to the national school of his village, and Hawkshead has only those few day scholars who may happen to live close by, with such boarders as the private connexion of the head master can gather. Forty or fifty years ago it was a thriving place with a market to which people of the surrounding dales brought their homespun yarns and sold them to the dealer from Kendal; now there is not a creature in the streets, and few cottagers along the lanes." [1]

Or again writing of the Bottwnog Free Grammar School:

"This is probably the most remote and secluded Grammar school, except that at St. Davids to be found anywhere in England and Wales. It lies far down in the peninsula of Lleyn, that

[1] Vol. xvii, p. 264.

projecting part of Caernarvonshire which forms the northern horn of Cardigan Bay, in a high hilly country, swept by keen sea breezes to which nobody seems to have come from the outer world since the days when pilgrims used to pass through on their way from Caernarvon to Bardsey Island."

The contrast between the Grammar schools in Lancashire and the Western counties struck him particularly,

"in Shropshire, Worcestershire and Monmouthshire, those grammar schools which have not sunk into parish schools, have preserved a distinctively classical character. Latin is taught to every boy. Greek to all who remain long enough in the school; arithmetic and even mathematics are looked upon as subjects of quite inferior importance; modern languages are little attended to; chemistry — physics — are scarcely heard of. But in Lancashire it may be said that the grammar schools have almost all of them undertaken to give those who seek it a commercial education."

What, however, was even more remarkable was the meanness, despite the abundant evidence of surrounding opulence, of these Lancashire Grammar Schools which were now endeavouring to adapt themselves to the needs of the new industrial society.

"The Lancashire towns, as everyone knows, are not the most beautiful in England; they have all the marks of having been built in haste and built with the sternest practical purpose. In spite, however, of the general air of ugliness, the public buildings are seldom mean, and even the mills and warehouses, as well as the private houses of the richer people are spacious, solid, and comfortable. Only one class of buildings remains uniformly mean, confined, unsuited to their purpose, and these buildings are the Grammar Schools. Out of some sixty or seventy there are but two (Preston and Lancaster) which both in point of elegance and commodiousness, can be pronounced altogether satisfactory."

The private schools were generally pronounced to be deplorable.

"Arithmetic, penmanship, possibly also French are assiduously cultivated : Latin is languid : even mathematics is pushed on one side. Not in more than three or four private schools in the whole country did I find that the main object of teaching was to invigorate the mind by these robust studies."

The private schoolmasters had declaimed against the tyranny of Latin and Greek, but had put nothing equally good in its place. Their arithmetic was not superior to that of the Grammar schools.

"Much is made of geography, history and miscellaneous information of diverse kinds but so far as I could discover not to any great purpose. The pupils had been taught a good many facts, but then only just the facts which a smartish boy picks up for himself, when he leaves school. Meanwhile the discipline and guidance, which the school ought to give him, had been neglected."

In general the balance of argument strongly inclined in favour of the fee-paying as against the gratuitous school :

"It is easy to conceive circumstances under which gratuitous education may be right and necessary. But looking at the phenomena as a whole, it cannot be doubted that most frequent and most glaring instances of inefficiency, neglect and general mismanagement are to be found among the free schools."

It should be remembered that Bryce is not here talking of elementary schools, attendance upon which is now compulsory, but of the old Grammar schools offering an elementary education often apt, because it was eleemosynary, to be little valued by ambitious parents.

Another conclusion which runs counter to current opinion was that the claim of the small school to excel, by reason of the facilities which it provided for "individual" teaching, was not substantiated.

"Among both the private and the endowed schools which I examined, the larger were almost invariably the better; and this not merely because good teachers succeed in collecting a greater number of pupils. There seems to be something depressing in the very atmosphere of a small school. . . . Individual teaching does not mean the bestowal of good private tuition on each boy. It does not even mean the supplementing of collective teaching by half-an-hour or so spent each day with the boy alone. It means the neglect of class teaching and the attempt to replace it by giving the fortieth share of a teacher's attention to each of the forty boys at once — the most wasteful and purposeless of all possible modes of teaching."

The two principal defects which struck Bryce in the educational system of Lancashire were the poverty of the education which professed to be commercial and the meagre opportunities for the education of girls. These blemishes were interconnected. The reason why the vast majority of parents especially of the commercial class were "indifferent to any education whose pecuniary value they do not see" was because the women, who alone have leisure, were empty of intellectual interests and attachments. The remedy was female education. Educate the women and in time the mothers of Lancashire would come to see that "nothing does so much harm to the education of the middle classes as the notion that there is such a thing as middle class education." He accordingly pleaded first for the establishment of schools for girls under public authority and supervision, secondly for changes in the curriculum of girls' schools (more arithmetic, Latin where there was a fair prospect of a girl being able to spend four hours a week on it for three years, English literature, elements of logic and political economy) and lastly for the opening of places of higher education for girls, since only so could the low standard of education among school mistresses be remedied. Many of these recommendations are now happily embodied in the educational practice of the country. And perhaps it would be well if the vital necessity of attending to a solid grounding in Arithmetic and Latin even in schools which profess to be commercial were more generally attended to than is now the case.

In one further point of great importance Bryce was a pioneer. He urged that any scheme of educational reform must be comprehensive, that it must regard boys' schools and girls' schools, elementary schools and secondary schools, night schools and day schools, technical schools and universities as part of a single plan. The Education Act of 1918 embodied this, the only fruitful and legitimate conception of his work which the educational reformer should have in view.[1]

The Report of the Taunton Commission is a landmark in the educational history of England. For the first time the country was apprised, upon official authority, and after enquiry into some eight hundred endowed schools, of its deficiencies in respect of secondary education. Now at

[1] Bryce's Report on Lancashire is to be found in Vol. IX, pp. 423-839 of the Report of the School Commission. See also Vol. XVII and Vol. XX.

last it learnt how scanty were the opportunities even in flourishing industrial centres open to boys and still more to girls for obtaining a decent education after the primary stage, how inefficient were many of the schools, how uneven their distribution, how archaic their methods, how wasteful the use of educational endowments. As a remedy the Commission proposed that if any town or parish should be disposed to rate itself for the establishment of a school or schools it should be permitted to do so. In these days it seemed a brave step to suggest that secondary education might be made a charge upon the public purse. The Commissioners shrank from recommending a compulsory rate, nor did they appreciate that if a scheme of secondary education were ever to be effectually built upon the support of public funds the local areas must be larger than the parish. It was not until the Act of 1902 that a great extension of rate-aided secondary education became possible; but the Taunton Commission had exhibited the evil and suggested the lines upon which it might be attacked.

At this time the public opinion of the country was still fluid and uncertain as to the main groundwork of educational policy. The principle of universal compulsion had not been introduced into elementary education, and influenced by the reaction against tariffs which had been proceeding ever since the publication of the *Wealth of Nations*, many good minds were induced to contend for a policy of laissez-faire in education. Of these perhaps the most distinguished was Robert Lowe, who argued that the only safe way of providing abundant and good instruction for the children of the upper and middle classes was to trust to the commercial spirit of demand and supply. Bryce came out in opposition with an admirable statement of the case for national organization :

"Instruction in England," he wrote, "is at present wholly unorganised. Endowed schools, proprietary schools, State-paid primary schools (national and British) lie scattered here and there where chance has placed them, each managed without reference to those of a different class and grade. Some neighbourhoods are overstocked with schools: others equally or more prosperous have no schools at all or none of the grade needed. The whole thing is a chaos and the first step to educational reform is to recognise the necessity of having all places of instruction organised upon some general and definite principles so as to form parts of an ordered and comprehensive whole."

Nor was it sufficient to correlate the existing schools.

"In every one of our great towns, in Manchester, Birmingham, Leeds, Liverpool, Bristol, Newcastle, Sheffield, there ought to be besides the schools an institution like a Scotch or German University, though not necessarily with so large a stock of professors, giving instruction of a high order in the most important branches of literature and science."

The main objects which Bryce here proposed were happily accomplished during his lifetime.

The work upon the Commission was only one of many threads of activity pursued between 1865 and 1868. Bryce still maintained his connection with Oxford, travelling down from London to lecture and keeping contact with a wide circle of historically minded friends. Articles were written for the *Saturday*, the *Cornhill* and other Magazines, a chapter was contributed (in 1867) on *The Historical Aspect of Democracy* to a volume of *Essays on*

Reform, the main purpose of which was to show that "the demand for a mere national Parliament is not a mere cry to which it would be folly and weakness to give way, or the expedient of a party anxious to attain power by the aid of popular agitation, but a conviction seriously entertained and capable of being supported by arguments worthy of the attention of those who wish to legislate deliberately and in an impartial spirit for the good of the whole nation." [1]

At the same time wider literary projects were entertained, one of which was an edition of Cicero's letters, a very serious lacuna at that time and one which Bryce, by reason of his lively sympathy with the social, legal, and constitutional aspects of Roman civilisation could have filled with great distinction. From this project, however, Bryce was drawn away by an offer from the Clarendon Press (March 1867) that he should undertake a History of the Empire of Germany during the Middle Ages. The terms were generous and the author of the *Holy Roman Empire* was clearly marked out for this great historical task. Cicero was accordingly put aside and it may be presumed that such leisure as the Education Commission, journalism, the bar, politics and travel permitted, were allotted to the new enterprise. The great history was, however, never destined to see the light. Fresh acquisitions of mediæval knowledge, and they were numerous, for Bryce continued to keep himself *au courant* to a remarkable extent with the march of German historical scholarship,

---

[1] Other contributors were G. C. Brodrick, R. H. Hutton, Lord Houghton, A. V. Dicey, Leslie Stephen, J. B. Kinnear, Bernard Cracroft, C. H. Pearson, Goldwin Smith, A. O. Rutson.

were woven into successive editions of the *Holy Roman Empire* but never embodied in a separate book. "When is Bryce's *History of Germany* coming out?" was a question asked in Oxford for many decades. But the classical history remained unwritten and mediævalists like Freeman derived little consolation for its loss from the successive improvements which were introduced into the Arnold Essay or from the appearance of three substantial volumes on the *American Commonwealth*. There was nobody, however, more acutely sensitive than Bryce to the law of diminishing returns in the field of erudition. He had said his say on mediæval Germany in the *Holy Roman Empire* and we may doubt whether the labour of writing another book largely covering the same field would have yielded him a proportionate income of enjoyment and interest or would have compensated the public for the loss of his many contributions to the literature of travel, jurisprudence, and political science.

The friendship with E. A. Freeman was very close in these years. The two men were drawn together, not only by their common interest in history and archæology but by a common method of approaching historical and political subjects. They were both romantic, interested in the epical side of history; both were nurtured in the literature of Greece and Rome, and concerned with the classical ideas of liberty, both too were attracted by the things which make history vivid and real, the topography of battles, the architecture and landscapes associated with historical incidents, as well as by the political issues of the past. Each saw in Austria the emblem of tyranny and obscurantism as well as the foe of nationalism and was passionate for the liberating movements in Italy and Hungary; each was greatly impressed with the worth of German character and with the historical achievement of the German nation. In their companionship, Bryce, as the younger man, was probably at the outset the recipient rather than the originator of intellectual impressions, but in temperament and proclivity there was a natural sympathy between them.

So in these years there are many traces of the association of "The Holy Roman" with Freeman. We hear of Bryce going down to Somersetshire to help Freeman in his election when he was standing in the Liberal interest for Mid-Somerset in 1868 and of a joint visit in the following year to the field of Senlac. And the friendship with Freeman naturally led to a friendship with Freeman's friend, J. R. Green, likewise an historian and a Liberal.[1] For all three history was not a dead thing, an affair of Babylonian weights and measures, nor yet a romantic interest only, a miscellany of delectable memories, but a guide to wise conduct and the only key to humane and intelligent policies. To this association of young Oxford historians there was added the impressive figure of Goldwin Smith, likewise a Liberal, whose clearcut views on every topic, expressed, even in the most unguarded moments, in language of the finest elegance and precision made him the arbiter of every conversation.

Two minor but not insignificant activities of this period here deserve a brief notice. In 1865 when occupied with

[1] The first time I ever saw him was in St. Phillip's Church at Stepney about 1866 and I shall never forget the impression made on me by the impassioned sentences that rang through the church from the fiery little figure in the pulpit with its thin face and bright black eyes. — *Biographical Studies*, p. 167.

the work of the Schools Commission Bryce had formed an acquaintance with Miss Emily Davies, the eminent pioneer of University teaching for women. Miss Davies supplied him with introductions to women teachers in the North and Bryce entered into correspondence with her on matters affecting girls' education. Two years later we find him criticising a circular which Miss Davies proposed to issue with regard to the establishment of a Women's College, if possible to be connected with the University of Cambridge. A question affecting the proposed Women's College which exercised Bryce was the statement in the Circular that the religious services and instruction in the proposed College should be in accordance with the principles of the Church of England.

"I need not tell you," he writes, "that I would far rather there was no intention of one denomination any more than another, but, of course, you have to look at the practical aspect of the plan and the feeling of the English upper class."

The College which formed the matter of this correspondence was opened at Hitchin in 1869 and removed to Girton in 1873. Bryce gave some lectures on Greek history at Hitchin and was an original member of Girton College. He was thus associated with the beginnings of the movement for giving a University education to women and was throughout his life an active adherent of the cause. There had been many highly educated women in Bryce's own family, not least his own mother, to whom he owed so much. He had thus from early youth been accustomed to the society of women who read widely and talked intelligently, and was never able to understand why the benefits of the highest forms of education should be denied to women, seeing that from his own family experience they were so admirably fitted to profit by them. On the other hand, he remained through life a convinced opponent of female suffrage. It was repugnant to his chivalrous conception of the other sex that they should be involved in the hard clash and sordid struggles of the political arena and to the end of his days he continued to doubt whether the extension of the Franchise to women was otherwise than a misfortune.

The other activity was related to the efforts of a young academical institution in the north of England to make good its claim to rank as a British University. In 1868, Bryce accepted the invitation of Mr. R. C. Christie to lecture on law at Owen's College, Manchester, and continued to deliver courses of instruction first as lecturer and then as professor until the end of the session 1873-4.

The recollection of his remarkable gifts was long cherished by his pupils. "He would lecture on Jurisprudence without a note," writes a correspondent to the Manchester Guardian. "Sometimes after stating matter which would occupy about thirty lines to print in your columns he would say 'Now, Gentlemen, that is a most important passage,' and proceed to quote it verbatim." [1]

He also prepared the draft constitution for an enlarged College upon which the Act that received the Royal Assent on July 4th, 1870 was based. Thus he had a direct and important share in the construction of the institution which, after further changes, became the Victoria University of Manchester.

[1] "Manchester Guardian." Jan. 27, 1923.

Nor were these the only services which he rendered to Owen's College. The Faculty of Law and Jurisprudence owes to him its first scheme of studies framed, as he pointed out at the time, "with a view to the practical needs of students rather than to scientific propriety." And when in 1874 the new Owen's College buildings were opened he contributed to the volume of Essays and Addresses, published in commemoration of the event, an essay on the Judicature Act of the previous year which, in the opinion of one of the best of judges, is in respect of lucidity of arrangement and force of critical comment surpassed by few of his writings. For Manchester and its people he acquired a great respect.

"Manchester," he wrote to his mother,[1] "has a very perfect idiosyncrasy compared with any other town I have seen; it is less bustling and crowded than London; but the people wear a greater look of earnest restlessness and resolution to get on, a sort of rude rough vigour, determined to jostle obstacles out of its way they have, such as neither the lean hungry-eyed Yankee nor the shrewd thrifty Scot equals, though each is perhaps as successful. England gets quite one half of its curiously mixed complicated character from these northern people."

One other friendship of peculiar intimacy during the sixties may here be touched upon. Henry Nettleship, gifted alike as a Latin scholar and a musician, had by one of those lapses of justice which occasionally occur in examinations, obtained a second class in Greats in the list in which Bryce had won the highest honours. The two young men were making holiday together in Gloucestershire when the news reached them, and the pleasure with which Bryce learnt of his own success was dashed

[1] May 11th, 1866.

with genuine grief at the disappointment of a friend. For some years Bryce and Nettleship appear to have corresponded with one another with the frequency which belongs to young and intimate friendship. Letters are received from Nettleship congratulating Bryce on his first cases at the bar, countering his arguments against Church endowments, and keeping him informed of the progress of Annan Bryce at Oxford. Afterwards the tides of life swept them apart, politics dragging Bryce one way, Latin philology, a mistress hardly less exacting, exercising her empire over Nettleship. They saw less of one another and they corresponded less, but while intercourse rooted in pleasure or in self-interest vanishes the friendship which is founded upon moral esteem, is as Aristotle observes, eternal.

The younger brother at Balliol who furnished matter for some of Nettleship's letters was destined to show ample evidence of the family ability. Indeed, up to a certain point the two brothers might have exclaimed with Horace "Utrumque nostrum incredibili modo consentit astrum," for each was a First in Greats and became President of the Oxford Union, each was an observant traveller, and each sat as a Liberal member for a Scottish seat.[1] John Annan, however, on leaving Oxford went into business and spent many years in India and Burma, paying the penalty, if such it be, which attaches to the transaction of business affairs but retaining through life a vivid interest in art and travel. To his elder brother he stood in a relation half fraternal, half filial, but of unbroken affection and esteem.

[1] J. A. Bryce sat for Inverness from 1906-1918.

CHAPTER VII

INTELLIGENT OBSERVATION

1864–68

A magnanimous soul is always awake. The whole globe of
the earth is but a nutshell in comparison with its enjoyment.
The sun is its lamp, the sea is its fishpond, the stars its jewels.

TRAHERNE.

To this period of his career belongs a holiday in
Transylvania with Leslie Stephen. Thirty-two
years afterwards in proposing Bryce as President
of the Alpine Club, Leslie Stephen, who claimed to be
'the creator of Bryce as a mountaineer' alluded humor-
ously to this expedition. 'I remember going with Mr.
Bryce on our first expedition together into the Carpathian
mountains, a wonderful region for political philosophers
and for all sorts of peoples, Magyars, Wallachians, Germans, and I know not what others, all there huddled
together in a manner which delights the intelligent observer. He observed intelligently until I succeeded in dragging him off into the mountains, not so high as the Alps,
but haunted by bears and wolves and more or less imagi-
nary banditti. Then he showed me that he was a thoroughly competent mountaineer quite able to keep me at
my full stretch when my powers were at my best.' Some
letters illustrating Bryce's power of 'intelligent observation' both in Transylvania and elsewhere during this
period of his life are here appended.

[119]

James Bryce

The first written to his sister Kate (April 14, 1864) describes Garibaldi's reception in London.

Monday last was really a wonderful scene here; the most striking that has been seen in London for many years, and one indeed which it would be hard to see anywhere else. At 1.30 P.M. I went with several friends to the middle of the broad street called Whitehall which runs from the Houses of Parliament to Charing Cross, and there we took up our position in the middle, just between the Horse Guards on one side and the old palace of Whitehall on the other. Even then the streets were lined with spectators, who increased steadily hour after hour, till by 4 P.M. the vast area was one mass of dense packed human creatures, most of them of the poorer classes, some women intermixed, all in the best humour, the street boys full of gibes at the occupants of the carriages who struggled through the crowd till the police at last stopped all traffic. Not till after five did the procession begin to appear, though Garibaldi had reached the station a mile and a half off at 2.30; and then what a strange sight it was: a string of dirty unshaven men carrying the flags and tawdry decorations of their trades unions and friendly societies; many temperance associations among them, Bands of Hope and so forth, shuffling queerly along with a mixture of conscious sense of dirt and self-importance at joining in such a ceremony. When these and some cabs and carriages with members of various committees had passed, all came to an end, and no Garibaldi. The impatience and uneasiness lest he should have been attacked by the Irish or have gone another way was frightful; we were scarce able to stand with fatigue, having been on our feet near five hours; it was growing dusk and we feared not to see him after all. At last after seven distant cheering was heard from the bridge; then the sounds of his band playing the Garibaldi hymn, then their well-known red shirts in the van, at last a four horse carriage in the midst of a shouting, swaying rushing mob which stopped the horses at every step. When he came in front of the palace out of whose window Charles I stepped to the scaffold, there was just sunlight enough left for us and the eager mass of spectators who crowded every window and house-roof and swarmed on statues and lamp posts to see above the throng a face the sweetest and gentlest I have ever seen, with the well-known felt hat, red shirt and grey cape, turning every way to acknowledge the rapturous welcome of the people who felt they had at last a hero of the people, a man who could be admired and loved for himself and his deeds alone, with no wordly power, no lofty connections among crowned heads, to detract from his own merits.

The next extract (March 8th, 1865) portrays a very different character.

Some days ago I went to Birmingham and saw Dr. Newman at the Oratory. He received me (introduced by a friend of his) very kindly, with a sort of grave sweet simplicity which coming from so old a man, has in it something inexpressibly touching; and we had a long conversation; he giving me lunch and showing me over his library and then chapel. He looks very aged, hair more white than silvery, body stooped, a very large and prominent nose and large chin, brow which seems good, though one can't see it for the tangled hair falling over it; an air of melancholy, as of one who has passed through terrible struggles, yet of serenity, as of one who had found peace. Not a priest in his manner — still an Englishman more than a R. Catholic. He spoke freely about Gladstone and the controversy, but we talked chiefly about old Oxford. On the whole, he quite came up to the expectations one had formed all these years during which one has been hearing so much of him. There was music going on part of the time; he appeared to enjoy it intensely, plays himself moreover.

Of his experiences during the Transylvanian expedition in the summer of 1866 Bryce writes home with his habitual gusto.

James Bryce

Hermannstadt,

August {13th
15th, 1866.

We are now in the country which is, according to Herodotus, inhabited by the Agathyrsi, who tattoo their bodies, and live on human flesh. Hitherto, we have met with no instance of either practice — on the contrary the barbarous people have showed us no little kindness, and we have met with more courtesy than one would often find in some civilised regions.

But the journey here — if we had not survived it, I could hardly have believed it endurable at all. From Pesth to Arad was a most tedious day of heat and dust; from Arad to Hermannstadt we were a night, a day and a night, 33 hours in all cooped up inside the post-waggon, the heat by day such as even the natives considered extraordinary; blinding clouds of dust all round us, and no possibility of changing posture. Before we got in here in the morning of the 12th, at four thirty A.M. the cushions seemed to have turned to boards and the waggon itself to have become an engine box, wherein we were to be shaken for ever. It is well over now — but perhaps we may find it as hard to get out of Transylvania as it was painful to get in.

Hermannstadt is a thorough German town, with narrower streets than the Hungarian Arad, its little beer-houses and conditories, its quaint old fifteenth century church, belonging by good luck to the Evangelicals, and its simple honest people going out in homely sad coloured dresses. Only on Sundays and holidays do the women come out in the gorgeous attire which their ancestors brought from Saxony hither, some six or seven hundred years ago. The town lies in an open plain some eight miles wide from low brownish hills on the N. to the bold high wooded ranges which form the Turkish frontier on the South. Down through this range the Aluta finds its way into Wallachia by the Red Tower Pass, and falls at last into the Danube. We walked out this afternoon some five miles from here to a village standing in a hollow at the N. foot of these

[122]

hills, or rather of their lower spurs, nestling under deep woods of oak and beech and other forest trees to us unknown. It is famous for its fortified church, a high-roofed building with a strong square tower, surrounded by a double wall, so that when an enemy approached, the people drove their cattle into the churchyard, placed their household stuff under sheds or in the church, and poured arrows on the foe from the narrow windows of the upper church storey. This was done in many of the Saxon towns, as well as in our little Heltau — for there was always fear of Tartars and Turks, and sometimes the neighbouring Romans would rise to attack the German settlers. The lad who showed us the church told us with some pride that in all Heltau there was not a Wallack nor a Catholic, all Saxon protestants. These Wallacks or Romans are said to be the descendants of the ancient Dacians, mixed with Slavs; they pretend themselves to be of Roman blood. Till 1848 they were the serfs of Hungarian nobles — and now that they are free and own their land they are almost worse off than before, being a lazy thriftless race, who spend their earnings in drink, and when any calamity comes on them, sell or pledge the farm to a Jew who turns them to shame before long. They have a vacuous, but otherwise not unamiable look — only quite wild — they look wonderingly at the stranger, but generally salute him by doffing their hat. Fancy living in a country where in every parish people speak at least three languages — perhaps four.

Of the social condition of the inhabitants I can't tell you much — as one sees only the outside of everything. The Germans here are much like Germans anywhere else — and stand by Austria, since she represents their nationality. There is no such hole of wretchedness and poverty in Transylvania as in the great Hungarian plain through which we came by railway and where Austrian soldiers were packing into the train weeping Slovak conscripts, round whom their sweethearts from the village were clinging. Even the dress is somewhat more Christian and less dirty in these parts than along the Theiss.

James Bryce

To-day (Tuesday 14th) is market day, and a great crowd of natives fills the open spaces of the town. The women wear sometimes very broad and shallow straw hats with flowers — but more often gay coloured handkerchiefs wreathed round their caps, and two aprons, a black one in front and a bright-coloured curtain-like one hanging down behind to the heels. We have just had a walk in the country, led by a gewisser Krabs, a bookhandler, who very civilly gave us his afternoon, and have returned in a peasant's waggon, not without jolting. First we saw a Wallack village, wherein not a man was to be seen — the women were all sitting at their house-doors spinning in the old fashion with distaff and spindles. The churches — Greek — are adorned outside with pictures of saints — especially George and Michael, and there is a profusion of little shrines all up and down the streets similarly decorated. Thence we went to a gipsy settlement, where half the people were living in holes, roofed over like a bee-hive with a mound of earth, wattle, and straw. The wild-looking children pursued us begging. Then last, after a lovely walk down a wooded glen — we reached a German village, where each house stood apart hidden by fruit trees and tall poplars from its neighbours, and whence we drove back hither in a peasant's waggon. You see what a catastrophe has befallen this sheet — I have no time to write a new one. To-day, August 15, despairing of the weather and of a peak named Csorta on the Turkish border which we had hoped to climb we start Northwards towards the gold-diggings and Klausenburg, whence I hope to write you. I enclose some sprigs of Asplenium septentrionale, found among the rocks here — and a pretty little flower from near Heltau.

Arad,
August 10th, 1866.

All things have alternatives, and so one must not expect every day's journey to be equally pleasant. From Vienna to Pesth down the river was pure enjoyment, from Pesth by railway hither by no means so. From 7 A.M. till 4.40 P.M. we dawdled along in a "gemischter zug" at a pace of some seventeen miles an hour, stopping ten or twenty minutes at each station.

The country is a plain throughout, a dead and absolute level such as I had never seen before except at sea, and far more dismal than the heaving waste of blue. Nearly half the land lies uncultivated, and the fiery sun has by this time destroyed the grass, so that it is a desert of dry bare earth — in fact a steppe, such as one reads of in Russia and Tartary. The people are more like savages than one would expect to find in Europe. Their dress is a loose linen jacket hanging down to the waist and below what looks like a linen petticoat but is really a pair of very loose linen drawers, descending to the knee. Ankle and foot are bare except that some of the richer sort wear huge boots of crumpled leather, laced up the leg with thongs.

Here in Arad — where we have had to stay a whole day, there being no room in the post to Hermannstadt on the night of our arrival — it is market-day, and the strangest variety of dresses and faces adorns the big open square in the centre of the town. There are Magyars who form the aristocracy here, with braided coats and jack-boots, Wallacks, or Roumans, as they are commonly called, a swarthy undersized race, with the linen dress I have described, and sometimes hung over it a dirty sheepskin; there are Jews in long black robes and broad-brimmed hats, the cutest looking and the dirtiest of all; and lastly there is a sprinkling of repulsive gipsies, their black hair dangling in wisp-like curls about their shoulders. As far as the laziness and the confusion go, one might fancy oneself in some country town of Ireland, but the scorching sun, the intense blue air in which the clouds hang like solid things, and the strange names on the gaily coloured houses make one feel at an enormous distance from home. I find myself in this enervating heat, where the huge plain is watered only by a sluggish muddy stream like the Maros here, realizing with painful intensity the fresh streams of Arran, or the delights of a plunge in Cardigan Bay on Pwllheli strand. This evening at seven we set off by the post on a tedious journey of two nights and a day to Hermannstadt in Transyl-

James Bryce

vania, where, however, we hope to be in a cooler atmosphere,
among the hills. Thence we think of moving Northwards to
Klausenburg, and so either back to Pesth direct or via the north-
most Carpathians, where we are told there is some very pretty
country and high peaks worth climbing, though not quite up
to the snowline. There however, as here, there is one sad draw-
back to travelling. The days are hot — the nights are not only
hot but rendered tedious by the combat one has to maintain
against the inhabitants. Their light infantry, like the Prussian,
is more than a match for the artillery of camphor and insekten
Pulver which we bring to bear against them. However, it is to
be hoped that after all this one will learn to appreciate more
the blessings of travelling in a civilised country.

Pesth itself, is a fine town'— happily altogether without
sights, except indeed the new suspension bridge which connects
it with Buda. We walked some three miles out to call on one
Baron Eötvös to whom Arthur Stanley gave me a letter; and
had from his house, on the top of the Schwannenberg, some
1,400 feet high, a splendid prospect of the bright city and the
windings of the stream with its long islands far away down into
the southward plain. The Hungarians are a courteous graceful
people, and among their women a wonderfully large proportion
of pretty faces. Their features are delicate, the complexion
clear — generally rather blonde than dark, their bearing full
of ease and withal somewhat stately. And the little round hat
or rather cap which forms the head-dress is absolutely bewitch-
ing.

Gyorgo Szent Miklos, Aug. 28.
Tusnud Bad, August 29.
Kronstadt, Aug. 31.

1866.

From Borszek, whence I last wrote to you, we drove down to
a village called Tolgyes, which you may probably find on the
map — close to the Moldavian frontier. Our object was a high
hill beyond the border, which we had seen coming from Toplitza
— and hoped to ascend. Everybody in Borszek crowded round

us, giving advice, and making statements wholly irreconcileable with each other respecting the distances and the accommodation. We had been introduced to a certain Graf who was lodging in the village, and he carried us round everywhere, all sorts of fellows offering letters of introduction, and proposing that when we came to such and such a place we should stay with them. One Moldavian boyard — the place is full of Moldavians and Wallackians — queer-looking customers — savage with a little French polish on the surface, gave us a letter to another — and armed with all these directions we drove off to Tolgyes, the frontier village, and put up at an inn kept by an Armenian woman — (there are lots of Armenians in these parts). Here we got hold of the Kaiserlich Königlich forester of the district, who agreed to accompany us to the mountain. Next morning we were off, got over the frontier with a passport — and drove down a long valley by the river Bistritz — and then up another to the foot of the Csaltho' — so the mountain is called — where in a delicious green meadow — under the deep pine woods backed by glittering crags lies a little convent of Greek monks. Terrible stories had been told us at Toplitza, Borszek, and Tolgyes respecting the banditti who infest these mountains, so that the forester brought with him two guns and a pistol. Here on the spot the danger seemed to become more imminent. A Wallack boy with the organ of wonder developed, as Mamma would say, to the exclusion of all others — came and told us — or rather the forester — for of course we could not understand a word — that the robbers had appeared that very day in this very forest, twelve or fourteen strong, and that they not only plundered, but also stripped and beat their hapless victims. The forester now became really frightened, and — especially as the day was hot, and he no climber, did not wish to go further. Luckily we were firm, and did not say a word that he could lay hold of, so on we went. He gave me with great solemnity a gun, put a cap on it, and slung it over my shoulder, the plant-book dangling in front. We had all our money about us, and didn't know that we might not be foolish in going on, but having already learnt to believe only one tenth of what we heard, we did not like to cave in — and the result proved this British instinct right, for we met with nothing more formidable than a superb eagle, who went wheeling round and round the crags of the mountain.

The ascent was not long — and the height may be 6,300 feet. The upper part is entirely conglomerate, which weathers white, and all along the ridge rises in grand pinnacles, whose bases are fringed by black pines. The day was not very clear, though bright, still the view eastward was very extensive and impressive from the very absence of any of those known objects which one usually catches in a mountain prospect. All round for twenty miles, towards E. and W. — for perhaps five degrees N. & S., one saw nothing but silent, forest-covered mountains, and deep valleys, all without a sign of life. Then beyond these to the east were rolling hills, finally subsiding beyond Piatia into the great plain of Moldavia and Bessarabia. The Pruth showed us a long bright line almost on the horizon — the guide pointing out the site of Jassy, beyond this more plains, all across the steppes of the Caspian to the Altai. It was strange to think that between us and them there was no hill. S. E. we strained our eyes for the Euxine, and assured each other that we saw it. N. W. and W. a boundless region of ridgy shapeless mountains rolled away, one over the other, far out of sight.

There is little beauty, or variety in the forms of the Carpathians, though this peak on which we stood is a notable exception — even the valleys are seldom picturesque — it is much more the vastness and solitude, and the exquisite richness of the lower wood — beech, oak and birch — that gives the scenery its peculiar charm. It seems — as Tennyson says — a land where no man comes, or hath come, since the making of this world. Geologically — I have of course been able to see very little. The watershed in one place where we crossed seemed to be of schist, in others of a granitic gneiss. On both sides there are huge strata of conglomerate, and here and there beds of limestone. The Borszek springs, for instance, seem to come up

at the junction of the schist and limestone. The singular thing
is that there has been so much volcanic action in many parts of
the mountain district, though its own structure is nowise volcanic. This is witnessed to not only by the hot springs as at
Toplitza — and all down the valley of the Alt — at Tusnud
Kovasna — and many other places — but also by the existence
of sulphur beds. One has recently been found N. W. of Borszek,
and to-day (Aug. 29) we have seen another in a region of extinct
volcanoes — in the valley of the Aluta. We got late last
night to this place. Turned in after a most fatiguing drive in a
jolting waggon, open to the sun, from Gyorgo Szent Miklos —
some forty five miles. This morning we started at $9\frac{1}{4}$ with a
Szehler guide, who knew — of course — no word of German.
Over a steep wooded hill we reached a singular little lake, sunk
deep among the hills, the crater of an extinct volcano, its stone
covered with a gravel of trachyte and that light whitish stone
of which one finds so much round Naples and Baiae. From
this it was a two hours march through delightful beech-woods
to Budas, where on the side of a high hill are two caves in the
same softish rock; in one of which sulphur is found, the walls
being coated with it, and the vapour within stifling. In the
other there is some sulphur too, though less, and an extraordinary quantity of carbonic acid gas, exactly like the Grotti
del Cane. We lit paper, which became extinguished as soon as
it reached the floor. The hills are covered so thick with wood
that the exact lines of craters are not easily traceable — still
one can see how they must have run. All round the country
teems with mineral springs. Close to this place — Budas —
are three or four quite distinct — one of what they call here
sauerwasser — bubbling up with carbonic acid gas — another
of some sort of salt — a third of iron and I think another with
sulphur. The wealth of all this region in natural productions is
inconceivable, but the want of communication makes it un-
available for commercial purposes. All the Hungarians declare
that Transylvania is going back, and of course lay the blame on
the Austrian Government.

CHAPTER VIII

OXFORD AND ICELAND

Why do we long to wend further
Through the length and breadth of a land
Dreadful with grinding of ice
And record of scarce hidden fire
But that there mid the grey grassy dales
Sore scarred by the ruining streams
Lives the tale of the Northland of old
And the undying glory of dreams.

WILLIAM MORRIS

ON April 11th, 1870, Bryce received a letter from Mr. Gladstone offering him the Regius Chair of Civil Law in the University of Oxford. The Chair, which was founded by King Henry VIII and occupied in the reign of James I by the illustrious Alberic Gentile, had become a sinecure so far as the substantial teaching of the Civil Law was concerned, and the heaviest duty of the Professor was that of presenting in alternate years the destined recipients for honorary degrees at the Encænia in complimentary Latin. For this minor but honorific duty Bryce was admirably fitted. His Latinity was easy and graceful and he had the happy gift of terse characterization which is expected on complimentary occasions and more exquisitely achieved in the Latin than in the English language. Orations which would have afforded scholars of greater leisure matter for

Mrs. Bryce, Mother of Lord Bryce

most anxious consideration were tossed off with brilliant facility in the odd corners of a day filled with other business. For his first Commemoration Ceremony, which coincided with the inauguration of Lord Salisbury as Chancellor of the University, he was called on to compose no less than fifty speeches — an exceptional ordeal — on eminent persons of very diverse gifts, including Canon Liddon, Matthew Arnold, Edwin Landseer, Sterndale Bennett, Robert Lowe, and E. A. Freeman.

"I was pressed very close at the last, having had other work in London till Saturday morning, and having had to examine all Saturday at Oxford for BCL, so that there was scarce any time to get twenty two speeches ready for Tuesday and twenty eight for Wednesday. I had to sit up till past one on Tuesday night (having been at the great Chancellor dinner at All Souls) and get up after hardly any sleep before six on Wednesday to set to work again at the speeches. I found myself both on Tuesday and Wednesday in excellent train and voice and was distinctly heard in every part of the theatre: though I tell it! it will please you so much that I must tell it, it was really I believe, a great success, and everyone (even old Tories who gnashed their teeth at my appointment) both in Oxford and since in London have been congratulating me on the whole thing. . . . Old Freeman was neither to hold nor to bind. It was great fun."

In 1873 Bryce had the pleasure (using for the first time the new Latin pronunciation) of introducing his friend, James Russell Lowell, the American minister, "in celeberrimâ illa atque nobis dilectissimâ academiâ Harvardensi olim professorem," and of pronouncing a eulogy on the *Biglow Papers*.

The substantial work of the Chair, for the University was now resolved to make it substantial, consisted in

the delivery of public Lectures, in examining for the
B. C. L. degree and for the Honours School of Jurisprudence (founded in 1872) and more generally in taking
a share in the direction of legal studies in the University.
In the revival of an interest in Roman Law Bryce was a
pioneer. "Till 1870," he says, "there was scarcely any
teaching in Roman Law and what little did exist in the
Colleges was confined to commenting on the solitary
book (*The Institutes of Justinian*) set for the examination.
No one had lectured on the Digest; no one had treated
the history of the subject." The decline of this, the earliest of all the subjects taught in the University, was an
indication of the remarkable isolation of England from the
general current of European legal thought and practice.
Bryce, who had sat at the feet of Von Vangerow in Heidelberg, conceived it to be part of his duty to awaken an
interest in the Civil Law not as an antiquarian curiosity,
but as a great power in the moulding of European thought
and history and in its relations by way both of contrast
and resemblance to the Common Law of England, which
it was stimulating and instructive to explore. To small
but select companies drawn by the fame of the lecturer
to the Hall of Oriel College he would discourse widely,
eloquently, learnedly, but always with clarity and power
upon those aspects of the science of jurisprudence which
were most interesting to the historian, the publicist, and
the traveller. The present writer well remembers how,
one Saturday afternoon, in the summer term, at an hour
when most undergraduates were amusing themselves on
the river or the cricket field, he was impelled by curiosity
to stroll into the dining hall of Oriel, where an audience

some twenty strong were listening to a brilliant speech delivered from a manuscript or from full notes but with a force and animation rare, if not unknown, in Oxford lecture rooms by an alert, wiry, grey-bearded man with clean-cut features and flashing blue eyes and an azure neck-tie. The orator was speculating upon the possible effects of English laws upon the immemorial structure of Indian society. At present, it may be, there were few obvious signs of change. Caste barriers and caste customs appeared to survive almost in their original strength, but who could say but that this ancient and imposing fabric was all the time being sapped by hidden rills of influence percolating from the West? Then came the simile which drove the idea home — the image of a ship imprisoned for months in an Arctic icefield finding itself suddenly, by reason of the accumulated influence of warm but secret vernal currents, floating in the open sea. So it might be with India. The solid crust of Hindu custom might crack of a sudden and the vessel of Indian society might be destined to accomplish the remainder of her voyage on the strange and shoreless ocean of Western Jurisprudence.

The general view which Bryce took of the scope and value of his subject was expanded in his Inaugural Lecture on the Academical Study of Civil Law. It was his object to show that the study of Roman Law was not only an essential part of the education of the historian but that it was of special value to lawyers not only by reason of the influence which it had exerted upon our own domestic law but also as furnishing the key to the comprehension of foreign systems of jurisprudence and the whole fabric of international law. It was easy for the

historian of the Holy Roman Empire to illustrate the
formative influence of Roman Law upon mediæval thought.
What was less obvious was its practical utility for those
who regarded law as a means of making a livelihood.
Upon this point, however, Bryce sounded no uncertain
note. Quite apart from its educational value as a study
calculated to form and strengthen the intellectual habits
necessary for success in life, he held that Roman Law
enabled the student to obtain more rapidly than would
otherwise be possible a grasp of our own legal system.
Moreover in the great but still unaccomplished task of
codification, the classic precedents of imperial Rome were
of indispensable use and incomparable importance.

After his appointment to the Regius Chair, Bryce
usually spent his week-ends in Oriel where his visits were
greatly appreciated by Fellows and Undergraduates alike.
" He brought with him," writes the Provost, " a breath of
fresh air from the outer world. He was conversant with
all the best in literature and politics, he gave us a sense of
proportion, a varied interest and much of his own enthusiasm. A Liberal through and through he showed how a
clear and critical knowledge of the past was consistent
with a full appreciation of its romance and a zest for
progress. A zest for education in all its branches, an
ever growing familiarity with foreign countries, an interest in science as well as in letters gave a wealth of matter
to his conversation, while his personal charm and ready
sympathy carried conviction for the younger members of
the Common-Room. With the serious it was the same.
He joked with Stubbs, discussed Ithaca with Monro and
was one of the few who ventured to play with Freeman."

Nor was his influence limited to the Senior Common Room. "He would," continues the Provost, "gather round him at breakfast the leading undergraduates and hold them spell-bound. He did not, as some talkers, lecture to the circle, but he had a consummate power of setting them at their ease, of drawing out their opinions of men and books, of catching the drift of the undergraduate mind. We used to say that when he went back to London, he took with him a clearer knowledge of Oxford, its standards and its judgments than we who lived here could claim to have." [1]

The year in which Bryce received his Oxford appointment was the Annus Mirabilis of the nineteenth century, marked as it was by the outbreak of the Franco-Prussian war, the completion of Italian unity and the Vatican Decree establishing the Infallibility of the Papacy. For some time Bryce dallied with the thought of going out to France as a war correspondent, but the plan was set aside for a journey which was destined to exercise a permanent influence on the course of his life and the nature of his interests and activities. In company with his friend, Albert Dicey, he paid his first visit to the United States.

There lived until August 1926 in the pleasant town of Cambridge, Mass., a famous American citizen over ninety years of age who retained a vivid memory of the descent of these two young Englishmen upon the soil of New England, and of their burning and insatiable curiosity as to

[1] Bryce was elected to a Fellowship at Oriel 25th April, 1862, vacated his Fellowship on marriage, was re-elected Professor Fellow 24th April, 1890, resigned 1893 and was made Honorary Fellow 12th October 1894. See, *The Provosts and Fellows of Oriel College* by G. C. Richards and C. L. Shadwell.

all things American. This was Charles Eliot, formerly
President of Harvard University and justly regarded as
one of the glories of American manhood, tall, erect, active,
a born leader of men, and, like Bryce, a denizen of two
worlds, the one academic, the other political. A friendship between two such intellectual and bodily athletes,
was soon formed and steadily maintained by intercourse
and correspondence until it was sundered by death.

It was the oldest, as it was perhaps the most intimate of
the many American friendships which Bryce was happy
enough to form during his oft-repeated visits to the
United States.

The travellers were well-equipped with introductions,
for Dicey's kinsman, Leslie Stephen was intimate with
the distinguished group of men at Harvard and Goldwin
Smith was already established at Ithaca in the lovely hill
scenery which is one of the delights of New York State.
So they met many arbiters of taste and leaders of thought,
Emerson and Longfellow, James Russell Lowell and
E. L. Godkin, Doctor Howe, the specialist in the teaching of the deaf and dumb, Oliver Wendell Holmes of the
breakfast table, and Oliver Wendell Holmes of the Com-
mon-law. With the last of these eminent men Bryce
kept in close touch for the remainder of his life.

"*Anima naturaliter Americana*" is a phrase which has
been applied to Bryce. There was indeed much in American life and society, as he first saw it, to attract his admiration and sympathy. Here he found great and unaffected
simplicity, an engaging spirit of equality and a quickening
sense of hopefulness, as inspiring as the dry, nimble air
and the stainless blue sky of an American Fall. Many of

the things which least appealed to him in English society were here absent, the intricacies and affectations of rank, the prominence of dogma and Church establishment, the wide powers and social prestige of the sporting landlord. Some things, on the contrary, which spoke to him, were plainly present. Bryce was a democrat and here was a democracy, the only great exemplar of democratic rule in the modern world; an educationalist and here was public education carried out on a mammoth scale. He fell in love with the United States. It was almost a case of love at first sight.

The idea of writing a treatise on the American Commonwealth had not yet occurred to his mind. Certain aspects, however, of American life and society had specially attracted his interest, and his impressions of these were given to the magazines upon his return. An article on *Some Peculiarities of Society in America*, contributed to the *Cornhill*, is a piece of light-hearted good-humoured observation (suggesting that the writer had had a very good time) of the ways of the American young woman and her chaperon; another on *American Experience of the Relief of the Poor* was written with the practical object of making known to British philanthropists a system of poor relief which had been found valuable in New York; a third on *Some Aspects of American Public Life* was directed to show that although corruption, vulgarity, and ignorance existed in America, they did not have the same importance as they would have in England because the best men did not go into politics. Moreover, the worst Americans never reached the highest places. "Out of the whole list of Presidents of the United States of

America there is not one on whose character for personal probity a stain rests." The main burden of his article was that America should not be judged by her politicians. The American people was one thing, the American Government was another. "Politics mean less and politicians count for less in the United States than in any European country. Their merits are less beneficial, their faults less mischievous, their whole sphere of action more restricted and less regarded than in England." Readers of Ambassador Page's striking letters will remember how, to his surprise and chagrin, he found that this distinction between the American Government and the American people was clearly established in the British mind. It had been pointed out by Bryce in 1871.

A visit to the Battlefields of France with his friend, Edward Bowen, the brilliant Harrow master and the writer of the Harrow school songs, occupied part of the summer of 1871. "It was a pleasure to be led over a battlefield by Bowen, for he had a good eye for ground, he knew the movements of the armies down to the smallest detail and he could explain with perfect lucidity the positions of the combatants and the tactical moves of the game." Between Bryce and this gay, light-hearted man of genius there was a bond of very deep sympathy. Three times in later years did they travel together in France and Germany, and it was while they were on their Easter holiday in 1901 that Bowen "died in a moment while mounting his bicycle after a long ascent among the lovely forests of Burgundy then bursting into leaf under an April sun."

Meanwhile the wish for a Parliamentary career was gaining ground. Somebody seems to have suggested that a seat might be won at Wick, a little town in Caithness at the extreme north of Scotland, where his grandfather had preached to zealous anti-burghers. The letter to his uncle John in which Bryce records a pious but not altogether disinterested pilgrimage to Wick is delightful reading:

Wick,
December 30th, 1871.

Dear Uncle John,

— Οικος εστι πολις ἐπ᾽ ἀριστερα
παραπλεοντι εἰς ᾽Ορκαδας νησὸυς
οὐτε μεγαλη λιαν οὐτε καλη, ουτε δη
αλλως μνημης ἀξια εἰ μη ὁτι ἐν αὐτῃ
συ αὐτος κ.τ.λ.[1]

It seems, I fear, that instead of seeing you this vacation I must content myself with seeing your birthplace; and odd enough it is that of all the family I should be the first to see it. Would that there were more to praise in it, but to me it is all unlovely save therein that it is your birth-place, and that I fancy you running about these bleak hill-sides, and gazing out on this cold, gloomy sea, this μεγα λαττμα πολιον as an eager child with wide and wondering eyes. A land that seems forgotten and cut off, swept forever by the wailing winds, beaten for ever by the melancholy surges, brooded over by heavy clouds rising for ever from the misty West — a land treeless and bare, where palisades of stone divide the fields, over which this winter sun casts but a faint and watery gleam and then hides himself again behind the darkening moor. Τρηχεῖ αλλ᾽ ἀγαθη κουροτροφος — a land where one may wonder that men should dwell at all, but where one feels that if they dwell they had need to be robust and strenuous, to wrest their life's means from unwilling Nature;

[1] Wick is on the left hand side as you sail towards the Orcades islands. The town is remarkable neither for size nor beauty nor otherwise memorable save that you yourself etc. (was born there).

and which one might, for its very sternness, get to love more than all the soft allurements of the South.

No one has anything to tell me of Pater's sojourn here — had I known in time I would have seen if you had known the house he lived in when you were born — it is that, rather than his life here that interests me, for he did not like the people. The congregation now meets in another church, built in a part of the town which did not exist at all in his day when Wick was a small place on the left or north bank of the river — and his church was at a spot called Newton — a mile or so out to the north or north east. An old woman died to-day at eighty who might have just remembered him as a child, but hardly that. No one else can I hear of.

The town is small, dark — built of the bluish grey Caithness flagstone — and not well kept — the people hardy and shrewd — mostly fisher folk, who have a struggling life of it.

Quod superest, there is no chance for me here at present. Samuel Laing, a former member, has resolved to stand, and will probably carry it against the briber Pender, spite of his long purse; there would be no opening for a third, especially as Laing's strength is in Kirkwall, where I could have best suited the people. However, I don't regret the journey, having seen the country and its people, the wild and once terrible Ord of Caithness, where Pater once got nearly lost in a snowstorm. I remember well his telling me the tale five-and-twenty years ago, and the town itself where you and Uncle Robert and I suppose, Aunt Jessie also saw the light. Enclosed are a few sprigs of withered heath from its rocks, the only thing I can find as a memorial at this season. The United Presbyterian congregation seems a pretty large one — but I could see no one in it old enough to have remembered Pater.

On Tuesday or Wednesday I hope to be at Blantyre again, but fear it will, after all this loss of time, be impossible for me to get over to you, but if I still can, will try — only don't expect me. A happy New Year.

The autumn of the following year brought with it a diversion from the law the more refreshing by reason of its being something of an adventure. Bryce had plotted a holiday in Norway with his friends, Ilbert and Mackay, but almost at the last moment, Mackay, having heard of a steamer which was to sail from Leith to Seydisford on the east coast of Iceland and to return to Reykjavik some three weeks later, diverted the excursion to Iceland. Here at least was a tempting prospect for young men who were still young enough and strong enough to enjoy roughing it for its own sake. And the Iceland voyage proved to be even rougher than was anticipated. Its early stages Bryce reported to his father (August 18, 1872) in the following terms:

We left Granton on the Thursday morning, as you doubtless gathered, and had it pretty calm up to the Pentland Firth, through which we passed early on Friday morning. Then a strong south wind sprang up, which carried us rapidly past Hoy, whose grand cliffs loomed out of the clouds upon us. By mid-day the sea had risen, and though the waves followed, the vessel began to roll a good deal, and did so even more next day, Saturday, which was mostly bright, with occasional showers, the wind having now got round to the West, and blowing very fresh. We passed not far W. of the Faroe Isles, but did not see them. The westerly wind had now carried the sea also round, and Saturday afternoon and all night long we rolled heavily, so that it was far from pleasant. Add to this that the saloon and still more the sleeping cabin was desperately close and evil scented, and you may fancy that we often vowed internally nothing should tempt us to visit Iceland again. High peaked mountains came in view about 8.30 A.M. to-day (Sabbath) and by 11 we were some six or seven miles from the coast, steaming along in the hope of discovering our fjord, where neither the

captain nor anyone else had ever been. We had merely the
chart to guide us and our guesses at identification of the points
and islands laid down on it. Fortunately these were pretty clear
— at 2.15 we turned to enter Seydisfjorde, and by 4 had cast
anchor at the head of it, some eight miles up from the open
ocean.

The coast is certainly very grand, and unlike anything I
remember to have seen. Lofty peaked mountains, faintly
sprinkled with snow (larger snow patches just showing themselves behind) run out in a succession of bold promontories, and
break down to the sea in tremendous faces, almost mural, of trap
rock, the upper part precipitous, exactly like the precipice of
the Storr in Skye, the lower an exceedingly steep slope of lakes.
Sometimes the cliff comes right down into the deep sea. A
faint and sparse green clothes the upper slopes of the hills, where
a peak rises behind the precipice, but for the most the mountains are altogether bare, and you can imagine nothing more
desolate or terrible than these grim pinnacles, and ridges,
crowned with fantastic tors and needles, rising out of a profound
and inky Arctic Sea. The whole aspect of the landscape is
chilling, desolate, lamentable. One felt that one had quite
passed away from the lands which Nature meant for man.

Inside the fjord the scenery is less dreary but hardly less
grand; the lower hillsides are clothed with grass and descend
in great steep sweeps to the deep dark blue water, not a trace
of cultivation, nor indeed of life at all till one gets near the top
of the fjord, where on the north side is a tiny church, a little
wooden shed about as big as the carriage house at Boweshill
with a neat two double cottage beside it which is doubtless the
parsonage. At the fjord head where we cast anchor there are
several houses scattered about, the smaller ones mere earth
burrows, rising little above the earth and covered with green
twigs, in which the natives live in smoke and filth inexpressible.
Beside it is anchored a British frigate, which to our great surprise steamed in just after us; she has been cruising all round
these coasts, looking after our fishing boats, it is supposed, but

practically amusing herself, for there seem to be few English boats up here. We go on shore and reconnoitre, trying in vain to make some arrangements about ponies to take us across the country, and at last seem likely (Monday morning Aug. 19) to come to an arrangement which is to include not only ourselves but two young Englishmen who have been passengers out along with us, named Marriott and Hornby, the brother of one of whom, who is returning by this ship, undertakes to post this letter to you. Over the worries and miseries of our bargaining for saddles, ponies, guides, etc. etc., I drop a veil; We have the sense of being horribly victimised, not so much by Icelanders, though they are bad enough, as by a Scotchman who has bought up all the ponies of the district and from whom we have to purchase what we need. After perils of the sea it is rather trying to have to undergo perils of our own countrymen likewise, but this is the common lot; we endeavour to be philosophical while they are screwing the uttermost farthing out of us, and making such a row at night in the saloon over their drink that we can scarcely get to sleep, and remark how keen and fresh the breezes are. Cold they certainly are; but it is pleasant to have daylight up till 11 o'clock — or rather 10.15 by Icelandic time, for we are far West of All Europe here.

At Akureyri, a hamlet of some fifty houses on the shore of the Arctic Ocean, whither they had ridden from their place of disembarkation, the travellers were met with the disquieting news that the return voyage from Reykjavik was not to come off. Could they catch the next mail steamer? Not, so they were informed, by the ordinary western route, but it might be possible to cross the central desert by a shorter, less known and more difficult route, which had not been tried for fifteen years or so and was supposed to be known to only one man in the whole countryside who bore the name of Sigurd, the hero of the Volsunger Saga. Of the journey across this appalling wilderness, Bryce subsequently published a description characterised by his usual felicity in recalling the emotions excited by the wilder aspects of nature.[1]

"There was not a cloud in the sky, not a bird, not an insect, not a floweret at our feet; only the blue dome of air raining down brightness on the black desert floor, the dazzling snows in front, and far away exquisite tints of distance upon the western peaks. And then the silence, what was ever like it? A silence not as of death but as of a time before life was."

It is hardly necessary to observe that Bryce brought to this, as to all his expeditions, a full cornucopia of the appropriate knowledge. "He had learnt," writes Sir Courtenay Ilbert, "all that was to be learned from Konrad Maurer and others about early Icelandic laws and institutions. He knew and loved the Icelandic sagas and would listen to long recitations from Ngala in an Icelandic rectory or farmhouse. In later days when Bryce was at Washington, President Roosevelt would draw up his knees and slap them with delight if he succeeded in eliciting Bryce's stores of knowledge about the sagas."

One interesting historical speculation suggested itself to Bryce's fertile and inventive mind as the result of his Icelandic visit. Why is the modern Icelander, despondent, sluggish, dilatory, so unlike the magnificent hero whose exploits are recorded in the sagas? The difference is far greater than that which divides the modern Frenchman or the modern Englishman from their mediæval prototypes, for the very qualities which are impressive in the Icelander of the sagas are conspicuously absent in the

[1] Reprinted in *Memories of Travel*, Macmillan Co. 1923.

Icelander of modern times. Was it the decline of piracy, or the extinction of the independent republic in 1262, or is something also due to the crushing influence of Nature? Whatever may have been the cause the result is certain. The glories of Iceland belong to days long past, and "The ghosts of these terrible heroes seem to stalk across the desert plains, mourning the downfall of their isle."

How the travellers were compelled to sleep in churches (there being no hotels in the island) how they bought a pony in Latin, or by what ingenious shifts they circumvented the difficulties of the Icelandic language were long matters of amused reminiscence. For Bryce the principal result of the Icelandic visit was a more profound interest in old Norse literature, not only for its own sake but also as supplying a key to the understanding of the Homeric poems as well as contributions to our knowledge of early English history. Indeed, in his view, the sagas belonged to the most attractive category of literature. Like the old Testament and the Homeric Poems and the *Divina Commedia* these ancient narratives depict the lineaments of a vanished civilisation, enabling us to form an idea of the passions and thoughts and actions of the men of old as well as of the ethical tone and social texture, of the laws and institutions and creeds of a remote age. There was something in the simplicity, in the breadth and the open-air breeziness of primitive literature which appealed to the spirit of Odysseus.

CHAPTER IX

Nos manet Oceanus circumvagus : arva, beata
Petamus arva, divites et insulas.

HORACE

1871–4

IT is difficult for Americans, who have little concern for
politics in their own country, to understand the
imperious force which drives men of high character
and wide ambition into political life in Britain. To serve
one's country at Westminster, to take part in the debates
in that classic assembly, the origins of which may be traced
back to the thirteenth century, to enjoy the influence and
the responsibility which attaches to the character of a
Member of Parliament, these are attractions which,
in the eyes of ambitious young Britons outweigh the
material advantages even of the most lucrative career
in industry, commerce, or finance. At Westminster great
issues of foreign and domestic policy are constantly de-
bated. Every year the panorama of contemporary world
history unrolls itself before the members. Every day
witnesses some episode in a conflict of parties which is
watched by the whole nation with an interest approaching
to that which is inspired by a contest on the race course
or the football field. If there is a social grievance to be
remedied, a foreign power to be encouraged or rebuked, a

[146]

great act of remedial legislation to be promoted, there is no place from which such objects can be more effectually advanced than from the front benches of the House of Commons. With every increment in the growth and industry of the British Empire in the world, the responsibility and reputation of this illustrious assembly was sensibly increased, and perhaps it had never stood higher, not even in the classic days of Charles James Fox and William Pitt, than during the years before the election of 1874, when the art of paralysing debate by obstruction was as yet undiscovered and Mr. Gladstone and Mr. Disraeli were at the height of their dazzling powers. During this year Bryce's life was full of multifarious activity. He was working hard at the bar, bringing out a new edition of the Holy Roman Empire, attending to the duties of his Oxford Chair and augmenting his income by contributions to the press. But at the same time he was turning over in his mind the prospects of a political career. "I have some idea of fighting Bouverie in the Kilmarnock Burghs," he wrote to his mother 20th March, 1873, "but still doubt whether it is compatible with practice at the bar and my Oxford Chair, and am excessively exercised to know which is the best course to take, whether abjure politics meantime and stick to the law alone, which hitherto has not been encouraging, or make Parliament one's first object. As respects money, which is of course a serious difficulty, my Chair and my savings together would give me enough to live upon."

The election of 1874 precipitated a decision. Bryce offered himself as a Liberal candidate for Wick and thoroughly enjoyed the fight ("another rattling meeting at

Dingwall last night; great enthusiasm, chairing to the hotel, speech from window, etc." . . . you will be pleased to know that I am the ladies' candidate everywhere, as well as the people's, especially the street boys who strut after me and cheer in all directions, whereas provosts, and bailies and such like are hostile with few exceptions"; but Mr. John Pender, his Liberal opponent, having the advantage of wealth and much influence was returned (857 votes to 730). The General Election indeed was disastrous to Liberals all over the country. Even in Scotland there was a loss of nine Liberal seats. In England and Wales the Tory majority was a hundred and five, in the new House of Commons forty-eight; but depressing as these figures were to the followers of Mr. Gladstone they did not represent the full measure of the disaster, for the Irish National Party, returned fifty-eight strong, now severed themselves from the Liberals and formed a separate Parliamentary organisation. The great Liberal chieftain went into retirement and for the time even the Liberal candidate for Wick Boroughs was compelled to lay aside his Parliamentary ambitions.

Travel is a regular part of the political equipment of a British statesman. There have been statesmen even among those who have risen to the highest eminence who have seldom or never crossed the Channel, but such insularity is rare. To learn something at first hand of the problems of foreign or imperial politics is generally regarded by industrious and ambitious young British politicians as a counsel of prudence which should be followed as far as circumstances permit. But Bryce did not travel in order to be able to make well-informed speeches on Foreign Affairs in the House of Commons. He travelled like Herodotus because he was filled with curiosity about the planet and the men and women who inhabited it. To James Bryce, said his witty friend William James, "all facts were born free and equal." And as when he read, so when he travelled, nothing was too insignificant to fix his attention and attract his notice. He is known to have had a train stopped that he might investigate a rare plant which his eager eye had detected nestling in some distant cranny, and while delighting in the form and colour of the landscape, he would be very careful to take note as a man of science of the geographical and geological foundation of the scene which he admired as an artist. He complained that his eye for colour was not good but it was certainly very far above the average. To climb a mountain if a mountain was in sight, to bathe in every notable river, to fish if occasion offered, were also habitual observances from which he derived great exhilaration. What he saw was the more tenaciously fixed in his memory by reason of the delightful physical experience which the vigorous exercise of his muscular powers provided for him. As a landscape painter in words he has few equals; and part of the joy of travel to him must have consisted in the ease with which he exercised this attractive gift and the great perfection to which, by reason of the fact that his emotion in the presence of scenes of natural beauty was deep, pure, and unaffected he succeeded in bringing it.

The August holiday of 1874 was spent in Norway with his younger brother Annan and Sir George Young. Some graphic letters to his father abounding in the detail most

likely to please the geologist, recount the experiences of
the party. The Romsdal more particularly impressed
the travellers. "The most striking and delightful feature
of all is the contrast of the intensely stern grandeur of
the precipices with the light green smiling levels of the
valley bottom and the tranquil splendour of the broad
river. The grandeur of this valley has taken us quite by
surprise, we had no notion that gneiss rock could assume
such spiry forms, break off in such monstrous mural
precipices. The grey whiteness is varied by huge black
drip streaks, so that oddly enough it looks exactly like
some of the great limestone cliffs of the Alps; and I was
often reminded of the gorge between Agordo and Belluno
which Ilbert and I descended in 1868."

On his return to London Bryce experienced a pleasant
surprise. A law case in which he was briefed necessitated
a voyage to Portugal in September 1874, and again in the
summer of the following year, and though the work of
examining witnesses would have been enough for most
men, it was not sufficient for Bryce, who contrived to
obtain a synoptic view of Spain and Portugal, to be cap-
tured as a brigand in the Portuguese mountains, to visit
Tangier and to write some vivacious letters home describing
his experiences, one of which might almost be printed, as
it stands, as a picturesque introduction to a geographical
description of Spain. To the sightseer, who after an uncomfortable night in a jolting diligence, gives up all hope of
breakfast in order to see a Cathedral, and is content at a
pinch with an allowance of two hours' sleep, many blessings
are vouchsafed beyond the reach of ordinary mortals.

Of the collection of letters relating to these experiences,

the following, written to his sister, may be taken as a good example : —

Tangier.
Oct. 16/75.

. . . I ran across the Straits to-day in a little steamer and landed here to find myself at once in the middle of the East and Islam, the Bible and the Arabian Nights. When the boat that brought us from the steamer neared the shore, a half naked crowd of swarthy, yelling Moors rushed into the water, seized us and carried us to land ; passing thro' the gate into the town, one seemed to have dropped into another world, faces, dresses, buildings, shops, speech, all utterly unlike anything one had seen before. Perhaps the real East is different, but this is at any rate very different from our West, and the strangeness is the greater because one is separated only by twelve miles of water from England in Gibraltar, and Catholicism in Spain. The town is a tightly pressed mass of low, white, flat-roofed houses, each with a sort of little tower rising from its flat roof, and thrown together apparently quite without order. The streets being short and crooked, running at all sorts of angles to one another, crossed by arches, or rather by houses built over them, and so narrow that two walkers can but just pass. No windows, only here and there little iron-barred apertures in the thick wall, the rooms seem to open off small interior courts, and some to have no light or air at all, but be merely vaults entered by a door. All are built of thin bricks, covered with whitewash, very solid ; the better ones have a Moorish horseshoe arch for their door ; the shops are mere stalls or recesses just big enough for a grave, silent man to sit crosslegged in beside his wares, and these are mostly all in one street. Three or four tall minarets, covered to the top with coloured tiles, rise from beside the mosques, plain square whitewashed buildings, with a court in the centre, into which one could just catch a glimpse passing by, for no Christian dare enter. A darting, screaming crowd fills the streets. Moors of all hues, some dark as a negro, some lighter than the Spaniards, but with much the same cast of face, tall

[151]

and sinewy, with a curious mixture in their faces of wildness (I mean "unculture," so to speak), and gravity, as if the least thing would make them furious but nothing would make them laugh; men whom you can imagine falling like wild cats on an enemy, and driving the Visigoths across Spain before their victims had awakened to know the danger. The better class wear a red fez and turban, with an ample robe of cloth, blue mostly, the poorer ones wrapped in a sort of loose white flannel overcoat, the hood of which they draw over their heads, or in a greyish or striped rough sack-cloth, their legs bare below the knee, to which short white drawers descend. They chatter Arabic with harsh voices and violent gestures. Besides these there are numerous Jews, mostly tall handsome fellows with a red sash fastening their long tightly fitting robe; beautiful Jewesses with splendid eyes and regular, not very aquiline features, who make up for the concealment which the Moorish women (who cover their mouths and foreheads) are forced to practise by displaying their charms in the house doors where they stand, all in white or light coloured European dresses with brilliant handkerchiefs tied round their heads and crossed over the breast. Lastly, not to mention the Spaniards, of whom there are a good many here, come the negroes, slaves from the Soudan, brought across the desert in caravans, and adding a deeper shade of colour to the whole strange picture.

It is the month Ramadan, when no Moslem tastes food from sunrise to sunset; and the moment the gun tells that the orb has disappeared, a sound of trumpets, bagpipes, tom-toms, rises up over the city, and everyone rushes to buy food at the stalls or fall to on what he has been cooking. The Jews too are keeping their Feast of Tabernacles; hence, I suppose, so many grey dresses on the women; one sees through the doors of their houses, which look much more comfortable than the Moorish, boughs twined up to make booths according to the precepts of Leviticus. We have just been up to the gate of the castle, which stands on a hill commanding the town and harbour, whereof it forms the north point. The mass of white roofs and little towers, pierced by the two minarets, lay below dazzling white in the moon, a few palms and fig trees sprang out of the country and a hum of voices, discordant sounds which could not be called music, rose from the streets, white figures lay coiled up sleeping in every corner — many of the Moors seem to have no houses to speak of: and beyond, the moonbeams lit up the bay and the opposite coast, and the distant hills of Spain, Gibraltar's square mass just visible in the distance, the light of Tarifa and the stars almost extinguished by the brilliant moon, whose radiance is something one has no idea of in our thick air; it is not perhaps brighter than Iceland on a frosty night, but softer far.

Strangest sight of all is the Sook or market place, an open hillside just outside the landward gate, covered for a quarter of a mile each way with a dense throng of jostling, chattering, screeching human beings, selling fruit, grain, sheep, oxen, crockery, driving their camels and donkeys through the crowd, cooking their food at little charcoal braziers, while on the outskirts are encamped as many more, in odd little tents of brown or bluish sackcloth laid across a sort of rafter, just big enough to hold two people, and open at the end; their camels crouched by them with legs doubled in, their donkeys standing patiently around, poor pensive little greyish or white fellows, like those on which Jair's fifty sons rode. It is all Arabian Night-like, even down to the fowls picking up the loose pomegranite seeds, as Jarjares the descendant of Ihlees did, when he transformed himself from a Jinnee into a cock — but you perhaps don't know that great work as well as Annan and I did, of whose childhood it was the chief delight. The country behind is covered with cactus or prickly pear, bearing a fruit the people eat greedily, aloe rising in huge prickly tufts and tree-like flower stems, and a variety of bushes unknown to me, but apparently differing little from those on the Spanish hills opposite. We went up to explore the tomb of a Muslim saint, a white dome enclosed by walls, but were warned not to enter the enclosure — the Moors here are fanatical Mohammedans,

[153]

and would think nothing of tearing in pieces an infidel found in their sacred places. Fiercest of all are the Riffs, a tribe who inhabit the coast from the Straits eastward, live in holes of the rocks, and murder any stranger they can catch on their wild solitary coast. It seemed strange to look at these picturesque hills and be told one dare not venture there on peril of one's life. Everybody talks Arabic and harsh enough it sounds, yet the voices are not so much harsher than those of Spaniards when excited. Nothing strikes one so much as distinguishing these Southern races, Spaniards even more than Italians, French or Portuguese, than their liability to anger, and to an excitement bordering on ferocity when they are angry. When in good humour, they are more courteous as well as far more dignified than our people. But indeed in many respects the Spaniards seem to have been affected by or retained characteristics of the Moors. There is the architecture of course, the style, the use of coloured tiles, the construction of the house. There is the harshness of voice, and the monotonous discordant singing, very wearying to even a dull ear such as mine. There is the love for gay colours and the use of the market instead of shops, tho' perhaps this belongs to all primitive peoples.

In one respect to see a real Moorish town has been rather a shock to me, for in Spain one gets a very high impression of the Moors from the remains of their splendid buildings, from their admirable system of irrigation now mostly abandoned by the lazy Spaniard, from their toleration of Jews and Christians, from the literary glories of the era of the great Cordovan Khalifs. Here however in Morocco everything is behind Spain, backward as Spain is. Is it that the African Moors have really gone back, or that the traces of Arabian rule in Spain give an impression above the reality, or that Moorish civilisation in Africa never reached so high a tidemark as in Spain? Nevertheless, barbarous as these Berbers are, they have some considerable virtues, are often faithful and honest, are generally industrious and frugal, and above all are sober — the Koran you know forbids all intoxicating drinks, and these people obey it much more strictly than the Osmanli of Turkey. The country too is very rich — and with better government and some roads or railways might become extremely prosperous. At present it exports a good deal of grain — wheat, beans, millet, and so forth besides wool, hides, wax, and cattle, and some of those pretty fabrics which you know by sight.

Tangier is said to have a wonderfully soft climate, excellent for consumption; and we met here two Scotchmen who were going to winter in it for that reason — poor fellows, they looked ill enough. The sea is delightfully cool and clear; we bathed in the morning to the wonderment of the crowds of country people driving their camels along the sands to market; who probably never had their clothes off in their lives. This want of cleanliness in town and people is one of the things that has rather turned me back from Islam, to which experiences of Spain, saint worship, images, Inquisitors, had been impelling me strongly.

The sail back along the coast through the Straits was delightful, the sea smooth, though, owing to the currents, it breaks everywhere in small waves, the sky bright, the water an exquisite deep blue, darker than the Mediterranean azure. Cape Trafalgar is seen to the N. W. 30 miles off, Gibraltar the same distance E. N. E. Ceuta and the other scenes of Portuguese warfare with the Moors, a glorious but useless crusade in which the strength of the little kingdom was wasted for eighty years, lie along the S. shore: one is in the middle of some of the greatest events of history — it was at Gibel al Tarik that the first Arab conqueror of Spain landed and entrenched himself before the great battle of the Gaudalete — and the scenery is worthy of the history. One feels, here, as we felt looking from Brunnen up that glorious valley which leads between the Uri Rothstock and the Brisenstock to the St. Gothard, past Altorf and the meadow of Grütli, as if Nature were in sympathy with man and had deigned to display her grandeur and beauty in spots which his deeds were to make for ever memorable.

Meanwhile what of the law? The Homeric Odysseus was not under the unpleasant necessity of satisfying Manchester solicitors, and some of Bryce's friends were beginning to doubt whether, in view of his multifarious occupations he really intended to stick to the bar. "The fact is," wrote Edward Donner (15 April, 1873) "the impression is all the time gaining ground here (*i.e.*, in Manchester) that you are always cutting off somewhere to lecture or to attend meetings, or to do something or other and that you don't intend to follow up the bar." Nor did the publication of a handy little book on "The Trade Marks Registration Act and Trade Mark Law (1877)," dissipate the impression. "Bryce," says his friend Frederick Pollock, "was a sound English lawyer" but long before he had reached eminence in his profession, he had transferred his allegiance to another sovereign.

CHAPTER X

ARARAT

And the ark rested in the seventh month, on the seventeenth
day of the month, on the Mountains of Ararat.

Genesis c. 4.

A thousand shadowy pencilled valleys
And snowy dells in a golden air.

TENNYSON.

In the late summer of 1876 Bryce started with his old
Oxford friend, Aeneas Mackay, for a voyage to the
Caucasus. The route lay through Petersburg and
Moscow to Nijni and thence by a river steam-boat down
the Volga past the glittering towers and domes of Kazan
to Saratov where they took the railway which carried them
all the way to the feet of the Caucasus, a distance of 1,100
miles, through dry, bare, dusty plains, through forests
of beech and then for an entire afternoon, night, and day
over the strange and solitary region of the Steppe. "Trav-
ersing this steppe for two whole days enables me to understand the kind of impression which Scythia made on
the imagination of the Greeks: how all sorts of wonders
and horrors, like those Herodotus relates, were credible
about the peoples that roamed upon these wilds: how
terrible to their neighbours, how inaccessible and uncon-
quered themselves they must have seemed to the natives
of the sunny shores of the Aegean."

The line came to an end at Vladi-Kavkas, important both as the fortress commanding the entrance to the Dariel military road and also as a trade centre for the distribution of goods coming by rail to the mountain regions in the South. Here the great range of mountains was close at hand. "An icy pinnacle soaring up into the air 14,000 feet above us seemed no further off than Pilatus looks from Luzern. It was Kazbek, the mountain where Prometheus hung in chains. Hither nymphs came to console him; over this desert to the north Io wandered, driven by the gadfly of Hera."

Henceforward it was necessary to take the road. Bryce and Mackay were fortunate enough to find two Russian ladies bound for Tiflis and after "a preliminary skirmish about English sympathy with Turkish cruelties," it was arranged that the two parties should join forces and hire a vehicle to carry them over the 126 miles of road to the southern capital. They crossed the famous Dariel pass, the wild mountain summits towering 7,000 or 8,000 feet above the plain, reached the watershed about 8,015 feet above the sea and descended from its open green pastures by a series of long zig-zags an almost precipitous mountain face to the pretty little Georgian village of Mlati and so on to Tiflis through deep richly wooded valleys, the southern luxuriance of which was a delightful contrast to the desolation of the steppes.

The capital of Transcaucasia ringed round by a circle of stern brown hills "where not a breath of air can reach you from the mountains you descry, where the sun's rays are reflected from bare slopes and white houses, where often not a shower will fall for months together" is not a pleasant place in summer. No traveller, however, could fail to find Tiflis interesting for the town itself was a museum; and its inhabitants "quite sufficient to keep curiosity alive for days and weeks together." Indeed, here was "a city of contrasts and mixtures," as Bryce afterwards described it "into which elements have been poured from half Europe and Asia and in which they as yet show no signs of coalescing." Or rather an amalgamation of cities, for in Tiflis there are three distinct towns, one Russian, another German, a third oriental, and at least six distinct nations. Here Bryce had many opportunities of inspecting members of the Armenian race whose cause he afterwards so strenuously championed in his own country. "Where there meets you a keener or more restless glance you may be sure," he writes, "that it comes from an Armenian eye." Indeed more than half the Russian employés in Transcaucasia were said to be Armenians.

"Sharp men of business they certainly are, thrifty, able to drive a hard bargain and sticking wonderfully together. Among them are several persons of learning and ability, and as their education improves and their wealth increases, the number of such persons is likely to grow; so that altogether one seems to see a considerable future before them."

September was not the season for society in Tiflis. The magnates were mostly away in the country and to their vexation the travellers found few of those men of letters and science to whom they brought introductions. Time, however, did not hang heavily upon their hands. Preparations had to be made for the journey to Armenia for without road passports and letters of commendation and an interpreter no progress off the great roads could be safely counted on.

On September 6th the two travellers rattled out of Tiflis in a comfortable tarantass (an oblong cart) *en route* for Ararat, the mysterious mountain which legend identified with those mountains of Ararat upon which according to the narrative of Genesis (viii. 4.) the Ark rested in the seventh month on the seventeenth day of the month. On the third day after a journey through the most brigand-haunted region of Transcaucasia they reached Erivan, the capital of Russian Armenia, "a thoroughly Eastern town with just a little Russian varnish in one or two of its streets."

Here Bryce, whose childish imagination had been fed by the Bible and the Arabian Nights, found even the most trivial details of external life fascinating.

"To see people sitting or sleeping on the flat roofs, or talking to one another in the gate through which a string of camels is passing, to visit mosques and minarets and bazaars, watch the beggar crawl into the ruined tomb of a Muslim saint, and ramble through a grove of cypresses strewn with nameless, half-fallen gravestones, to stand by the baker or the shoemaker as he plies his craft in his open stall, and listen to the stories told by the barber, even when one does not understand a word, with the sacred mountains of the Ark looking down upon all, this seems like a delightful dream from far-off years."

Both in Tiflis and all the way along from Tiflis to Erivan the travellers had been enquiring about Ararat, the side from which to approach it, the modes or chances of ascending it. Little, however, could be learnt except that they must make for the frontier station of Aralyk, lying on the right bank of the Araxes about twenty-four miles from Erivan. Accordingly on the morning of September 9th, they drove off from Erivan under the blazing sun, with a good stock of provisions in the tarantass. After five hours of driving and changing horses twice they came to the banks of the Aras, "pontem indignatus Araxes," and drove through this historic, but very shallow and muddy river, here as wide as the Thames at London Bridge. On the way back seven days after in accordance with his almost invariable practice Bryce gave himself the pleasure of a plunge into these famous waters.

The two Ararats together form an elliptical mass of about twenty-five miles in length from north-west to southeast and about half the width. Out of this great mass rise two peaks, their bases confluent at a height of 8,800 feet, their summits about seven miles apart. The higher or great Ararat is 17,000 feet above the sea level, the lower or little Ararat 12,840 feet, the little Ararat an elegant cone, the great Ararat "a huge broad-shouldered mass, more of a dome than a cone supported by strong buttresses and throwing out rough ribs or ridges of rock, that stand out like knotty muscles from its solid trunk." Bryce was well posted in the latest geological account of the structure and history of Ararat and in his vivid book, *Transcaucasia and Ararat*, one of the classics of travel, abridges from various scientific journals the views of Herman Abich, the only geologist of eminence who had carefully examined the mountain. It may be sufficient here to say that both peaks are entirely composed of igneous rocks and that Bryce was able to confirm the German geologist's statement as to the absence of any crater on the summit of great Ararat. "It would, however," as he observes, "be rash to infer from this that no crater ever existed for many volcanoes may be cited where the central crater has been almost or quite obliterated. The fires of Ararat have in any case been long extinct. Indeed no record exists of an eruption in historical times."

Two phenomena, however, were distinctive. The first was the great height of the snow line on Ararat (nearly 14,000 feet), a circumstance to be attributed to the low rainfall of the area and to the geographical position of the mountain massif which is isolated, rising from the great Araxes plain, which, with its bare mountain rim to south and east, may be likened to a huge cauldron of hot dry air which is continually rising up the sides of the Ararat and melting the snows which are deposited upon them.

The second phenomenon is connected with the same upward rush of air. The summit of the mountain is generally during the summer and autumn months clear during the night and till some time after dawn. Then as the plains begin to feel the sun and the heated air mounts and reaches the snow region it is condensed into vapour and forms clouds. The mountaineer therefore, who wishes for a clear view from Ararat must arrange to be on the summit in the early morning.

Those who desire to read a full description of this great mountain, the lower peak of which was the meeting point of the Russian, Turkish and Persian confines, must have recourse to the pages of *Transcaucasia and Ararat*. What principally impressed Bryce was not any special beauty of detail, for the mountain is dry, bare, and woodless besides being generally uniform in structure and in the columns of its volcanic rock, but the sublimity of this huge yet graceful mass when seen from the plain below. At one glance the eye could take in every zone of climate and vegetation "from the sweltering plain to the cap of dazzling silver suspended in the sky."

In spite of the persistent superstition of its inaccessibility Ararat had been ascended more than once, the first time (so far as records go) by Dr. Parrot of Dorpat in 1829, the second by Sparsky Aftonomof in 1834 and the third by Herr Abich in 1845. Moreover, General Chodsko while conducting the triangulation survey in Transcaucasia had spent three days on the top in a tent pitched on the snow. Lastly a party of Englishmen had reached the summit from the Turkish side in 1856. Nevertheless the general belief in the neighbourhood was that no human foot since Father Noah's had ever trod the sacred summit.

At 8 A.M. on the morning of the 11th of September, Bryce and Mackay set out from Aralyk to ascend the mountain. In view of the fact that they were neither of them in hard physical training and that they had been travelling continuously in sweltering heat, cramped up in a carriage and short of sleep, they were making a considerable call upon their reserves of strength. The party consisted of nine persons, six soldiers of a Cossak detachment who had been furnished them by the Russian Commander at Aralyk, the interpreter, and the two mountaineers. They were all mounted and Bryce and his friend

in addition to pistols stuck in their belts, brandished
heavy ice axes, the management of which, together with
that of a bridle and a big white umbrella required some
dexterity. The heat was terrific but the air fresh and
stimulating and the sight of the jutting peak above
"seemed to shoot a thrill of coolness through our burning veins."

At the beginning all went well. The climbing party
reached the Well of Sardarbulakh, the only high permanent camping ground on the mountain (7,514 feet) in reasonably good time, but henceforward difficulties began to
accumulate. The horses could go no further, the Cossaks refused to carry the few things required for a bivouac
and it was, therefore, necessary to secure Kurds for the
purpose, a slow business, and to conclude a bargain with
them, which was even more tedious. So much time was
lost in these proceedings that Bryce suggested that the
party should remain and sleep at Sardarbulakh and make
a start upwards as soon as the moon rose, shortly after
midnight. The plan of operations was accordingly modified. Supper was prepared and after a meal of boiled
mutton and milk and some of the inevitable tea they
lay down for a little sleep.

"The silence of the mountain was astonishing. No
calling of torrents to one another, no rippling of rills or
rustling of boughs, not even the noise of a falling stone,
only the whistling of the West wind, the home wind, over
the pass."

About 1 A.M. the party were afoot, the Kurds leading,
and made straight across the grassy hollows which trend
upwards towards the great cone. But the Cossaks and

Kurds were impossible. They loitered and after every ten minutes' walking they would sit down smoking and chattering for seven or eight minutes. At 3 A.M. the morning star rose behind the Median mountains, shedding a light that almost outshone the moon and then an hour later it began to pale in the first faint flush of yellowish light that spread over the Eastern heaven. They were still far from their objective and meanwhile the precious hours during which a clear view can be reckoned on from the summit were receding and the travellers had to expect a fresh obstacle in the shape of mountain clouds.

They breakfasted at about 12,000 feet and here Mackay who carried more weight and had felt the want of training on the way up gave in, and decided to halt, leaving Bryce to proceed unaccompanied to achieve the ascent. What he then accomplished will always stand to his credit, not indeed as a great feat of mountaineering, for the climbing difficulties were not exceptional, but as a triumph of nerve and enterprise and physical endurance. He had no real guide, for the Kurds and two Cossaks who accompanied him to a height of 13,000 feet knew nothing about the mountain, or about climbing, and were not properly equipped for the work. Moreover for the last part of the journey he was absolutely alone. The thinness of the air caused breathlessness, which began at 13,000 feet and continued, growing worse as he mounted to the top and forcing him at every two steps to stop for breath. Moreover, the clouds had begun to settle down, so that the summit was invisible and its whereabouts had to be inferred from the direction of the ridges running up the face of the cone. It was a desperate race against time.

At 3 P.M. come what might, he would have to turn back if he was to reach the camping ground by daylight. The question was could he reach the summit in time? When it wanted barely an hour to the moment when he had determined to turn back, the rock slope came suddenly to an end and he stepped out upon the a most level snow at the top of it coming at the same time into the clouds and feeling the bitter cold of a violent west wind.

For five or six minutes he walked over the soft snow, following the gentle rise of its surface and trailing his ice axe behind him. Then to his astonishment the ground began to fall away to the north. A puff of wind blew the mists aside and showed the Araxes plain at an abyssmal depth below. It was the top of Ararat. Or rather it was one of two tops, the second of which some thirty feet the higher was reached at 2. 25 P.M. Bryce had won the race against considerable odds by 35 minutes.

A few days later he visited the Armenian monastery of Etchmiadzin near the northern foot of the mountain, and interviewed the Archimandrite. "This Englishman," observed the interpreter, "says that he has ascended the top of Massis (Ararat)." The venerable man smiled sweetly. "No," he replied, "that cannot be. No one has ever been there. It is impossible."

The return journey from Poti (on the Phasis of antiquity) to Constantinople by the Black Sea was for Bryce full of instruction for he was here brought into direct contact with the paralysing effects of Turkish misrule. And accordingly when towards the end of the year war seemed impending between Russia and the Turks and fears were

entertained that England, under the leadership of Disraeli, might undertake the defence of the Sultan, Bryce
threw himself into opposition to the foreign policy of the
Government. A body called the Eastern Questions Association had been formed to combat the pro-Turkish
schemes attributed to the Prime Minister, and of this from
the first Bryce was an active member, serving on a sub-
Committee of five who were appointed to draft the
manifesto convoking delegates from all parts of the country to an Eastern Questions Conference which met in
December. Indeed since he was the most politically-
minded member of the sub-Committee which met at his
house, it may be suspected that he took the largest share
in drafting the appeal.[1] What ensued has been amply
recorded in the pages of Morley's *Gladstone* — a Conference at St. James' Hall (Dec. 8th) attended by representatives of men of every type and from every part
of the Kingdom, a great speech from Mr. Gladstone then
in the full glow of his passionate advocacy of the Bulgarian cause, and a clear intimation to the Prime Minister that on no account would the nation tolerate being
drawn into a war on behalf of Turkey. The first shots
were fired in the political campaign which ended in the
fiery explosions of Midlothian and the Liberal triumph
at the polls in the early spring of 1880.

The tide of passionate feeling on the Near Eastern
question which brought Gladstone back into office,
steadily swept Bryce forward into an active political life,
and since the question of the hour was one upon which
he had thought much and possessed unusual knowledge,

[1] Other members were William Morris, J. R. Green and Stopford Brooke.

it was inevitable he should be a candidate for Parliament in the election of 1880.

In those strenuous days one sad thought was mingled with much exhilarating and buoyant activity. In 1877 Bryce lost the father to whom he was so deeply attached and to whom he had recourse in all the difficult turns of life. After the death of her husband Mrs. Bryce moved south to Streatham where she kept house with her daughter, Kate. The elder sister, Mary, lived with Bryce in Norfolk Square and in Bryanston Square, which became the scene (1875 to 1889) of much agreeable hospitality, the meeting ground of politicians and lawyers, artists and men of letters, not to speak of friends from the New World, from the continent of Europe and from various parts of Asia. So passed many pleasant years of domestic happiness, while political storms raged outside, the five members of the family bound together by the closest ties of intimate affection, and the revered mother, so strong and piercing in her intelligence, being regarded by her gifted son as an oracle, whose counsels even in the most important questions of political conduct could never be safely neglected.

In 1879 Bryce was elected to the Alpine Club. At that time his mountaineering achievements included the ascent of the Schreckhorn, Monte Rosa, the Pelmo, and the Marmolata in the Dolomites, Hekla in Iceland (with Ilbert), and Ararat in Armenia, the last a remarkable feat by reason of the fact that he climbed the last five thousand feet alone and enveloped in a thick mountain mist. He had also scaled, again with Ilbert, the Maladetta and the Vignemale in the Pyrenees and in 1878 had

clambered among the steep cliffs of the Tatra which divide
Hungary and Transylvania with Leslie Stephen. His
mountaineering record then, even if it contained fewer
peaks of the first order of difficulty than are now often
achieved by young aspirants to the Alpine Club, was distinguished for an unusual variety and betokened a love
of mountains for themselves and apart from their function in providing an exhilarating form of exercise. "He
took," observes Mr. Douglas Freshfield, "peaks as they
came — they were like fences in a day's hunting — the
most enjoyable incidents in journeys that were crowded
with objects and interests picturesque, historical, political. It was for him an important recommendation to a
country that it should provide climbs even if they were no
higher than Croagh Patrick and Croaghun, up which he
used to drag his panting officials, when he was chief
Secretary in Ireland." Ice, snow, and hard rock were of
course the supreme luxuries.

Thus his mountaineering expeditions were of the most
catholic description. They included the ascent of Mauna
Loa in the Hawaiian Island, of Machaca in Basuto Land,
of Myogisan in Japan, of all the rocky hills in Mount
Desert Island in Maine. In 1883 he wrote an address on
North America as a field for mountaineering, for he was
anxious, like a good sportsman, to spread the knowledge
of any regions likely to delight the heart of a climber.
Nor was his interest in a mountain confined, as is the case
with some excellent climbers, to the character of the climb
itself, the state of the rock, ice or snow, the nature of the
handholds or footholds, or the discovery, in the case of a
new ascent, of the easiest route to the top. A mountain

provided other interests, notably geological, upon which his curiosity was actively exerted. And it may be worth adding that his observations made on the Ararat climb as to the influence of altitude on respiration, namely that the rise from 8,000 to 14,000 feet is often more felt than the rise from 14,000 to 20,000 are in accord with the accepted view as to the importance of habituation in adjusting the lungs to a rarified atmosphere.[1]

[1] The triple-peaked Mt. Bryce in the Canadian Rockies was named after the conqueror of Ararat in 1898.

CHAPTER XI

PARLIAMENT

The new Parliament will be tested by its acts. It will not draw
its inspiration from me. No doubt it will enact changes that
will be denounced as revolutionary, and then recognised as innocent and even good. But I expect it to act in the main on well-
tried and established lines and do much for the people and little
to disquiet my growing years.

W. E. GLADSTONE, 1880.

GLADSTONE'S Midlothian campaign of 1879, if it
did not make a Liberal victory certain, was in any
case the means of diffusing through the country a
great flow of Liberal enthusiasm. The Jingo policy of the
Times was sharply challenged and when the elections
came in the Spring, they showed that for the time being
the sentiment of the country was on the side of the Ideal-
ists. Bryce stood in the Liberal interest for the Tower
Hamlets and was helped in his election by Albert Dicey
and by his two sisters. Gladstone was the hero of every
contest during that month of March, but in the Tower
Hamlets a good deal of fervour was left over for the Liberal candidate, who won some reputation at the time by
addressing the German bakers in the constituency in their
own tongue. "The people down here," Bryce wrote to
his mother, April 2nd, 1886, "are wonderfully excited.
I never saw such cheering and handshaking. It really
makes me quite ashamed of myself to be the object of
so much enthusiasm."

[171]

James Bryce

In the midst of the contest a letter of good-will came from J. R. Green.

Hotel Quirinale, Rome.

"I cannot but send you one word of good wishes, dear Bryce, before the Tower Hamlets speak their "Yes" or "No." On all personal grounds you know how warmly I long for your success: and on public grounds I long for it just as warmly. If I have sometimes pressed you to come and take the place as historian which you could take if you would, and have sometimes grumbled at politics for robbing us of the one writer who could do the work of Gibbon in a nobler and larger spirit than Gibbon's, it has not been from any underrating of the field you have chosen nor of your powers in such a field. Politics is the noblest and most useful work that a man can undertake, and in a State like England, where the destinies of nations yet to be are moulded by our statesmen it is the work whose issues have no rival in their importance. Perhaps I am fanciful and 'Johnny-esque' in longing to see English politicians rise to a higher point of view than those of the day, in wearying of leaders born seventy years ago, and whose view — however widened by a sympathy with great and free things — is still necessarily bounded by the world into which they were born, or in longing for younger men who will realise the World of *fifty years to come* and let Europe alone sink into its coming littleness! In that greater World, how odd, how ludicrous, will be the spectacle of a Germany and a France, each passed by in the race of nations, still growling and snarling over their little Alsace! To me all these Bismarks and Dizzys and Andrassys are alike anachronisms, men living in a world which is passing away, and whose mighty schemes and mightier armies are being quietly shoved aside by the herdsman of Colorado or the sheep-masters of New South Wales.

If it were not for the thought of this, I could not bear to look on the world about me, to see these Italian boys torn from their peasant homes in the Abruzzi and prisoned in their barracks when every arm is needed to *make* Italy — I could not bear this

[172]

Europe, echoing with the tramp of armed feet. But in this dead Rome I gather courage at the sight of another world that is passing away, and I look across the Atlantic and the Pacific to a new world and a better.

But all this is just what I meant *not* to say. What I wanted was simply to wish you success, and to wish it with all my heart."

The result was satisfactory. Bryce was returned at the head of the poll with a majority of three hundred votes, and so in his forty-third year entered Parliament.[1] Among those who wrote to congratulate the new member were Jowett, John Morley, and William Morris.

The Tower Hamlets division was a poor region of Eastern London with a voting list of 44,000 which in 1880 was reckoned a large and populous constituency. Bryce told the House of Commons later on, when the question of election expenditure came up for consideration that he had come into the constituency sixteen months before the Election and during that period had only spent £50 or £60.[2]

In any case, it is always an advantage to represent a working-men's constituency, not only because such constituencies most accurately represent the needs and desires of the population, the greater part of which is compelled to earn its living by manual toil, but also because it is the poor who most immediately and poignantly feel the pressure of bad legislation and are most conspicuously benefitted by the wisdom of Parliament. To represent a poor constituency is, therefore, in

[1] The members were — Bryce (L) 12,020, Raikes (C) 11,720, Samuda (L) 10,384, Lucraft (L) 5,103.   [2] June 24, 1883.

itself a valuable part of the education of a member of the British House of Commons.

It is not, however, every able and industrious man who is able to conquer the attention of this fastidious assembly and though Bryce was always, and indeed could hardly fail to be a valuable member, he never succeeded in rising to the highest Parliamentary eminence. Those who read his speeches in the columns of Hansard and have no personal experience of the ways and affections of the House of Commons may find it difficult to explain why Bryce did not reach the first rank. His speeches are ably constructed, well argued, couched in good perspicuous English and always full to overflowing with accurate information. He never rose without saying something which was a distinctive contribution to the debate. He was never fumbling or uncertain. There was always the sense of an active and athletic mind behind anything which he said. Nevertheless he was not a Parliamentary success. He was considered to be too academic and professorial. Irrelevance is often a very valuable element in oratory but it must be the right kind of irrelevance. It must be the irrelevance which amuses or excites, not the irrelevance which merely instructs. Now when Bryce became irrelevant from the House of Commons' point of view which is always that of the practical man who wants to get on with the business, and never that of the man of science who desires to investigate causes, it was into the didactic form of irrelevance that he lapsed. This he did not from ostentation or conceit, for no one was simpler or less vain of his acquisitions, but from the momentum of his own personal interest and out of a certain lack of susceptibility to the needs and interests of his audience. Thus in a speech on Irish coercion he would lay down the general principle that no democratic community ever succeeded in governing another democratic community by force. Then he would stop to ask whether the case of Switzerland and the Sonderbund did not constitute an exception to the general rule and would stray off the main road to explain to the House why the case of the Sonderbund was not apposite. Now it is highly probable that only five percent of the honourable members had ever heard of the Sonderbund and that even to this small minority the case of the Sonderbund had not suggested itself as an exception to the general rule about democracies. And then when the Sonderbund had been disposed of, they would be asked to consider another possible exception, the case of the Northern and Southern States of the American Union, which again had not occurred to them, and would be told the many reasons which made this exception also inapposite. A man of the quick instinctive House of Commons temper would not allow himself to drift so far away from the prevailing mood of the assembly. Even if these objections did happen to occur to his mind, he would leave it to one of his audience to make them by way of interjection. But Bryce, who was above all things an historian, desired to tell the truth, the whole truth, and nothing but the truth; and so Chamberlain, who was concerned to disparage him and knew how little the House of Commons thinks of academic intellects, was always careful to allude to him as Professor.

Thus men with only a fraction of Bryce's intellectual power were more successful than he in the cut and thrust of Parliamentary debate. A certain lack of pliability, an insistent voice, a temperament somewhat deficient in the good-humoured composure which is one of the most valuable of Parliamentary gifts, a turn of phrase incisive rather than humourous, a prevailingly serious outlook coupled with the defect to which allusion has been made of excessive indulgence in historical disquisitions and analogies, these little blemishes of manner and method concealed from his fellow Members of Parliament the remarkable qualities which belonged to him. In England public men tend to be estimated by their Parliamentary equipment. Bryce was not a first class Parliamentary figure. Neither in the House nor in the country did he exert the authority which belongs to a man whose word is decisive in the shaping of political opinion. For this reason the estimate which was formed of him by the general public was surprisingly below his real deserts.

'I knew Bryce' writes Lord Gladstone, 'when I was an undergraduate at Oxford and under the spell of his "Holy Roman Empire." It so happened that we both entered the House of Commons in 1880. He was always a true and most kind friend to me and I watched his political career with keen interest.

He sat continuously for twenty-six years: he spoke on a great variety of subjects — in substance and argument, admirably; he was a Cabinet Minister in three administrations. Debates were enriched by his great stores of knowledge and trained powers of thought. In office he was business-like and thorough. His fame as a writer added dignity and authority to the House. Yet he never reached the Parliamentary status expected by his friends.

Why was it? Distinguished men frequently fail to rise to expectations from lack of certain essential qualities. The explanation in the case of Bryce is, I think, quite different.

The strength and reality of his political convictions brought him into public, largely as a matter of duty at the age of forty-two. He did not sit through debates studying speeches, absorbing the political and social atmosphere and so identifying himself with the inner life of the House. His dominant interests and engagements were usually elsewhere, and he gave that impression. The House of Commons is rigid in limiting its full favour to those known as House of Commons men. Bryce did not receive its *imprimatur*.

He entered Parliament somewhat late in life, as a student and writer, with his mind already absorbed in a wide range of interests and work. Before the proofs came from the printer, a new book was on the anvil. He was in this way intellectually independent of the House of Commons. Excepting office periods his political work seemed in a certain measure to be a side issue — at least in the sense that he did not give his whole mind to it. His life was fashioned when he entered the House, and had he changed it for the sole purpose of a Parliamentary career the result is a matter of speculation.

It is often said that the busiest men never seem in a hurry. Bryce at any rate was an exception. He did not work through others. His extraordinary energy kept him constantly and personally occupied. When he had finished one thing he was already in a hurry for the next. Men who wished to have a talk with him in the lobby found him with his pockets bulging with papers. He was always most courteous but he induced the feeling that he was really thinking of his next subject.

Bryce's great charm was a simple directness of purpose, and his main purpose in life was not a career in the limelight, but unceasing endeavour to give to the nation and the world the produce of his own intellect, training, and experience.

In later life many of the defects of parliamentary style which were noted by his contemporaries in the House of Commons disappeared and he became one of the best and most graceful public speakers in the country. Indeed those who only heard his oratory after his return from America will be at a loss to account for the somewhat disparaging estimates which were formed in earlier days of his Parliamentary efforts. Much practice had given him not only ease and fluency but a remarkable command of striking and appropriate vocabulary. No one, not even Mr. Gladstone, had a happier gift of quotation or a more copious supply of illustrations drawn from the past. The sense of strain which marred his earlier efforts passed away. He spoke as if speaking were as pleasant and natural a function as breathing itself and established without difficulty and from the first that pleasant bond of spiritual sympathy which unites the true orator with his audience.

Even an active back-bencher may find hours when he can safely retire into the seclusion of the House of Commons Library and write between the Division bells. Bryce made full use of such intervals of leisure. He worked at his books, he wrote for the Press. One of his many occupations during the eighties was to contribute a London letter to the New York Nation 'the best weekly not only in America but in the world' then edited by E. L. Godkin, a remarkable Irish Protestant who brought into the profession of American journalism a rare force of intellect and integrity of character. Here Bryce was able to expand himself at will. Now he would describe an exciting Irish debate, now analyse the character and claims of rival party leaders, now expound Gladstone's Irish Land Legislation or the defects of English Parliamentary Procedure. His topics, however, were not always political. There are literary and historical diversions and among these a pleasant moralising article suggested by an academic ceremony in Edinburgh which showed his American readers a new facet.

It may be asked why Bryce should have put so much good work into an American weekly at a time in his career when the advancement of his reputation with his own countrymen might have been expected to be a predominant consideration. The answer may partly no doubt be found in his admiration for Godkin as a man, but still more in his belief in the value of the service which Godkin with 'his passion for truth, his hatred of wrong and injustice, his clear vision, his indomitable spirit' was rendering to the improvement of American public life. It was Bryce's belief that Godkin's weekly was a strong influence for good with University men in America and that through them, it was destined to refine, elevate, and direct the opinion of the nation. In such a task he was proud to co-operate.

One great advantage belonged to Bryce as a beginner in Parliamentary life. He came into the House as an acknowledged expert in the affairs of the Near East. His travels in Russia and the Caucasus, his first-hand knowledge of the conditions which prevailed along the northern shore of Asia Minor and in Constantinople enabled him to speak with authority upon a large field of public policy with respect to which opinion was still imperfectly or erroneously informed. Three conclusions in particular, each of them rejected by a great number of his compatriots had been burned into his mind.

The first was the fundamental error of regarding Russia as a serious menace to the British Empire. In contradistinction to the view first instilled into the mind of the country by David Urquhart and afterwards expressed in the Crimean War and in the whole course of Disraeli's foreign policy that Russia was the eternal enemy, immense, formidable, unsleeping, Bryce who had seen something of Russian Government and Russian human nature held that as compared with Great Britain Russia was formidable neither in power nor in moral influence. She was far less powerful in attack than she was generally believed to be, and in modern warfare, which was above all things a matter of money and science, was probably less strong than the weakest of the three other great military states of the Continent. He argued, therefore, with great good sense (March 23rd, 1881) that we should not complicate the defence of India by retaining our troops at Kandahar out of fear of Russia. The great Empire was weak at the heart. The temper of its people was sluggish and fatalistic, not given to concerted and organised enterprise. Its own internal problems were quite sufficient to occupy its energies. The experience of the great war abundantly confirms the correctness of Bryce's diagnosis.

The second conclusion held with tenacity and passion through the whole course of his public life was the hopelessness of the Turk. Wherever the Turk had ruled, he had spread desolation. The provinces of Asia Minor, once the scene of a brilliant civilisation, had been emptied of their arts and science, their commerce and industry by the lethargy, the incompetence and the caprices of a barbarous master.

"I despair," he writes (*Transcaucasia and Ararat*, p. 378) "of conveying the impression of melancholy which the coast of Asia Minor makes upon the traveller whatever are his political or religious prepossessions. Here is a country blessed with every gift of nature, a fertile soil possessing every variety of experience and situation, a mild and equable climate, mines of tin, copper, silver, and coal in the mountains, a land of exquisite beauty, which was once studded with flourishing cities and filled by an industrious population. And now from the Euphrates to the Bosphorus all is silence, poverty, despair. There is hardly a sail on the sea, hardly a village on the shores, hardly a road by which commerce can pass into the interior. You ask the cause and receive from everyone the same answer. Misgovernment, or rather no government; the existence of a power which does nothing for its subjects, but stands in the way when there is a chance of their doing something for themselves."

Like many of his contemporaries Bryce held the view that a power so manifestly feeble and corrupt was soon bound to disappear. "There is no denying," he said, July 23rd, 1880, "that the existence of Turkey as an Empire will be limited to a very few years."

[181]

The third conviction, held with no less zeal and persistence, was that the British Government had a solemn responsibility towards the Christian subjects of the Porte. It was owing to the intervention of the Tory Government of Great Britain and out of the prevailing suspicion of Russian designs that the Treaty of San Stefano had been set aside, under which Russia would have undertaken the protection of the Christian subjects of the Ottoman Empire. We could not, therefore, look on with folded hands while these miserable populations, whom for our own assumed convenience we had robbed of the shelter which was proferred them, were subjected to the numerous occasions of pillage and violence incidental to the life of Christian communities under Turkish rule. We were bound to co-operate with the other Powers of Europe to secure for these poor people such help as might be possible. It was all very well for America to stand aloof. In his first important speech in the House (April 2nd, 1880) Bryce contended against Sir Wilfrid Lawson's non-intervention motion, that such a course was impossible for us.

More particularly was he concerned to argue the case of the Armenians, the most laborious and energetic and as they were then, the largest of the Christian communities in Asia Minor. Under Article 61 of the Treaty of Berlin the Porte had undertaken to guarantee the security of the Armenians against the Circassians and Khurds whose periodical diversion it was to pillage and slaughter this indispensable but unpopular race of money lenders, traders, and peasants. How was this undertaking being fulfilled? Was the Turk in fact doing anything to redeem his pledge? Again and again in questions to ministers and as occasions offered themselves for the treatment of foreign affairs in debate Bryce returned to this theme. He became in fact the principal advocate of the Armenian nation in England, the founder and first President of the Anglo-Armenian Society, the member for Armenia in the British House of Commons.

It was, indeed, mainly due to his efforts that public attention which had been absorbed by the wrongs of the Balkan Christians was directed to the even more calamitous situation of the Christian subjects of the Porte in Asia Minor. He helped to draft the Armenian appeal and the Memorial from the Committee of Armenian residents in London which was circulated at the St. James's Hall meeting on December 8, 1876. Two years later he organised a meeting on behalf of the Armenians at the Jerusalem Chamber in Westminster over which Dean Stanley presided and which was addressed by Lord Shaftesbury and Lord Lansdowne. Thereafter no Armenian visiting London failed to call on him, and since all information bearing upon the situation of the Armenian people was immediately brought to his notice, he was able, from his place in the House of Commons, or in contributions to the Press, or as a speaker at public meetings, to remind the country of the obligations which had been undertaken for the protection of the Armenians under Article 61 of the Treaty of Berlin and of our national duty to see to it that these obligations were fulfilled.

The popular prejudice against the Armenians, as a race of usurers battening on the necessities of the poor, awoke no echo in his heart. He did not stoop to discuss this disparaging and superficial opinion. Had he done so he

would have contended that the nation was not to be
condemned because here and there in the Levantine
towns the Armenian excelled in the art, condemned by
Aristotle, "of making money breed money." What he
saw in the Armenians was a capable, intelligent race of
singular tenacity, which had never entirely come under
the Roman Empire, which had been converted to Christianity in the fourth century and ever since maintained
its fidelity to Christian teaching amid manifold persecu-
tions, a race of peasants and traders who from time to
time had furnished illustrious statesmen and generals to
Byzantine Emperors, Ottoman Sultans, and Russian
Tzars, a race with an ecclesiastical literature and a sense
of culture unique in Asia Minor, but condemned by the
paucity of its members and by its geographical dispersion
to serve an alien master. He was not then content to
rest the Armenian case either upon the claims of humanity, strong as these undoubtedly were, or upon our debt
of honour under the Treaty of Berlin. These circumstances, sufficient in themselves to enjoin compassionate
solicitude, were corroborated by the historic merits of the
Armenian people as he saw them. He thought them the
best race in Asia Minor, superior in tenacity of will and
capacity for moral and intellectual progress to their neighbours, Turks or Khurds, Tartars or Russians. If Asia
Minor was ever to be regenerated from barbarism, the
work must devolve on the Armenians. Some day he
believed that this would happen, for he did not scruple to
affirm in one of his latest writings (1910) that there was
no abler race in the world.[1]

[1] The American Commonwealth, ed. 1910, Vol. II, p. 453.

He was not blind to the difficulties of a problem which the statesmanship of Europe has pitiably failed to solve. He realised that annexation to Russia, though it would be a boon to the Armenians as compared with the position in which they then found themselves, would neither be a good thing for the annexed provinces nor for Russia herself. The erection of an independent Armenian principality in Armenia proper, the country round the Upper Euphrates and Tigris was an alternative superficially more attractive. It was doubtful, however, whether the Armenians, despite the capacity for self improvement of which they had given recent evidence were fit for self government or capable of self defence. Moreover even if they were able to maintain themselves against the untamed Khurds and their other Moslem neighbours, Russia would certainly oppose the creation of a state to which her own Armenian population would necessarily gravitate, and whose existence would deprive her of the influence which she exerted as Patriarch of the Armenian nation.

There remained then the less heroic expedient of attempting, despite many failures of the past, to improve the Turkish administration of these provinces. A faint ray of hope emanated from the Lebanon where, after the massacres of 1860, the European powers had succeeded in securing more tolerable conditions for the Christians of that mountain region by the expedient of local Christian Governors and mixed courts and by the establishment of a local police force of all races coupled with the exclusion of the Turkish soldiery. Something on the same lines might be contrived for the Armenians. The problem was not so much to issue reforming ordinances as to secure their proper execution, to check the corruption and partiality of the judges and to bridle the extortions of the tax-gatherers. As he truly observed, "It is not merely, perhaps not so much, an honest purpose and good laws that are wanting to the Ottoman Administration: it is force and power. . . . No amount of supervision and reporting will get over this fatal weakness."

In his first Parliamentary session (July 23rd, 1880) he put the Armenian case, as he conceived it to be, with great force to the House, recalling the grievances of the Armenians, reminding the House that they did not ask for independence but only for protection from murder and spoliation, and urging the appointment of a Christian governor as in the Lebanon. The problem was urgent, partly because of the geographical contiguity of Armenia to Russia and partly because Armenia was the only country in the Asiatic territories of the Sultan which held out great hopes of future growth and development. He concluded by enlarging upon the brilliant qualities of the Armenian race and of its widespread influence as illustrated by the careers of such men as Loris Melikoff and Nubar Pasha. But the House of Commons has never succeeded, despite a long array of earnest and eloquent advocates, in being stirred to its depths by the woes and tribulations of the Armenian nation. That race has had the misfortune to be judged by the traders whom it sends into the towns and these do not generally appeal to the travelling Englishman who, for the most part, forms the opinions of the House of Commons upon alien races. No British election has been fought on the Armenian question, no British Government has been materially advanced or imperilled by its handling of a problem so remote and so difficult. Yet there can be little doubt but that the movement in favour of Armenia, of which Bryce was a lifelong and enthusiastic supporter, did make a wide appeal in the country and that its reverberation in America, now embarking on the field of missionary enterprise in the Near East, was considerable and of great importance as an influence moulding the attitude of the Western democracies to the problem of Turkish mis-rule.

As a young member of Parliament, Bryce was responsible for the passage into law of a useful little measure dealing with the parochial charities of the City of London. These presented a problem well calculated to engage the interest and attention of one who was alike a student of historical survivals and a democratic reformer. The City of London, once a crowded centre of population, had in recent years become a congeries of huge business premises animated by day but, when business hours were once over, emptied of their great army of managers, foremen and clerks, and given over to comparative solitude. Here was indeed one of the rare illustrations of Goldsmith's line,

" Where wealth accumulates and men decay,"

for while the opulence of the city was rapidly growing, its population had sunk to 52,000. Meanwhile its parochial charities (the City possessed no less than 61 churches) represented a lavish income, ill administered by a miscellany of trustees, churchwardens and vestries, who expended part of it in demoralising doles and some of it on purposes entirely obsolete, such as sermons of thanksgiving for the defeat of the Spanish Armada or the frustration of the Gunpowder Plot.

The object of Bryce's Bill was to remove the traditional restrictions which confined the benefits of these charities to the City and to make them available for the poor of London under schemes to be devised by a Board of Commissioners. The charitable fund of the City was to be rationally employed for the benefit of four million souls instead of being absurdly distributed among the poor of a population of 52,000. In two excellent Second Reading speeches (for two bills were successively considered in two successive Sessions) Bryce commended the general principles of his measure to the House and subsequently obtained no little credit for the skill with which he piloted the second of his Bills through Committee against some determined obstruction from the City members.[1]

The new Member for South Aberdeen was not destined to languish for long upon the back benches. The Election was held in December, 1885. In the following February Mr. Gladstone invited Bryce to undertake "the very important duty of representing the Foreign Department in the House of Commons as Under Secretary of State." So at the age of forty-eight Bryce became for the first time a Minister of the Crown. For the leader of his party Bryce cherished a profound, but as the preceding sketch will have shown, not an undis-

---

[1] The Schemes under the London Parochial Charities Act of 1883 were not altogether satisfactory to Bryce. He wanted to help "the very poor" with recreation grounds, public baths, workhouses, and convalescent homes. The Schemes provided for encouragement to be given to new Polytechnics, excellent institutions which the City Companies, in Bryce's view, might be trusted to help.   Speech of March 20th, 1890.

criminating devotion. He admired his dauntless courage, his vast span of intellectual interest and sympathy, his stately simplicity, his extraordinary gifts as orator and parliamentarian and his burning sympathy with the oppressed. The intrepidity with which Mr. Gladstone staked his political fortunes on Irish Home Rule, when it was doubtful whether the party would follow him, struck him as one of the most courageous acts in our Parliamentary history. But he was not blind to defects on the side of political leadership, literary skill, or scholarship, overshadowed though these deficiencies were by the commanding gifts which enabled Gladstone to interpenetrate the history of an epoch with the force of his personality. Their acquaintance seems to have begun at least as early as 1873 when we find Bryce invited to the famous Thursday breakfasts and favoured with postcards on Armenia. From that time forward the intimacy grew,[1] ripened by many common interests and more particularly by reason of their equal attainments in the fields of Homeric and Dante scholarship.

"I think," writes Mr. Gladstone (March 25th, 1874) "the text of Homer well worthy the kind of extraneous illustration which you propose to supply from Icelandic sources." And when Bryce got into Parliament the opportunities for such literary intercommunications multiplied. "Once in the lobby of the House of Commons seeing his countenance saddened by the troubles of Ireland, I told him, in order to divert his thoughts, how someone had

---

[1] Bryce's first visit to Hawarden appears to have been in January, 1884. He writes to his mother that his host "displays a range of knowledge of poetry and literature especially classical and ecclesiastical, which makes me despair."

recently discovered that Dante had in his last years been appointed at Ravenna to a lectureship which raised him above the pitch of want. Mr. Gladstone's face lit up at once and he said, "How strange it is to think that these great souls whose words are a beacon light to all the generations that have come after them should have had their cares and anxieties to vex them in their daily life just like the rest of us common mortals."

With Lord Rosebery, his chief at the Foreign Office, Bryce's relations were always happy and cordial. Foreign Secretary and Under Secretary were alike conspicuous for an incorrigible love for good letters, and exact information. Lord Rosebery's interests however were not conspicuously mediæval, and he was amused one morning when, in the height of an international complication, with the British fleet blockading Crete, Bryce rushed into his room in the Foreign Office to communicate the momentous news that Hodgkin's Cassiodorus was at last published.

Lord Rosebery's advent to the Foreign Office was generally expected to portend an improvement of the relations between Britain and Germany. "As to Foreign policy and Lord Rosebery," wrote Max Müller to Bryce, "all I know is that he has been for some time *le bien Desiré* at Berlin. If England and Germany begin to understand each other again, we may still hope to see the end of the present state of military vandalism which beats anything in the whole history of the world, even the fifth century." Such expectations were not destined to be realised. The brilliant Foreign Secretary was hardly established in the saddle before the Liberal Government, depending as it did on a small and precarious majority, and pledged to the unpopular policy of Irish Home Rule experienced a decisive defeat in the House of Commons. Bryce's first term as a Minister hardly amounted to six months, for the Government fell in August, and in the ensuing General Election the Liberal Party was decisively beaten at the polls.

No Parliamentary observer would ever have described Bryce as other than a strong party Liberal. On all the great issues which divided Liberal and Tory during the seven and twenty years of his Parliamentary life, he took without faltering the Liberal line, to the surprise of some critics, who wondered why a man so learned and cosmopolitan should have been content to deviate so little from the straight way of party orthodoxy. But if Bryce gave to Gladstone his consistent support, his case was not singular. Most of Scotland, almost every member of the Free Churches in Britain, a very large proportion of University intellectuals were in the like position. The Liberal creed, as it was then expounded in Parliament and the country, was an inspiring body of doctrine, equally acceptable to the idealist and the professor of economics, and appealing to the great fund of generous sentiment which is characteristic of British youth. While its general aim was the steady elevation of the masses of the people, it was compatible with a strong, and even passionate devotion to Parliamentary traditions, and with an emphatic repudiation of policies savouring of Socialism or revolution.

One central tenet in Bryce's political creed was illustrated in a discussion in the House of Commons (May 17,

[191]

1889) on the Reform of the House of Lords, a perennial subject of academic debate, introduced on this occasion by the lively and iconoclastic spirit of Henry Labouchere. Bryce spoke strongly in favour of a Second Chamber but "it must be strong if it is to be useful and representative if it is to be strong." The present House, being based on the hereditary principle, was neither. It was necessary, therefore, that it should be reformed, not in the interests of a political party but because it is desired to give stability to the whole structure of government, to save the country from sudden impulses, and in the happy words of Mr. Lowell, " to let the government carry out the people's will and not the people's whim." Mr. Balfour, rising in reply, congratulated the member for Aberdeen on "his extremely Tory speech." In his old age, Bryce was appointed Chairman of a Conference to deal with the Second Chamber question, and drafted a report on the Reform of the House of Lords, which embodied the principles contained in the "extremely Tory speech" of his middle life.

Among the minor measures of the session of 1889 was a bill for the reform of the Scottish Universities, the main features of which, seeing that it was proposed to appoint an executive Commission with large powers to add new subjects of study, to permit the recognition of extra-mural teaching and to carry out many other useful reforms, were welcome to Bryce. There was one question, however, which in his eyes was so important that it should be dealt with by Parliament itself without delay, and not referred to the Commission. This was the question of the religious tests which were at that time imposed on professors.

They were of two kinds, a declaration imposed on Chairs other than those of Divinity, that the professors would never endeavour, directly or indirectly, to inculcate any opinions opposed to the Divine Authority, or exercise the function of their office to the subversion of the Established Church of Scotland, and a narrower theological test, subscription to which was required from the holders of the Divinity chairs. Bryce opposed both these tests. The declaration was "absurd, trivial, ridiculous" and should go. The retention of the tests for theological Chairs was hardly less objectionable. The examples of Germany, Italy, and America showed that there was no necessary connection between the existence of an established Church and its possession of theological chairs at the National Universities. Moreover, in Scotland the imposition of these tests was peculiarly impolitic, partly because the Established Church of Scotland was in a minority, both in respect of students and in respect of ministers, and partly because the theological differences between the three Protestant Churches in Scotland were exceedingly small. Hence the hardship was greater. The appointing bodies might safely be trusted with the duty of making suitable appointments.

The government so far conceded to this pleading as to abolish the lay tests. For the Divinity Chairs, however, the tests were retained. "I do not know what the honourable member means by free theology," said Mr. Balfour.[1] Bryce did not enter into the metaphysics of the question, but as a practical man he was certainly right in his surmise that the appointing bodies might be trusted

[1] July 2nd, 1889.

to choose with discretion and that the area of suitable choice would be widened by the removal of these vexatious restrictions, and the dignity of the Chairs enhanced.

One literary enterprise belonging to the summer of 1885 deserves a brief mention here. As far back as 1872 J. R. Green had discussed with Bryce the prospect of founding an English Historical Review, but the scheme failed to mature principally from lack of financial support, until thirteen years later a famous publishing firm came to the rescue. With the aid of Messrs. Longmans all difficulties were smoothed away and on July 15 Bryce invited a small company of historians to dine with him at Bryanston Square to discuss the policy and management of the new publication. At that symposium there were gathered among others Lord Acton, Dean Church, Mandell Creighton, R. Garnett, Adolphus Ward, Robertson Smith, and F. York Powell. "We spent" writes Mr. R. L. Poole, "a long evening and settled the general policy of the Review."

Bryce, unable to undertake the editorship himself, suggested Creighton for either and contributed to the first number of the Review which appeared in January, 1886 a prefatory note in which he pointed out that it had "long been a matter of observation and regret that in England, alone among the great countries of Europe there did not exist any periodical organ dedicated to the study of history." Neither in Britain nor in the British Dominions nor in the United States was there an organ concerning itself "with history in general or appealing to an audience of the whole race." There was then clear need for such a journal. But how was history to be defined? "As the

record of human action and of thought only in its direct
influence upon action." Essays on controversial questions would be admitted but not if the questions were
argued with reference to the controversies of the hour;
and an effort would be made to provide in each number
some articles or reviews which an educated man, not
specially conversant with history, might read with
pleasure and profit. In a characteristic sentence Bryce
continued 'so far from holding that true history is dull,
we believe that dull history is usually bad history.'

So the English Historical Review appeared, heralded
by a tremendous salvo of learning on German Schools of
History from the pen of Lord Acton. Bryce was but a
rare contributor, but in 1907 when newly appointed to
the office of Chief Secretary of Ireland he presided over a
dinner in Balliol Hall given to Mr. R. L. Poole, to cele-
brate the twenty-first anniversary of the Review. 'The
question is often asked,' he said, 'whether History is a
science or an art. You might as well ask whether the sea
is blue or green. It is sometimes the one and sometimes
the other.'

Among the friendships formed in the early years of his
Parliamentary life and vigorously maintained one in particular deserves mention. Both on grounds of historical
interest and political sympathy Bryce was greatly drawn
to Lord Acton. We find him introducing Acton to Creighton, associating Acton with himself in the foundation of
the Historical Review, sending him to cheer up J. R. Green
during his last visit to Mentone and conversely we find
Acton consulting Bryce as to the acceptance of the History Chair at Cambridge, keeping him posted in the

latest intelligence of Mr. Gladstone and equipping him with elaborate notes on the Berlin savants in view of an approaching visit to that city. Who should be invited to write for *the English Historical Review*, who for the *Cambridge Modern History*, who should fill this chair at Cambridge or that at Oxford, should not de Francqueville have an honorary degree, was Helmoldt's method sound or unsound? These and such like learned matters are freely discussed between the friends. There is also inevitably much correspondence about Irish Home Rule, a scheme which Acton stigmatises as "necessary, dangerous, unhopeful" but supports notwithstanding with lessons drawn from the history of Belgium, Poland, Hungary, and Bavaria. Nor was gossip excluded. By a curious exercise of patronage Mr. Gladstone had in 1892 made his learned Catholic friend a Lord-in-Waiting to Queen Victoria and the letters from Windsor where the days passed pleasurably but "with a want of intellectual stimulus quite astonishing" are here and there spiced with the entertaining tittle tattle of a court. The historian, however, will note with regret that Bryce was unable to accept the invitation to contribute to the *Cambridge Modern History* that article on Rome under Sixtus V which Acton had reserved for him as peculiarly fitted to his historical sympathies and genius.

CHAPTER XII

IRISH HOME RULE

Only an infinitesimal portion of the soil belongs to the descendants of those who possessed it before Cromwell, and the division of classes which was begun by confiscation, has been perpetuated by religion and was for many generations studiously aggravated by law.

LECKY

THE Liberal party, fresh from its inspiring victory at the polls, was confronted at once with the menacing spectre of Irish discontent. Agrarian crime in Ireland, coupled with Parnellite obstruction at Westminster, compelled English politicians however distasteful the prospect might be, to make Ireland their main preoccupation. In the course of four troubled years the Liberal party, after losing the gloss of its early popularity over the Transvaal and Egypt, was finally shattered on the rock of Irish Home Rule.

The process which converted the Liberal Party to accede to the demand for Irish self-government has been very well described by Bryce, who as a young member of Parliament took a minor but active part in this critical transformation. By birth, religion, and family connections, as well also as by the quality of his temperament,

[197]

nobody was less likely to sympathise with the Catholic Irishmen of the south than a Scottish Presbyterian, born in Belfast; and Bryce became a Home Ruler, not because he liked Home Rule, but because he saw no other way of handling the Irish question which was not more objectionable. The Session of 1880 began the process, impressing as it did upon the mind of the new member three important facts, first that the Irish nationalists were a foreign body, second that the House of Lords regarded Ireland from the point of view of the English landlord and third, that the House of Commons cared so little about Ireland that it scarcely resented the rejection by the Lords of so important a remedial measure as the Compensation for Disturbance Bill.

In the next year Mr. Gladstone came forward with two measures, a Coercion Bill and a Land Bill. Bryce voted reluctantly for Coercion, hoping that its ill-effects would be more than overbalanced by a generous measure for the relief of the Irish peasantry. He noted, however, that the Irish party was often outvoted on amendments to the Land Bill, and that the measure itself was seriously injured by the House of Lords. "The two facts," he wrote, "which stood out in this eventful session were that even in legislating for the good of Ireland, we were working against the wishes of Ireland, and second that at the end of a long session, entirely devoted to her needs, we found her more hostile and not less disturbed than she was at the beginning."

The impression was deepened by the experiences of the next session which was darkened by the Phoenix Park murders and by a new Coercion Bill. "It is from this year 1882 that I date the impression that we formed that Home Rule was sure to come. 'It may be a bold experiment,' we said to one another in the lobbies, 'there are serious difficulties in the way. . . . But if the Irishmen persist as they are doing now, they will get it.'" The comparatively quiet session of 1883 did nothing to weaken the force of these gathering impressions. There was on the contrary a steady increase in the numbers of Nationalist Members returned from the Irish constituencies and a growing habit of co-operation between the Nationalist and the Tory opposition. Among the young Liberals the conviction began to spread that if Home Rule was not granted by the Liberal party, it would certainly come from the Tories.

What, however, made the grant of self-government to Ireland inevitable was the passage of the Franchise Bill in 1884. Not only because henceforward the Irish Nationalists were inevitably destined to hold the balance in English politics, but because in face of so large a parliamentary party as the Irish had now become, it was impossible to attempt to govern Ireland on the Crown Colony plan. Bryce, who as early as 1882 had come to the conclusion that if Irish discontent did not abate, some change would have to be made, now came to the conclusion that Home Rule in some form was imminent, and at Easter 1885 met a number of Ulster Liberals in Belfast, warned them of what was coming and urged them to prepare some plan for safeguarding the interests of the Protestant part of Ulster. "They were startled and

Even in the khaki election of 1900, when the charge of pro-Boer was brought up against him, he won through by the courage and conviction with which he laid his unpopular views before the Constituency.

It was natural that he should have been asked to stand for the Lord Rectorship of the Aberdeen University. The office is a coveted and honorific distinction involving no more labour than the preparation of an address, and if the election could have been made on academic grounds Bryce would have been glad to stand. By ancient custom however Rectorial elections in Scotland have been political contests of the ordinary type; and since Bryce thought it unsuitable that the highest office in an ancient University should be so awarded he declined to stand for the Rectorship either there or elsewhere whenever he was approached.

In ranging himself with the Home Rulers, Bryce was taking the most difficult and anxious decision in his political career. Yet though he would blame no one for not being a Home Ruler, for himself he could see no alternative. Writing to his Uncle John, May 17th, 1886, he says: —

"It is inexpressibly grievous to me not to have your agreement in the course I have taken, but I can assure you that every week has made me feel my own conscience more clear in the matter. I see nothing for it at all except a scheme of Home Rule with an Irish Parliament. No one here among Hartingtonians or Chamberlainites proposes any alternative scheme which will hold water for a moment, or offers any prospect of bettering the lamentable state of Ireland. You greatly overestimate my influence with Mr. Gladstone and in the party, but I have strongly urged the case of Ulster with him and Lord Spencer, and they would, I believe — this, of course, in confidence — agree to some plan, were any proposed by the Ulstermen, but the latter, in spite of my repeated entreaties, will propose nothing . . . we are going to be beaten, but I believe it is in a good and righteous cause, the cause of peace and friendliness between two peoples, and I never felt more strongly that the Christian principles which ought to underlie all Statesmanship dictate this course to us. My mother, who, as you know from her strength of mind, is more likely to influence me than I her, quite agrees with me."

In the last years of his life Bryce wrote a review of this stage of his career, which since it expresses with great fidelity the way in which the Irish problem appeared to him, not only as it first revealed its difficulties to the young member of Parliament, but also in the retrospective contemplation of extreme old age, may be printed here :

"Though my Father and Mother settled in Glasgow in 1846 we had all kept up close connection with Ireland, for five of my uncles lived there and four of my aunts, and I frequently crossed over to pay them visits, sometimes spending a week or two at Christmas and in the summer. Ulster affairs had a great interest for us, and my Mother always continued to feel herself Irish. Of the rest of Ireland we knew and heard very little after the failure of the rebellion of 1848. But in 1860, being then at Oxford, I went on a reading party with three English and two Scotch friends to Glengariff and Killarney. The country was then in a wretched state of poverty and general backwardness, but it was pretty quiet — quite quiet in Cork and Kerry, and fairly so in Tipperary, Clare, and Galway, where there was always some agrarian crime. But all ideas of insurrection, if they had not died out, had gone underground or to America. In the succeeding forty years I made two or three journeys in the West for the sake of scenery and antiquities, but did not study social and economic conditions till the winter of 1880, when hav-

ing been elected for the Tower Hamlets, and there being a great
deal of disorder and crime in Ireland, I felt it a duty to learn
directly what was going on. I went to stay for a day or two with
my friend William Brooke in Dublin, then went out to Westport
in Mayo, and from there across to Leitrim to stay with my friend
Colonel ffolliott.

"The Land League Campaign was in full swing and was
accompanied by many outrages. I talked with some Land
Leaguers, including some priests, and realised the gravity of the
situation. Some were very bold and confident, talking even of
restitution in respect of unjust rents. It was plain that drastic
legislation was needed to give the tenants security, and this was
demanded in Ulster also, though there were no outrages there.
An atmosphere of unrest and suspicion pervaded the whole of
the west. In getting across from Castlebar to my friends the
ffolliotts I had to stop at a place called Frenchpark to get a fresh
horse and car, and was told there was not one to be had in the
town. At several places where I enquired the answer was always
the same. At last I let drop, as if casually, the name of Mr.
John Dillon as an acquaintance of mine, whereupon the sky
cleared at once and the horse and car were forthcoming in ten
minutes. Parnell, and some of his colleagues, were being prose-
cuted before the courts in Dublin on a charge of sedition or some
such offence, and I went to the Four Courts to look on at the
trial. The Government were driven to take some steps, but
everyone knew there would be no conviction. When soon after,
in the House of Commons, the Coercion Bill was being discussed,
I tried to speak in the long debate, but was, of course, not
sufficiently known to have much chance. Once near the end of a
night's debate I rose along with Willis, a well-known common
law barrister of that time; but the speaker, after hesitating for
many seconds, called Willis and my chance was gone. Like
nearly all the young Liberals of the more advanced type, I was
reluctant to vote for the Coercion Bill. We ultimately did so,
with few exceptions, on two grounds which are worth mentioning,
for such things do not always get into histories. One was that

James Bryce, LL.D., Father of Lord Bryce

Irish Home Rule

John Bright (whom we considered our leader and thought we were safe in following as he had been a warm friend of Ireland) supported the Bill. He was then in the Ministry. Forster's authorship of it did not equally influence us, for although we had praised him for having taken the Irish Secretaryship at a time of great difficulty, our confidence in him had been shaken by his handling of the Education Bill of 1870, and by what we thought his weakness in the Eastern crisis of 1876–7. The other ground was that we wanted to have a very strong Land Bill for Ireland, and thought we could screw this out of the Government by making it a condition of our voting for the Coercion Bill. Looking back, I think we erred in voting for the Coercion Bill. Its principle was wrong and it did not have the effect which Forster expected. The scene of the passage of its Second Reading, at the end of a sitting extending continuously over three days and two nights, was the most exciting and (with one exception — that which saw the free fight of 1893) the most painful in all my Parliamentary recollections. It now seems to me to have marked the end of an epoch, the end of the old, dignified, constitutionally regular, and gentlemanly House of Commons, in which everyone was on his good behaviour and felt the force of great traditions, and even wearisome obstruction was tolerated for the sake of letting it be felt that the minority always had a chance and full opportunity secured for the expression of opinion. The Speaker is not to be blamed. The stoppage of business by the Irish party had become intolerable and practically the whole Liberal party, as well as the Tories — much more anxious than we to pass the Coercion Bill — thought the Closure inevitable. I was struck by the great reluctance which Mr. Gladstone showed when he had to propose it. No one was more penetrated by the old traditions, and he doubtless felt that the House of Commons would never be again what it had been before. The Closure was inevitable, though nobody supposed that it would be so freely used as to enable many clauses of Bills to be passed with practically no discussion. All other Assemblies have now had to adopt it. It has helped to reduce the credit and character of representative government; but representative government could not have continued longer without it. The ultimate cause was the change in the composition and spirit of the men who formed the House of Commons. The proximate cause was the discovery which Parnell and some of his colleagues had made of the weak side of the House of Commons. Ireland was avenging herself and she has continued to do so.

"The Coercion Act failed, for the situation in Ireland grew worse rather than better when one after another of the responsible leaders were imprisoned under it. At last Mr. Gladstone, seeing this, took the bold step of releasing Parnell under an arrangement which the Opposition called "The Kilmainham Treaty," because Parnell had undertaken to do his best to pacify Ireland. The Opposition were furious. Arthur Balfour talked of the Prime Minister or the Government — I forget which — as having descended to infamy, an expression which caused a coldness between him and Mr. Gladstone which lasted for some time. Driving home from the House in a hansom with Goschen he talked to me with great bitterness and said that if Disraeli had been living he would have risen to say, 'The House has just witnessed the humiliating spectacle of the Prime Minister of England defending a bargain of dishonour with the suspects of Kilmainham.' Gladstone used afterwards to express his surprise at the reproaches made to him. He would say he had no right to keep the men in prison when that was no longer needed for the peace of the country. There was no bargain in the matter. When any one of his colleagues inadvertently talked of the Kilmainham Treaty he did not conceal his displeasure.

"Concurrently with Parnell's release W. E. Forster resigned the Chief Secretaryship. His position had been made very difficult by Chamberlain's efforts to oust him. Whether Chamberlain desired to succeed him, I cannot say offhand. Some said at the time that he was disappointed at not being asked by Mr. Gladstone to do so. But he did not like Forster whose Education policy in 1870 he had denounced. He thought he was mismanaging Ireland. He incited John Morley, who was then editing the

Pall Mall Gazette to criticise severely Forster's conduct of affairs, but whether he actually revealed what passed in the Cabinet is more than I can say.

"Forster wished to be armed with stronger powers against disorder and when these were refused he went, and Frederick Cavendish (whom few had thought of) was appointed. It was said and generally believed that the post was offered to Dilke either then or shortly afterwards, before Trevelyan took it. Frederick Cavendish on the afternoon of the day he landed in Ireland was murdered in Phoenix Park. The impression made when the news spread over England next morning was greater, I think, than that of any event I can recall — perhaps even greater than the news of Abraham Lincoln's assassination in 1865, and the news of the entry of the Germans into Belgium on August 4th, 1914. I happened to be in Oxford on Sunday, the fourth of May. It was brilliant weather, and those who had come down from London for the week-end, as well as the resident dons, could be seen moving about all day long, gathering into groups and all talking of the same theme. No one then knew that Lord Frederick had been killed merely because he was in company with Mr. Burke and tried to defend him. The horror and anger were unspeakable and they fell upon the Irish generally, for nobody knew of the existence of the small violent group (the Republican Brotherhood) which had plotted and carried out the crime. Nearly the whole House of Commons went down to Chatsworth to the funeral three or four days later and the same evening Mr. Gladstone brought in a Bill which was commonly called the Crimes Bill full of stringent provisions directed against offenders in Ireland. I remember that Arnold Forster (the nephew of Forster's wife, and his adopted son) said to me in the Lobby, not being then a Member, that W. E. Foster would have remained in office if he had been allowed to have so strong a Bill. It was, of course, the murder that had made all the difference. When the Bill came into Committee some few of the Liberals thought it too severe, and fought some of the clauses, but were, of course, defeated, for the current of feeling ran very strong. Among these were Horace Davey and myself. It was easy for me to do so, for I was entirely free, but Davey's position was different, for he was in the running for the next vacancy among the Law Officers and might have feared to injure his chances by resisting the government in the matter. He was, however, a very high-minded and courageous man, not to be deterred from doing his public duty. I do not think that in reality he did suffer, for several times during the debates I thought I discovered that Mr. Gladstone himself disapproved of parts of the Bill and would have been glad to see them pared down.

About this time or a little later I began to perceive a change in Mr. Gladstone's views. Though he had consented to two severe Coercion Bills — the former less severe but more constitutionally indefensible than the latter — he disliked Coercion in principle. His love of liberty was repelled by it. It seemed to him to lead nowhere, and he was beginning to look out for some path that would lead out of this interminable morass. He made a speech — I think in 1883 — which already showed me that his mind was turning in that direction of Home Rule — was at least considering that as a possible solution. But though some of his phrases made the Irish Tories prick up their ears, the House generally did not see what was passing beneath the surface and his words which might have warned them, were soon forgotten. Early in 1885 I gathered from some conversation with Herbert Gladstone that his father's mind was moving more definitely towards some large concession to Irish demands. In the Easter of that year, being then in Scotland, I crossed over to Belfast to visit my eldest uncle, then eighty-six years of age, and while there was entertained to lunch by the Ulster Reform Club. There were then in Belfast, and in Ulster generally, plenty of Liberals of the old type — not exactly Radicals but strong on suffrage extension and on Ulster Tenant Right. In making a short address I told them that they must expect some conces- sions to the demand for Home Rule. Liberal opinion in England was inclining that way. The Government was supposed to be

convinced that the present system could not go on, and though
nothing was settled, or might be soon settled, as to what should
be proposed, they would do well to consider the subject and see
in what way the interests of Ulster should be protected. I did
not indicate anything like the Home Rule scheme of 1886,
having no idea that Mr. Gladstone would be likely to go so far,
but the little that I did say was received with some surprise but
complete incredulity. They had not known how British Liberal
opinion was moving, and they thought so ill of the Home Rule
party and all its works, that they refused to imagine any 'rap-
prochement' between it and the Liberal Government.

"In private conversation it was the same. I could make no
impression on them. In the summer, after the defeat of the
Liberal Government in June, I drew up a short memorandum
with some suggestions for a limited self-government in Ireland,
and gave it to Herbert for his father. Herbert remarked on
reading it, 'He has gone a good deal further than this.' The defeat of the Government and the way in which it happened had
already made a difference. I had spent Whitsuntide on the Lake
of Lucerne with my sister, Kathleen, and reached London on my
return on the morning when Parliament resumed. In the afternoon, having occasion to go upstairs to a Committee Room, I
saw the Tory Whip, Rowland Winn, walking up and down in
close conversation with someone else not quite so tall, and, in
passing them, perceived it was Parnell. When I came a little
later out of the Committee Room, they were still pacing to and
fro, seeming to talk earnestly. I was surprised but did not guess
all that the confabulation meant. Going down to the House that
evening at 10.30, from dining with Lord Granville, I felt as soon
as I entered the Chamber that curious sensation of an electric
tension in the air which one always feels in the House when something momentous is about to happen. Every seat was full,
members were standing at the bar, Mr. Gladstone was speaking,
and with a manner that showed that he felt a crisis at hand.
There was some anxiety in our lobby which grew more intense as
the last of our men were passing the tellers, and we perceived

that the Opposition Lobby was not yet empty. When the paper of numbers was given to Rowland Winn there was wild excitement. Randolph Churchill sprang upon a bench and waved his hat. There was a note of wild triumph in the cheers. As we streamed out to go home, I was struck by the look of satisfaction that Harcourt wore. He and one or two other Ministers were glad to be out of it. One heard afterwards that there had been a long struggle in the Cabinet and a compromise displeasing to both sides. But it was not merely because this crash ended the contest that some of the Ministers were pleased. They wanted to make a new departure, with more elbow room.

"Rowland Winn's talk with Parnell was now explained, for the whole Parnellite party voted with the Tories. There had evidently been a bargain. What was the consideration for the support the Parnellites gave? Some weeks afterwards Hicks Beach and Churchill reversed Lord Spencer's action as Viceroy in the case of the Maamtrasna murder. Someone said, 'The game of Law and Order is up.' For five years the Opposition had been denouncing the Irish members and urging the Government to stronger measures. Now they turned round upon the Government and threw over Lord Spencer in a matter where most people thought his action entirely justified. This more, perhaps, than any other incident carried Mr. Gladstone into Home Rule. He implied to me more than once that he doubted whether he could have taken up Home Rule as a practical proposition without Spencer's support; and Spencer's experience in this case convinced him that it was impossible to govern Ireland successfully under an English party system which permitted a reversal of policy from English partisan considerations. Not that Spencer resented the conduct of the new Government from purely personal reasons, he was quite above that, but he thought it a crucial instance. The Maamtrasna Debate was a turning point in history.

"In the electoral campaign of 1885, Gladstone made one or two speeches which indicated to those who knew his mental habits in what direction he was moving. Feeling sure he would go pretty far, I felt safe in saying in my Election Address at Aberdeen that, as regards Ireland, the further we go towards self-government the better, subject to the supreme control of the Imperial Parliament. However, most of my friends did not so interpret, or wish to interpret our leader's words, and committed themselves pretty decidedly against Home Rule. Harcourt was among these, and in referring to the Tory co-operation with the Irish Nationalists, and to a speech of Lord Salisbury's in which he seemed to hold out hopes of an arrangement with the Irish, Harcourt said, 'We will leave the Tories to stew in Parnellite juice,' words with which he was frequently taunted eight months afterwards. The Tory leaders were thought to be endeavouring to find a way of meeting the claims of Ireland, but more will be known on this subject some day. I went to Ireland in the autumn of 1885, and being in Dublin, called upon Lord Carnarvon (who was then Viceroy) and lunched with him at the Vice-regal Lodge. Without asking any questions, I gave him an opening for saying something about the Irish situation, and though he said nothing explicit, nothing that could have done harm if I had imprudently repeated it, he left me with the distinct impression that he was in communication with the Irish leaders and had hopes of arriving at a scheme which they could accept. This was subsequently practically admitted. He was not well treated by the Cabinet who threw him over and left him to be censured by the party for action which his colleagues had virtually sanctioned. He was too chivalrous ever to complain during the rest of his life. I have often tried to persuade his widow to let the facts be fully made known, but she has been unwilling to have revealed anything which she thinks he would not have revealed, sharing and respecting his sensitiveness.[1]

"Returning from Dublin, I found myself in the same steamer to Holyhead with several of the Irish leaders, including (if I remember right) Sexton, Dillon, and Healy (they were not yet alienated from one another). They were jubilant over the result

[1] A full account of the life of the Fourth Earl of Carnarvon by Sir Arthur Hardinge was published by the Clarendon Press, Oxford, in 1925.

of the General Election, which, leaving the Liberals slightly inferior in numbers to the other two parties put together, gave the Irish party the deciding voice. I do not remember the language they used, but the substance was, 'Now we have your English parties at our mercy; one or other will have to do our bidding, for we can keep out, or turn out, one or other'. I told them they were a bit too confident. The English are not very easily driven and there may be more resistance than you expect.

"It was curious to observe that the Irish, although masters of English Parliamentary politics, did not understand English character any better than the English understand the Irish character. Immediately after returning, I saw Herbert Gladstone who had come up to London, apparently to reconnoitre, and who disclosed what were believed to be his father's intentions in a speech which made an immense sensation at the time. This was the famous flying of the kite. It seemed to me at the time a mistake, for coming so soon after the election it was construed as a bid for the Irish vote, and what was supposed to be Mr. Gladstone's conversion to Home Rule was attributed to his discovering that the Irish held the balance of power. In reality, his slow conversion had been almost completed in the previous summer. It was right for him to wait to see how the Election went in Ireland and to keep his decision in suspense till it was plain that the Parnellites were going to have a large majority. But he ought to have somehow prepared the nation — and especially his own party, and especially the leaders of that party — for the new policy, rather than let his view get out in a casual uncertain way. His own friends were disquieted and did not know where they were, and the Opposition began to draw their ranks together. The new Parliament met in an eager and excited frame of mind. It was a Parliament with plenty of talent and an ardour even beyond its talent. The Whips told me that they found it difficult to restrain the new members in trying to turn out the Government forthwith. They had not long to wait. The Government were prepared to be turned out upon some Irish issue, but Mr. Gladstone apparently thought it better to choose another which would avoid the necessity for an Irish debate; and he did it on an Amendment to the Address moved by Jesse Collins, regretting that nothing was said in the Queens' Speech about small agricultural holdings. Mr. Gladstone made a speech in the Debate in which he emphasised the high importance of the question in which, so far as I remember, he had never shown interest before and never showed interest again. He might have spared himself the trouble, for his majority was certain, but he seemed to me to be acting from habit, under the idea that he must make a strong speech because a momentous result was to follow.

"When the new Ministry was in course of formation — I think on the day after the Division — he was sitting on the Front Opposition Bench in a long and earnest conversation with Hartington, who sat erect, stiff, and stolid, saying very little while Mr. Gladstone plied him with argument. One knew how much was going to turn upon that talk and felt the significance of Hartington's unyielding look. When I was offered the Under-Secretaryship in the Foreign Office, which (as I afterwards heard) was going to have been offered to me if the Ministry had remained in the previous summer, for Edmond Fitzmaurice was going to retire on the ground of health, I hesitated at first about accepting it, feeling doubtful whether I could support so large a Home Rule Bill as I conjectured Mr. Gladstone would propose. However, as the Bill was not to come on till April, there was more than two months to think the matter over, so I accepted, reserving a final decision. Reflection during the two months that followed convinced me that no measure short of Home Rule would solve the Irish problem, and when the time came I had no hesitation in remaining in the Government.

The scene when Mr Gladstone introduced the Bill was one of tense excitement. The attendance was so large that when all the galleries had been filled it was necessary to place chairs from the Bar forward towards the Speaker, and when these were filled there were still members standing. The speech was one of his best efforts, rather too long, but well-constructed and luminous. He began by saying that he approached the question as being primarily one of social order. That which had most impressed him in the troublous days from 1880 to '83 was the difficulty of maintaining order in a country where the people were, if not in sympathy with lawlessness or crime, yet either unwilling or afraid to help the Government to suppress it. This thought was at the bottom of his policy. By this time he had begun to study Irish history of which apparently he had known very little, and he worked himself up to a fiery heat of indignation when he read of the cruelties with which the insurrection of 1798 was suppressed. The Bill went slowly on its way; the Ministry willing to allow a long debate because they thought time and discussion were on their side, but the result seemed to prove they were mistaken.

"The elements hostile to Home Rule on the Ministerial side organised and consolidated themselves, Chamberlain being most active in directing the process. Yet he seemed or professed to hesitate more than once before finally deciding to throw his whole weight against the Second Reading. The best speech made against the Bill was, to my thinking, Hartington's on the First Reading. A great effort was made by Gladstone when the danger of defeat was imminent to rally the wavering Liberals by a party meeting — I think at the Foreign Office. He made an effective speech and seemed to carry nearly everyone with him. Some of his statements reassured the doubters and were taken as pledges that their objections would be fully considered, and we of the Government left the meeting hopeful. When the House met the same afternoon, the Tories who had heard of the meeting and had been alarmed at the prospect that the waverers were returning to the Ministerial flag resolved (it was said at the suggestion of Churchill) to bring the subject up by moving the Adjournment. Their cue was to taunt Gladstone with having gone far in the way of concession, and they attacked him in a way which provoked his anger, and, as it seemed to me, disturbed his judgment. In repelling their charges he seemed to virtually withdraw or minimise the concessions he had made at the meeting, partly, I think, out of pride, partly because he did not wish to awaken suspicions among the Irish. The result was to lose all that he had gained by the meeting. The waverers fell away from him. I felt from that evening that we should be beaten.

"The Irish Land Bill, which was meant to strengthen the Home Rule Bill by removing the fears of the landlords and their friends that they would be dispossessed by a Home Rule Parliament, did not improve our position. The landlords were not appeased and some Liberals were repelled. Trevelyan, who had resigned when the Home Rule Bill was brought in, said to me that he disliked the Land Bill the worst of the two, and my recollection is that before the Home Rule Bill went to a division it was practically dead. When asked to speak in the debate about a week before the division I inquired whether I might say that if the House of Commons did not accept it, Ministers would be ready to take the opinion of the country. Mr. Gladstone assenting, I did make the statement, but by the time the division had arrived, and still more after the division, hope of success with the country began to wither. Gladstone himself was sanguine, excited by his own passionate belief in the cause, and by the enthusiasm of the local leaders who were following him. However, before the polling began, I felt, and I think most of my friends felt, that we were marching to defeat. The bulk of the influential local men, the men of wealth and standing in trade and manufacture, were mostly against us. I do not speak of the landed gentry, for nearly all of them had left us before, some on the Eastern question of 1876–78, some like the Duke of Argyll and Lord Lansdowne on the Land Bill of 1881. Defeat came on the 10th June, a year and a day after the Liberal Government had been turned out in 1885. So suddenly did the Election come, that I was unopposed in Aberdeen. There had not been time to arrange for a contest. It was my only unopposed election. But many of my oldest and best supporters, including my predecessor, old Dr. Webster, had fallen away, and some of them continued bitter for years afterwards. Well do I remember a conversation with Mr. Gladstone in his house in Downing Street after I had returned to London from having spoken in five or six constituencies after my own return. We were alone. He was not depressed or dejected by the result — I never saw him really dejected; he had too much spirit for that — but he was rather saddened, and looked at the future with apprehension. He delivered to me, sitting in front of him, a short speech almost in his House of Commons manner, grim and emphatic, chiefly about Chamberlain. Its exact phrases escape me, but the substance was that Chamberlain was a most dangerous man, restless, ambitious, unscrupulous, and that the country would suffer from him. 'It does not much affect me,' he said, 'but those of you who will be in public life during the next twenty years will have experience of the mischief he can do.' There was not in his words a note of personal hatred, but there was the sternest condemnation I ever heard him utter of anyone.

"Looking back on the history of this first act of the Irish drama, round which British parliamentary politics revolved for nearly fifty years, one can see that four capital mistakes were made. The first was that Gladstone did not allow the country, and even most of his Cabinet colleagues, to know his intentions, or rather to know into what purposes his intentions would crystallise, if the event happened which was at least highly probable, viz. the complete victory of the Parnellites at the General Election of 1885. When the event happened, and they began to learn what his purposes were, they were not merely startled, many thought themselves ill-treated, and this sense of injury contributed to make some fall away and others follow him grudgingly. It shook, to some extent, the faith of the country in the solidity of his judgment. He was accused — unjustly, no doubt, but plausibly — of having changed his principles for the sake of regaining office. Even when it was known that he had written to Salisbury offering to support him if he would take up the Irish question and try to effect a settlement — taking the subject out of party politics — this offer did not remove the impression I have stated.

[216]

"Secondly, the way in which the announcement of his change of attitude was made — what was called the flying of Herbert Gladstone's kite — was not judicious.

"Thirdly, he ought not to have brought forward the Bill so early in the new Parliament. The House of Commons was not prepared for it, still less was the country. His own party had been opposing the Irish demands for five years and were now suddenly asked to concede them. Not enough time had been given them for education. The curve was too sharp, and some of the cars ran off the rails.

"Fourthly, when discussions outside and the debates in Parliament had made it plain that the Bill, if carried on the Second Reading, could be carried only by a very small majority — and most of us did not expect it to be carried — he ought to have admitted that the country needed more time to consider the subject, and given an assurance that if the Bill were carried on Second Reading he would go no further with it in that Session. Had this been done the chances are that the great rupture in the party might have been avoided, that rupture which threw the Liberals into Opposition for six years, sent an important section of them permanently into the Tory camp, and led to so many other regrettable errors in British policy. He very nearly saved the Second Reading by the Foreign Office meeting, but under the taunts of Hicks Beach and Churchill he just missed the chance. In that two hours' debate the fortunes of England and Ireland were turned aslant from the path that led to peace.

"Gladstone was unusually calm and collected in a crisis, complete master of his judgment as well as of his eloquence, but on this occasion he was taken unawares, and without actually losing his temper he lost some of his prudence and composure. To have suggested that he was clinging to office for the sake of his salary was more than he could bear, as the tones of his voice in answering the charge disclosed. The idea sometimes occurred to me that the appeal which the Irish question made to his emotions told unfavourably on his power of seeing facts as they were. He did not understand that other people were not morally touched by the sense of the wrongs Ireland had formerly suffered which had penetrated his own heart.

"I have not dwelt on his failure to appreciate one of the greatest obstacles in his path — the resistance of the Protestants in the north-east of Ireland — because his ignorance of that part of Ireland was shared by his colleagues and indeed by most English politicians. I tried more than once to make him understand how serious this difficulty was, how amazed the north of Ireland Liberals were at the sudden change of front, and what obstinate opposition they would offer. He always replied, 'Let them make some suggestions as to what safeguards they want.' This they always refused to do, and tactically they were right. The result was to drive them into the arms of the Orangemen and practically to extinguish Liberalism in the North of Ireland. The Tory Opposition soon perceived that the Northern Protestants — Presbyterians as much as Episcopalians — were to be their best allies. The Presbyterians counted far more than the Episcopalians, because they could and did appeal to the Scotch Presbyterians and the English Nonconformists who had hitherto been the staunchest battalions in the Liberal army. It need not be supposed that the English and Scotch Tories felt acutely the wrong supposed to be inflicted on the northern Protestants, but that wrong proved to be, as time went on, the strongest card in their hand and they played it effectively. It must be remembered that these Northern Protestants had a strong logical case. They were as distinct from the rest of Ireland except as regards the Land question, as Ireland was from England, and could, therefore, claim that the principles which Mr. Gladstone used to show that Ireland required separate treatment could also be used to prove that the Protestant — the 'loyal minority' as it began to be called — were also entitled to be separately treated. I had, at Mr. Gladstone's request, written an article on the Irish question in the autumn of 1885, indicating arguments that pointed to Home Rule; but in stating the case had been obliged to admit that the objection Ulster would make presented a serious difficulty. That part of my article was sometimes brought up against me, and the only answer I could make — it was not a sufficient answer — was that the Ministry had asked Ulster to say what she wanted, and that Ulster had refused.

"The result has proved that it would probably have been better to have left the north-east counties out of the Bill. The Parnellites might have refused the Bill upon those terms, but they could hardly have refused to agree to special provisions for Ulster, amounting to a sort of autonomy; and if these had been offered to the Ulster counties and refused by them Gladstone's position would have been a great deal stronger logically, and the English Nonconformists and Scottish Presbyterians would have been conciliated. However, this is one of the cases in which it is easy to be wise after the event.

"I tried privately to get some of the Belfast Liberals whom I knew personally to make suggestions for the amendment of the Bill, but they refused absolutely. Their blood was up. Disliking and despising the Parnellites, they thought themselves betrayed into the hands of the enemy.

"The rout of the Liberal party, and the proof that was soon given that the important Liberal Unionist section of the majority in the new Parliament was likely to co-operate steadily with the Tory section, and that co-operation would eventually pass into union, showed that the Liberal party had received a grievous wound from which it did, in fact, not recover until the election of 1905, by which time new forces were beginning to appear. The future historian, if he honours the memory of the Ministry of 1886 by saying that it fell valiantly for a cause which the subsequent course of events has approved, may also say that it was the beginning of the end of the historic Whig and Liberal party which dated from the Civil Wars. The Whig element represented by a large part of the landed aristocracy, had now almost entirely passed into the Tory camp; so had a considerable section of the Nonconformists. In the Irish Coercion Bill which the new Tory Ministry carried through in the session of 1887, the Liberal Unionists, with scarcely an exception, supported the

Government, and were logically right, because the Government presented their Bill as the only alternative to Home Rule. This attitude was maintained all through the Parliament, and there would probably have been very little growth of sentiment favouring Home Rule in the electorate at large, but for the charges which the *Times* newspaper brought foolishly and managed stupidly in its campaign against Parnell."

From this statement it is clear that Bryce was never an enthusiastic Home-ruler. He did not like Home Rule, but thought that all other Irish policies were even less promising. Nor did advancing experience invest the prospect of Irish Home Rule with added lustre. In the Spring of 1893, happening to be Minister in attendance on Queen Victoria in Italy, he disclosed something of his uneasiness to his friend Dr. Randall Davidson, then Bishop of Rochester.

" In the last week of March," wrote the Bishop,[1] " I had several walks and long talks with Bryce including a full afternoon on the hills above Fiesole. The whole of that day he was full of the problems of Irish Home Rule. I thought him definitely less hopeful on the subject than he had been a few years ago, and he was obviously more vexed than he cared to own at Mr. Gladstone's attitude in throwing scorn upon the fears of the 'property classes' as represented by London bankers and others. He had tried to talk things over quietly with the Queen but found the pitch had been queered by Mr. Gladstone's sermonising to her with the futile endeavour to convert her to his opinions. This had only irritated her and made Bryce's position in talking it over with her difficult. I asked him to tell me frankly

[1] Now (1926) Archbishop of Canterbury.

what in his opinion was likely to be the outcome of the struggle. He replied that he did not at all expect this Home Rule Bill or anything like it *ever* to become law. 'It will, I suppose, come to a compromise some day as other things have done. Perhaps the Tories will introduce a sweeping Local Government Bill which we shall be bound to accept though I do not myself think that would work nearly as well as the complete Home Rule scheme we have drafted.' He added that he thought it not improbable that some force might have to be used before the controversy is over. On the whole he left on my mind the same impression as in our many talks seven or eight years ago at Windsor on the subject, namely that he is a Home Ruler *in despair*, adopting it as the least of a choice of evils and being far from hopeful as to the results. He has quite dropped the position he used to take at Windsor when the first Bill was introduced, namely that it was impossible to give Home Rule without first settling the Land question."

To the present writer he once observed that he could never blame a man for not being an Irish Home-ruler. Ulster was for him throughout the formidable obstacle, for he knew Ulster from the inside, and remembered that the Protestant Settlement in North Eastern Ireland was older than the Voyage of the Mayflower.

CHAPTER XIII

THE AMERICAN COMMONWEALTH

An American is the born enemy of all European peoples.
ADET, 1746.

We are participants whether we like or not of the life of the world. The interests of all nations are ours also. We are partners with the rest. What affects mankind is our affair, as well as the affairs of the nations of Europe and Asia.
WOODROW WILSON.

1883–8

IN the course of 1881, Bryce was offered and declined the post, subsequently held by his friend, Courtenay Ilbert, of Legal member of the Viceroy's Council of India. To a lawyer, interested in the many delicate problems which arise out of the interfusion of Eastern and Western civilisation few posts could be more attractive than this high office associated with the illustrious names of Macaulay, Maine, and FitzJames Stephen. But there was one decisive reason against acceptance. Bryce felt that he could not leave his mother. As for the East, it was precisely in the opposite direction that his thoughts were turning. The idea of a great book on the American Commonwealth was slowly growing up in his mind.

As we have seen, Bryce paid his first visit to America with Albert Dicey in 1870. He was then thirty-two years of age in the full tide of youthful vigour. He saw much, he theorised boldly and, as he tells us in the Introductory Chapter to *The American Commonwealth*, threw half his bold generalisations overboard after a second four months' tour in the autumn of 1881. This second visit covered much new ground, for Bryce crossed the Continent to the Pacific States and also visited the Southern States and Baltimore. A third visit followed in 1883. Here too while many places were revisited new ground was broken. There was a voyage over the Northern Pacific Line to the States of Washington and Oregon, followed by a visit to the Hawaiian Islands; and again reason was discovered for much revision of earlier conclusions. "Though the two later journeys gave birth to some new views, these views are fewer and more discreetly cautious than their departed sisters of 1870." It was on the third journey, fifty years after the appearance of De Tocqueville's *Democratie en Amerique* that the big book took shape in his mind and that he definitely began to collect material for it.

From the pages of the *American Commonwealth* we can gather something of the manner in which these notable visits were conducted, how ceaseless and well directed were the interrogatories of the traveller, how wide was the span of his interests, how inexhaustible his appetite for significant detail.

"Having constantly enquired in every State I visited wherever the system of popular elections to Judgeships prevails how it happened that the Judges were not worse I was usually told that the bar had intervened to prevent such and such a bad nomination." That phrase "having constantly enquired" is very typical. The interrogatory was constant, systematic, unlimited. Anyone might be put under contribution. The waiters in a Denver hotel are called upon to explain how they expend their autumn and winter savings and their answer illustrates the restlessness of the West. A conductor on a New York elevated railway is asked how he is able to enforce the rule against smoking. He gives a reply which illustrates the American idea of equality. All forms of printed matter, good, bad, and indifferent, are laid under contribution.

"A perusal of the literature which the ordinary Americans of the educated farming and working class reads and a study of the kind of literature which the Americans who are least coloured by European influences produce, lead me to think that the Bible and Christian theology together do more in the way of forming the imaginative background to an average American view of the world of man and nature than they do in Protestant Europe."

With similar diligence the historian of manners counts eighteen advertisements of soothsayers in a single issue of a San Francisco newspaper, carefully notes the rate of interest on debts secured on what are thought to be safe mortgages in Walla Walla and discovers all about the young women who wait at table at his hotel in the White Mountains in 1870.

"The bird of Minerva," says Landor, "flies low and picks up its food under hedges." Bryce, hurrying over the continent in the fastest trains which American railway enterprise provides, picked up much of his food in the smoking cars. Here no travelling American citizen could hope to escape the thrust of his keen and pleasant inquisition. Add to this the impression left upon a quick eye and a receptive mind by the spectacle of American institutions in action. Now he is present at the admission of new voters to the New York roll ("droves of squalid men who looked as if they had just emerged from an emigrant ship"), now at a Democratic Convention in New York State ("a universal *camaraderie* with no touch of friendship about it; something between a betting ring and the flags outside the Liverpool Exchange"), now he watches the House of Representatives at Washington, "its noise like that of short sharp waves in a Highland loch, fretting under a squall against a rocky shore." Or to descend from the high plateau of constitutional observation to facts and influences not less significant, he detects in the dollar bills of Wisconsin, "a marked smell from the use of skins and furs from the newly arrived Swedes and Norwegians."

Meanwhile, as he travelled about he was gathering round him numbers of American friends, university men, lawyers, politicians, captains of industry, journalists, for he was, as the Americans say, "a good mixer" and found his feet at once in any society. The hospitality of America to English visitors is almost unbounded and to a visitor so curious about American institutions, so friendly and simple and transparently sincere and, above all, so strongly inclined by the natural proclivity of his mind and temperament to take a cheerful view of American civilisation, no door was closed. He went everywhere and saw everything. If he plied his American friends with questions, they were not less ready with answers. Having himself seen life in so many aspects, he lost no time in reaching the point of junction and common experience between himself and those with whom he was thrown even into the most fleeting and casual association. He could talk to lawyers of the law, to politicians of politics, to University men of academic affairs, to journalists as an old and tried member of the craft, to Mr. Theodore Roosevelt, "one of the ablest and most vivacious of the younger generation of American politicians" of the Icelandic sagas, than which no topic was more acceptable, and to the Germans of Milwaukee in their native tongue on the history of their native country. Nor were his American friendships the friendships of convenience. When Bryce took to a man, he never dropped him, and the great and ever extending fabric of his American associations was sustained by a vast and intimate correspondence.

The impressions gained in the three visits to America were thus fortified or revised by the letters of American friends or by personal intercourse with American visitors to England; and though the current of his activity was often deflected, now by politics, now by academic work at Oxford, now by holidays in the Alps or in Dalmatia and in Egypt, America remained the great intellectual interest from the first visit in 1870 until the publication of *The American Commonwealth* in 1888. Neither the Home Rule Bill, nor the Under-Secretaryship of Foreign Affairs, nor the excitement of the election of 1885, when he was returned for South Aberdeen, suspended his work of preparation for the *magnum opus*. The Home Rule Bill, however, was a blessing in disguise. The years 1887 and 1888, when the Liberal party was in opposition and no great opportunity offered itself of distinguished work in politics, were almost entirely devoted to finishing the book.

The American Commonwealth

The object which Bryce had in view was "to present a view of the United States both as a Government and as a Nation." It was no part of his design to draw from American experience lessons applicable to domestic problems in Great Britain nor again to use America as an argument for or against democratic civilisation. His aim was, so far as possible to present an objective account, uncoloured by party bias, of the whole political system of the country in its practice as well as its theory, to describe "not only the National Government but the State Governments, not only the State Governments but the party system, not only the party system but the ideas, temper, habits of the sovereign people." Now this was at once an original and an extraordinarily bold conception. The Federal Constitution has been often analysed and described. Many a traveller again had recorded fleeting impressions of American society gathered in the course of a short visit, but nobody had yet attempted to compare both the federal and the state institutions of this vast commonwealth with their practical results as exhibited in the working or to make a systematic and comprehensive study of the social habits of the American people. De Tocqueville's classic book was a *tour de force* of a different kind. The young Frenchman — and it is well to remember that De Tocqueville was not thirty years of age when he published *Democratie en Amerique* — analysed democratic phenomena in America with an eye to a practical purpose. He regarded democratic civilisation as inevitable; he saw it established on a wide scale in America, and he believed that what was then to be observed in America would in all probability be hereafter observable in France. Rarely, if ever, has a book on social philosophy, written by so young a man, shown an equal measure of penetration: but on the side of knowledge De Tocqueville was admittedly defective. He had never been in England, and how much of America is incomprehensible without a knowledge of the English roots from which self-governing institutions spring! Again his acquaintance with America was almost confined to the New England States. The importance of the American party system, the rôle of the State in the fabric of the federal constitution, the influence of localism in the working of American institutions, no one of these features essential to a full understanding of American democracy was clearly present to De Tocqueville's mind. So while his book is a mine of profound and ingenious observations it does not give, nor yet set out to give, a full and comprehensive portrait of American conditions as they existed in 1833.

Now Bryce's *American Commonwealth* is by the confession of all those best qualified to judge an amazingly accurate picture of the American democracy as it presented itself to the eye of a brilliant and scrupulous observer in 1888. If in originality of thought and finish of style it falls short of De Tocqueville's masterpiece, it has qualities equally rare of another order. No task in reality can be more difficult than the attempt to draw a living picture of a great and complex society, in its strength and weakness, its trials and achievements, its aspirations and failures, its manifold energies and hampering limitations, to see institutions never as mere documents but always in terms of the men and women who work them and to hold the balance even between impressions of good and impressions of evil, making deduction where deduction is due, and preserving throughout a proper sense of proportion.

All this is difficult enough. Hardly less exacting is it to carry through so large an enterprise under the empire of the idea that truth must never be sacrificed for effect, and that no labour is too great for the attainment of the real facts as opposed to the specious impressions and easy generalisations which confront every social enquirer.

By common confession the least original, though not by any means the least instructive or valuable part of the *American Commonwealth* is the sketch of the National Government in the first volume. Americans already knew a great deal about their Federal Constitution. What they did not possess and what was a matter of very great difficulty to supply was a synoptic view of their thirty-eight State governments in their principles, their framework and their practical working and a clear account of their party system in its organisation and actual operation. Both these wants Bryce supplied with a copious generosity of illustration which laid even the most instructed of his American readers under a deep obligation. The second volume, in which these matters are handled, has thus become an original authority, to which recourse is and will continue to be made when information is required with regard to the questions of which it treats. Not many people are likely to take the trouble to read the hundred and five State constitutions, patiently dissected by the British traveller. They will be content to take their knowledge of State politics and of the party machine as they existed in 1888, from the pages of Bryce.

The general impressions of the social, religious, and intellectual life of the American Nation which are contained in the third volume, while demanding less that was recondite in the way of research and investigation acquire a peculiar value, not only by reason of the detachment of the author, but also because they supplement and in large measure correct the dark and sinister forebodings which are inevitably aroused by a contemplation of the defects so unsparingly revealed in the description of American political life. The timidity and corruption of State legislatures, the enormous mass of ill-digested legislation, the Spoils system, the party boss, the deplorable failure in many cases of City Government to reach a respectable standard of probity, the evidence of corruption in the State Judiciary, the general contempt for the political class, all these circumstances tend to create in the mind of the unprejudiced reader of the second volume of Bryce's *American Commonwealth* a feeling of depression and disappointment. And this feeling is the stronger by reason of the obvious desire of the author to be fair to America, to notice whatever merits there be, and only to censure blemishes when truth compels, and in the measure supported by a careful estimate of the facts. But against these ugly circumstances are to be set on the one hand the excellence of the general frame of Government and on the other the amiable and in many respects admirable qualities of the tone and sentiment of the American people. It is in this connection that the third volume of the *American Commonwealth* is of special and indeed of original value. It sets out, without exaggeration and with all the advantages which a wide knowledge of other peoples and lands is able to supply, the good qualities of American civilisation, the all-pervading zeal for education, the widely-spread sentiment for religion, the great efforts made in humane and philanthropic causes, the pleasant and unaffected relations between the sexes, the unexampled diffusion of happiness and material well-being through the whole community. The deficiencies of the Governments are compensated for by the private virtues of the people. Indeed the final conclusion is one of which America, seeing that she is fully entitled to the verdict, may be rightly proud. It is this: "That America marks the highest level, not only of material well-being but of intelligence and happiness, which the race has yet attained."

Neither in America nor in Britain does the famous Federal Constitution of 1789 enjoy quite the same repute now as belonged to it when Bryce painted his full-length portrait. Time has revealed many defects which previously had gone unnoticed or little heeded. The sacred document is less sacrosanct. Amendments have become more frequent. But when Bryce was writing his book, the veneration of Americans for the framework of their Federal Constitution was almost unbounded. What miraculous prosperity had been achieved under its shelter! What shocks it had endured and nevertheless come out whole and entire! Even the cruel war between North and South had only left it stronger than before. Bryce caught the prevailing admiration for the work of the Philadelphia Convention and spread it far and wide. "After all deductions," he concludes, "it ranks above every other written Constitution for the intrinsic excellence

[231]

of its scheme, its adaptation to the circumstances of the people, the simplicity, brevity, and precision of its language, its judicious mixture of definiteness in principle with elasticity in details." That is very high praise, the more valuable seeing that it is freely acknowledged that this excellent frame of government has been found compatible with evils which might well be mortal to a European state, but in the sheltered position of America are no worse than "a teasing ailment."

It should not be inferred that in his treatment of the familiar theme of American Federalism, Bryce was merely content to echo the opinion of American publicists. He made real contributions of his own. The distinction, now so familiar, between rigid and flexible constitutions had been worked out in an Oxford lecture in 1884, and is helpfully employed to point the contrast between the British and American policy. The chapters again which deal with the Federal Courts state the position of the Judiciary under the Constitution with a force and clearness which had not previously been equalled. And quite apart from these portions of the work which demand the technique of the constitutional lawyer, there were certain general contributions to thought about America which as coming from so distinguished a student had, at the time at which they were made, the value of discoveries. That the points on which the American Constitution had been most successful were those on which it had been most artificial, that of all democracies America was the least democratic, that the division of opinion in America was vertical not horizontal and finally that the Americans are at bottom a Conservative nation, these and other observations which may be quoted were at the time real contributions to correct thinking. Here, for instance, are two passages about American Conservatism, which are characteristic of Bryce's political insight:

"They are conservative in their fundamental beliefs, in the structure of their governments, in their social and domestic usages. They are like a tree whose pendulous shoots quiver and rustle with the lightest breeze while its roots enfold the rock with a grasp which storms cannot loosen."

"In 1861 they brushed aside their darling legalities, allowed the executive to exert novel powers, passed lightly laws whose constitutionality remains doubtful, raised an enormous army, and contracted a prodigious debt. Romans could not have been more energetic in their sense of civic duty, nor more trustful to their magistrates. When the emergency had passed away the torrent which had overspread the plain fell back at once into its safe and well-worn channel. The reign of legality returned, and only four years after the power of the executive had reached its highest point in the hands of President Lincoln, it was dropped to its lowest point in those of President Johnson. Such a people can work any Constitution."

The publication of the *American Commonwealth* was not merely an event in the annals of literature. It was a political landmark. "*On ne saurait voir,*" writes De Tocqueville, "*de haine plus envenomée que celle qui existe entre les americains des Etats Unis et les anglais.*" That envenomed hatred between the Americans and the English, which De Tocqueville observed in 1833 had been largely dissipated when Bryce embarked upon his American enquiries. The settlement of the Alabama claims, the democratisation of England, the growth of literature and science in America, the ocean steamers providing as they do increased facilities for mutual intercourse, all these causes had contributed to establish more cordial relations between the two peoples. But the new friendship was still young and tender, and in many regions of American opinion the old prejudice still flourished lustily. The appearance of the *American Commonwealth*, so generously welcomed by American publicists and men of letters, sensibly advanced the march of reconciliation. Here was a book so accurate and well-informed that no American student of the institutions of his country could be dispensed from reading it, and yet entirely devoid of that note of condescension which Americans had so much reason to resent in the commentaries of European visitors. Moreover, though it was full of criticism and dry detail and repetition and in no sense aimed at being what the *Holy Roman Empire* certainly was, a work of art, it was marked by other qualities which America valued, absolute fairness, a real concern for American welfare, and a suffusion of that buoyant hopefulness which is characteristic of the American outlook on life and perhaps the most acceptable quality which an English book about their own country can possess for American readers.

From the first the book was a great success. Lord Acton, Woodrow Wilson, Frederick Harrison united in its praise. O. W. Holmes wrote to congratulate the author on his 'noble and brilliant success' adding that in a popular sense it could hold its own with Robert Elsmere, 'the best seller' of the season. What was sometimes lamented was the lack of historical background, which had been rigorously excluded by considerations of space. The book was a photograph taken and exhibited by a political philosopher, not a history, a picture of what was, not an account of how it had come to be. But as a picture it was generally praised, though E. L. Godkin would have liked more boldness and less caution.

"It may be doubted," wrote Frederick Harrison, "if there yet exists for any country in the old world a portrait so thoughtful, searching and complete, so suggestive of the character and with its life history so graven on the face as that which Mr. Bryce has now given us for the New World." And the portrait had a preceptive value. An American writer happily observed that the three volumes "forced upon every American reader a conviction of his responsibility, not of his good fortune alone."

Theodore Roosevelt wrote (Jan. 6th, 1889) with characteristic generosity.

You must by this time be tired of hearing your book compared to De Tocqueville's; yet you must allow me one brief allusion to the two together. When I looked over the proofs you sent me I ranked your book and his together; now that I see your book as a whole I feel that the comparison did it great injustice. It has all of Tocqueville's really great merits; and has not got, as his book has, two or three serious and damaging faults. No one can help admiring the depth of your insight into our peculiar conditions, and the absolute fairness of your criticisms. Of course there are one or two minor points on which I disagree with you; but I think the fact that you give a good view of all sides is rather funnily shown by the way in which each man who refuses to see any but one side quotes your book as supporting his. I was rather amused to see that the *Spectator* considered that the facts you gave told heavily against Home Rule — because our State Legislatures were not ideal bodies — and that similarly *The Saturday Review* had its worst suspicions of democracy amply confirmed.

I was especially pleased at the way in which you pricked

certain hoary bubbles; notably the "tyranny of the majority" theory. You have also thoroughly understood that instead of the old American stock being "swamped" by immigration, it has absorbed the immigrants, and remained nearly unchanged. Carl Schurz, even, hasn't imported a German idea into our politics; Albert Gallatin had nothing of the Swiss in his theories; our present Mayor Grant, of Irish blood, will rule New York, whether well or ill, solely by American precedents.

But I do not think that the Irishman as a rule loses his active hatred of England till the third generation; and I fear that a good deal of feeling against England — mind you, none whatever against an Englishman — still foolishly exists in certain quarters of our purely American communities. But they are perfectly ready to elect Englishmen to office; relatively to the total number of immigrants, many more English than Irish are sent to Congress for instance.

Did you notice that this fall we, for the first time in five years, beat the Irish candidate for Mayor in Boston, because the Irish were suspected of hostility to the public schools? Though they warmly protested that the accusation was untrue.

These eulogies did not turn the author's head. When the *American Commonwealth* was published in December, 1888, Bryce was touring in India and eagerly drinking in impressions of a civilisation as different from that which had so closely occupied his thoughts during the past two years as could be imagined. On his return in February, 1889, he wrote the following letter to his mother regarding the reception of his book.

Oxford.
February 24, (1889).

Among English voices, sights and occupation India is already fading away like as a dream when one waketh; yet perhaps it is rather as when one puts away a subject into a dark corner of one's mind, not to be bewildered by thinking longer over it, yet knowing one can draw it out again. People ask me but few questions touching it: how little curiosity except over the personal matters of the moment there is in the world!

I have been set to thinking how little love of enquiry for its own sake there seems to be in the world by the compliments paid me by the newspapers and by friends or acquaintances on the "impartiality" as they call it of my U. S. book. Trevelyan for instance said, "How difficult you must have found it to avoid indicating your own feelings on questions and to maintain the same tone, with nothing sensational from the beginning to the end." As people say this, I suppose they express the usual tendency: but in fact this detachment never cost me any trouble or even thought at all: it came of itself without any exertion: whereas the difficulties of arranging topics, of varying manner of treatment, of settling what to say about such matters as Public Opinion and the Merits of Democracy, of avoiding (which I I haven't quite done) that lapsing into platitudes which you and Papa used to make merry over thirty-five years ago — all these were serious, and made me more than doubtful of any merit for the book beyond that of a careful collection of relevant facts.

The reception given it, now that I realise it from the reviews and what friends tell me, is far beyond what I could have expected. What most surprised me is to be told by so many people, not all of whom can be flatterers, and many of whom have no special interest in history or politics, that they find it so interesting, and can read all of it with enjoyment. I tell Minnie to keep my head from being turned with these compliments: yet though the praise is more than is good for one, there comes also a sense of humility in thinking how far one comes short of keeping in actual life and political action on the sort of level which people seem to find in the book, and which indeed I have wished to place it on. Like the owner of the blue china, I feel called on to try to live up to it: and even, though conscious of so many deficiencies, in a way encouraged to try to use to better purpose and with more constancy such knowledge as I have gathered,

and such influence as the acceptance of the book may give me.
One would like to draw from success something better than the
mere pleasure of succeeding. Of that, the best part by far is
your gratification, and that of the girls and Annan. I am indeed
more glad than I can tell you to have been permitted to procure
this enjoyment for you — to whom with Papa I owe most of
whatever taste or turn for literature I have.

There is one respect in which the *American Commonwealth* differs from most modern works on sociology. It
is written almost entirely from personal observation and
from evidence collected orally or by letter from individuals,
and only to a small extent from books. His own estimate
given to Mr. James Ford Rhodes was that five-sixths of
the three volumes was derived from conversations with
Americans in London and the United States and only one-
sixth from books. It may well be asked whether since
the days of antiquity there has been any important historical work written so largely from the talk of living
men. The historical material, out of which Herodotus
composed his immortal history, was of the same quality,
less critically sifted indeed, but governed by the same
view that everything in the world is interesting and many
things entertaining. Both Herodotus and Bryce must
have had something of the same genius for asking questions and for obtaining answers.

Now it is clear that people were ready to amuse Herodotus because they realised that he was a vivid, amusing
man, easy and anxious to be amused and instructed.
And they were ready to confide in Bryce because they saw
that he was a vivid, truth-loving man who wanted to be
told the truth and would respect a confidence. Dr.

Hadley, Emeritus President of Yale University, has put this very well:

"The most salient feature in his work, as I saw it, was his thirst for truth and fearless pursuit of it. The fact that he so obviously wanted to know the truth as other people saw it, made them ready to tell him the truth as they saw it without reserve. His thirst for information was the best possible credential with all men who had real information to give. They told him the truth because they saw that he would use the truth in the way they desired — would try to understand their point of view and not to distort."

The result is that while so many historical works are the product of reading, the *American Commonwealth* has the value of an original source. It is a picture of America at a given point of time painted with the fresh colours of contemporary life.

All this makes it very questionable whether Bryce was wise to attempt, in later editions, to bring his book up to date. Things change very fast in America and a picture which was true in 1888 was no longer a likeness twenty-five years later, so that the more verisimilar the original portrait the more injury it was likely to suffer from the superimposition of certain features of a likeness taken at a later date. The later editions of the *American Commonwealth* contain much material that is new and useful, but the additions belong to a different book which has never been written, and which no pen, now that the questioner is gone, and many of the questioned, can ever write.

From the first the book enjoyed a character of authority which the lapse of time has apparently done little to impair. In American Universities and High Schools it is still an accepted classic supplying in a convenient and trustworthy form a basis for the study of American institutions. Two anecdotes will illustrate its influence. Once when the Bryces were going from Boston to Mount Desert in a steam-boat Bryce fell into conversation with a young fellow traveller and the talk chancing to turn on a point of American Constitutional law, a difference of view disclosed itself. Neither disputant ceding ground, the boy who had fought his end with surprising tenacity played his last card. 'But, Sir, I know I'm right, Bryce says so!' To which Bryce with great amusement felt obliged to tell him that he was Bryce and that his young friend had mistaken the meaning of the passage.

The scene of the second anecdote is laid in the Balkans. In the autumn of 1889, Mr. Stephen Bonsal, an American author, obtained permission to visit a prison known as the Black Mosque in Sofia, in order that he might interview a Bulgarian guide who had fled with some of his money and all his papers, and had since been arrested. 'While I was having my talk with the artist, Trykuvich'; writes Mr. Bonsal, 'I caught sight even in the perpetual twilight which reigned, of a huge ladder or rather of two or three ladders spliced together, which reached to the top of Mosque Minaret where, several bricks having been knocked out, a splash of sunlight intruded. Crouching in this bright sunlight was a little old man intent on reading a volume which was evidently to him in a foreign tongue as he would constantly stop and look up a word in a dictionary which he carried in his ragged coat. When word was passed to him that the visitor was American the old man basking in the sunlight hopped down with

surprising agility and showing me the book said in broken
French "See! I am learning English to read about your
country. The other prisoners are so interested that they
allow me to monopolise the sun spot all day provided that
in the evening I tell them all that I am able to dig out
about the wonderful government of your happy land." And
the book he held up was a well worn copy of the *American
Commonwealth.*'

It will readily be imagined that a book like the *American
Commonwealth* was not kept up to date without considerable labour. The second edition which was issued in the
autumn of 1889 was a reprint of the first save for the
omission of Mr. Goodnow's chapter on the Tweed Ring
in New York City which had given rise to litigation.
But the third edition, of 1893 was the result of a complete and thorough revision and took stock of the
constitutional changes in the States since 1889. Finally
when Bryce had been three years at the British Embassy
in Washington, he brought out a new edition completely
revised throughout with additional notes on recent
tendencies in legislation and on recent legislation regarding
Primaries, together with certain entirely new chapters
dealing with subjects which had been omitted in the earlier
editions or had come into increased prominence since.
Here are to be found his reflections on the latest phase of
the migration into the United States, on foreign policy
and industrial expansion, on the development of the
States since the war and on the present and future of the
negro. A special chapter is devoted to the remarkable
growth of the Universities during the last generation and
to the great place which seats of learning now occupy in

American national life. The later editions then, and more particularly the latest of all cannot be neglected by the student of American affairs. They contain much matter that is both new and valuable, but the new matter belongs to a new America differing from the America which was so faithfully described in the first edition, by innumerable modulations of tone, colour, and substance, by such distinctions in fact as transform the tissue of a living social organism in periods when the human mind makes swift conquests over nature and applies these with an incessant use of courage and ingenuity to the arts and conveniences of life.

CHAPTER XIV

IMPRESSIONS OF EGYPT AND INDIA

In these Four Things, Opinion of Ghosts, Ignorance of second causes, Devotion towards what we fear and taking of Things casual for Prognostiques consisteth the Natural Seed of Religion.

T. HOBBES.

DURING the concluding stage of his work on the American Commonwealth and again immediately after the book was finally disposed of Bryce took holiday in the East. His traveller's impressions of Egypt in the days of Sir Evelyn Baring (afterwards Lord Cromer) and of India in the early years of the Vice-royalty of Lord Dufferin are set down in a series of letters written mainly to his mother and sisters, some of which are here printed.

(To his Mother)

Cairo,
Dec. 25th (Christmas Day), 1887.

. . . Friday 23rd. I landed at Alexandria at 8 A.M., saw what little there is to see in that famous city — of all cities famous in history it contains least to recall the great men and events connected with it — nothing of Alexander himself, nor of the Ptolemies, nor of Julius Caesar, Antony, Augustus, nor of the great school of Grammarians; nor of the poets, Theocritus, Callimachus and their fellows; nor of Origen, S. Athanasius, Cyril,

[243]

Hypatia, and the Monophysite leaders; nor of Amru and the Mohammedans. Even the site is changed, most of the modern town is on what was the channel between Pharos and the mainland.

Lawn tennis goes on briskly in the hotel gardens. I have no very distinct impressions yet — the Egyptian Pharaohs of the IVth and XIIth and XVIIth dynasties jostling in one's mind the great mosque-building Sultans of the 14th Century, and the problem of how we are to get out of the country. It is the first time in history that a people or a Sovereign has wished to be rid of Egypt. Since Cambyses every great Power has wished to take it, and it has always been under some foreign dynasty or other. Now, at last, a race of conquerors desires to abandon it. But the rest of the world doesn't believe that we do. Of course all the English here and the native Ministers, such as Nubar and Artyn, say we can't, and wish us to stay.

The mixture of different ages and races produces something of the same confusion of impressions that one has at first in Rome. From the Citadel of Cairo the Western range of hills is studded with pyramids all belonging to an immensely remote heathen age. Then, leaping over the centuries from the Persian Conquest to the Arab, you come to Mohammedan buildings, the Persian, Greek, and Roman periods having left few visible external marks, tho' they were full of great events. Mohammedanism may be an improvement on the Old Egyptian religion, morally, but it is a far less interesting study. I have been to-day in the Museum, where these extraordinary religious rites are set forth in stone and on papyrus. One is struck by the influence they had in some things on the Hebrews — and in other points by the absence of an influence one might have looked for. The Egyptian religion turned almost wholly on the future state, of which one hears in the Old Testament so little. The animal worship is one of the less pleasing aspects, yet here there is some playfulness — Min would have liked a pretty little bronze group, 3,000 years old, in which a kitten is putting its paw against the old cat's cheek.

Impressions of Egypt and India

To his Mother
Memphis,
Dec. 27th, 1887.

To-day we have been seeing not so much Memphis, the ancient capital of Egypt, supposed to have been founded about B.C. 5,004, *i.e.*, 1,000 years before the creation of the world according to the old Hebrew chronology, but the cemetery of Memphis, a range of tombs, some with pyramids built over them, in the Desert behind Memphis. The city is absolutely and utterly gone, without a trace, tho' as late as the twelfth century it was a splendid mass of ruins. It was nearing its fall when Herodotus saw it in B.C. 540, being then already much older than Rome is now. There is a prophecy of this fall somewhere in Jeremiah, who was about sixty years or so before Herodotus. Now only palm groves, fields of deep black earth, with ponds left by the receding Nile, groups of half naked peasants hoeing the ground, camels bearing bundles of maize stalks along the raised tracts, children screaming Baksheesh, Baksheesh, and here and there a mound full of fragments of pottery and bits of stone, that may be chips from some temple or statue. It stretched eight miles, with a population probably larger than Glasgow. What they shew you now are tombs — we went into three, but in a crowd of tourists one finds it hard to see adequately, and still harder is it to receive impressions.

Dec. 29th.

Yesterday we sailed up river without stopping, there being no antiquities nor other objects of interest on the banks. It is pleasantly lazy, and the passengers are on the whole a pretty good lot, with a fair variety of experiences and interest. Very oddly, one of them is an Indian officer, a certain Col. Evans, who made the ascent of Ararat as far back as 1885. As there are probably only five or six people living who have done this, 'tis a strange coincidence that two should be on the same vessel. Mrs. Ogle and I talk a great deal about the respective characters and charms of her Muff and our Totem, and sympathize with that part of the Egyptian religion.

To his sister, Miss M. Bryce

Siout.

Dec. 30th, 1887

People in Cairo have been very friendly and attentive. I had a pleasant dinner with Sir E. Baring on Xmas Day. Have just now had an interesting talk with an American Missionary here, who agrees with Nubar that our soldiers have behaved admirably in Egypt; and thinks the people are already much the better for our administration; tho' whether they thank us for it is another matter. Doubtless the best thing for Egypt is that we should stay for twenty years at least. But whether the best for ourselves?

To his Mother

Thebes.

Jan. 2nd.

We have just reached this famous city after a delightful sail up from Denderah, whose temples we saw this morning. They are late, of the times of the Ptolemies and the Roman Emperors; it is curious to come down to these very modern times, which one knows from Rome and other parts of Italy; and to realize that the Egyptian religion was still going on, and in external appearance much as it had gone on two thousand years earlier — and that all this strange mixture of mystic theosophy with a rather repulsive animal worship and apparently a good deal of practical sensuality, was in full life at the time of Christ's life and the first preaching of Christianity. In fact the Egyptian religion from about 70 B.C. diffused itself a good deal over the world. Ladies worshipped Serapis in Rome, and all sorts of nasty rites went on for a couple of centuries in Italy among people who had lost interest in their own old religion. Like most of the other cities, this city and its temples stood on the edge of the Desert. Strange that in Egypt you step out of your

[246]

house into a wilderness of stone and sand, which stretches twelve hundred miles west to the Atlantic. The presence of this awful unexplored and unexplorable waste and silent land must have had a great effect on the mind of the people, even more than the melancholy Ocean has had on the Irish and the Hebridean Scotch.

Thebes (Luxor) Jan. 3rd.

Nothing I have ever seen in the way of ruins makes so profound an impression of strength, grandeur, melancholy, and destruction. All Egypt is a land of death, this city most so. Temples that seemed built for eternity are in ruins, statues which our strongest engineering machinery could not move, lie overthrown and shattered. All the vast city, except a few temple columns and walls, has been swept away; only the bright coloured paintings remain in the now despoiled and empty rock tombs of the Kings, and the brown river flows softly, murmuring to itself, and glowing golden under the evening light, serenely careless of all that passes on its banks. Such colours as those of the sunset Nile are worth coming all the way to see.

What makes the whole so awe-inspiring is that these monuments and the whole race they belong to seem so utterly out of relation to or in connection with the modern world. In Greece and Italy you feel that the names and ideas and literature have survived to us and become part of us. Here all has gone, as much as if it belonged to the moon, with no link to join it to our life and ideas.

The religion rather repels me, and one is glad the Israelites did not draw more from it. The vastness of the works and the constant representations of the power and severity of the sovereign Pharaoh and his great ones make one feel as if there must have been great suffering, great tyranny over the multitudes of slaves. From the beginning this world has been made for the Few. Will Mr. Saunders or any one else succeed in getting more out of it for the Many?

The art and architecture have the common fault of monotony.

[247]

James Bryce

Just as one sees the same sacred subject repeatedly, incessantly, in the fifteenth century pictures of Italy, so here Isis, Osiris, Amru Ra, and the other gods in their symbolic forms. Invention was as rare, perhaps rarer, in the early epochs as the annual Academy Exhibition shows it to be now. The temples, however, are less barbarous than one expected, and bear a comparison even with those of Greece. Our mediæval churches seem to me incomparably superior to either. What is, perhaps, most striking — tho' it has often been remarked — is the wonderful progress the arts had made. The Egyptians were as much more civilized, in that sense, than Abraham, as the English settlers in America were than the Indian tribes.

To Annan Bryce

Syene, borders of Nubia.
Jan. 8th, 1888.

From Thebes upwards one sees only Ptolemaic and Roman temples — of course all in the old Egyptian style and mythologic decorations, tho' the columns have been markedly influenced by Greek models. Esneh, Edfou, Kum Ombu, are all late but fine works. I was not prepared for the amount of activity in building and vitality in the old religion so late into imperial times.

Syene (Assouan) has practically nothing to shew in the way of antiquities. It is Nature that rivets you, a very striking and peculiar Nature. A granite ridge which has been moving towards the Nile from the N. E., between the river and the Red Sea, here strikes the stream, and closes Egypt. You feel as you approach you are coming to the end of everything, the mountains rising grimmer and darker, tho' not yet high, and the river seeming to spring out of them. The rapid — for of course the Cataract is only a rapid — is very stern and grand with black piles of granite rising above the swirling flood, and the desert sand on each side framing the picture. It is like nothing else I know, save that the stream and rocks somewhat resemble the Duro rapids above Oporto. But here the Desert enhances the effect immensely. There is a town with a small body of Native troops. All the English troops have now been withdrawn to Cairo, there is no force between here and there, near six hundred miles, and only a small detachment at Wady Halfa (2nd Cataract), watching the hostile dervishes who watch us there.

There is a retired Colonel who confides to me, when a little in his cups, that Gladstone is mad, quite mad; of course he's mad; and his wife, a vigorous good-natured rather clever outspoken 'campaigner'. There is a young Yankee Jew whose shrill voice is heard talking bad French from stem to stern. But on the whole we are an uninteresting company, who agree reasonably well and strike out nothing dramatic. . . . This is the spot where the priest of Sais said that the Nile rose between Krophy and Mophy.[1]

To his sister Miss K. Bryce

Wady Halfa,
Second Cataract.
Jan. 12th, 1888.

This day has brought me to the furthest point of my southward journeyings, already far beyond Herodotus and most of the ancient travellers (who stopped at Elephantine (Assuan), but not as far as one Roman general of Augustus, who pushed on to Gebel Barkal (Napatu) beyond Dongola, and made Queen Candace of Ethiopia sue for peace. Here is a garrison, four thousand strong, of Egyptian troops, commanded by British Officers; here is the only place in the world where England is at war. The Dervishes, as they call the Mahdi's followers, are only six miles off, and threatened an attack this morning; they are about five thousand, but might at any moment receive reinforcements; and attack seriously. Of course the forts here could easily repulse them, and the Egyptians smash them in the field, however, the disagreeable result is that we are not permitted to go as far up as we had intended — to the famous rock of Abu Sir, eight miles off.

[1] See Herodotus II c 28.

whence you look S. over the vast Nile plain, a desert of rock and sand with the river's silver thread winding through it, and see two mountains marking the site of Dongola, a hundred and fifty miles away. Tomorrow we turn back northward, I reluctantly, for the undiscovered always beckons one forward, and albeit there is not much of antiquity or of history or of beauty in this vast Sudan before us, or all the way up the long river course till one reaches the great lakes of the Equator. Now we know all this course, tho' only within the last twenty years; but how mysterious did the Nile seem to the ancients, who saw its vast stream, swelled by no affluent, come down to them out of a torrid desert, in which a few savage and nameless tribes were scattered here and there.

Nubia, as they call the country above the First Cataract (Assuan), looks on the map as big as England, but is really about as big as Middlesex, for it practically consists, so far as human habitation goes, of a strip of land on each side the Nile, which the inundation reaches or which can be irrigated from the river, a strip nowhere over two hundred yards wide on either side, and sometimes restricted to the sloping river bank, or disappearing altogether where the sands or rocks of the Desert come right down to the river. Both sides are desert, pure, unmitigated desert, without so much as a weed nestling between the stones. And the whole population from Assuan to Wady Halfa of this big country is about forty thousand people. How they live off so small a cultivable territory is a marvel. They are almost savages, but industrious savages, tilling this strip with great care, planting their lupins and lentils neatly in rows on the bank and working hard in raising water by their primitive machines. They are nearly black, but not negroes; women often with fine eyes, sometimes good features, always white teeth; but disfigured by golden nose jewels and by the plastering with castor oil of their hair, gathered into thick mats like Totems.

One has a curious sense here of the retrogression of civilisation. Ethiopia stood higher forty centuries ago, even thirty centuries ago in the days of Rameses II, than she does now. Her people were more numerous, richer, furnished with better temples, and practically no worse a religion than they have to-day. One has, of course, far less sense of an interesting and enlightened Past here than in Egypt, the civilization of Ethiopia was always a borrowed, an outgoing, a very inferior civilization to that of Egypt. But the fall has been relatively as great.

One of the great interests of the last few nights has been studying the new stars that rise in the Southern sky, and especially the Southern Cross, which I have twice risen and come on deck at 4.30 A.M. to observe. It is quite beautiful, less splendid than Orion or the Bear, but full of grace and symmetry. . . . the lowest star is the brightest.

Luxor.

Jan. 18th, 1888.

. . . I am as far back as Luxor on the return trip, and think of staying there a week, partly for rest, partly to let the great Theban temples sink better into one's mind. I hope to be at Cairo by the 28th and to leave for England possibly 30th, more probably on Feb. 3rd, via Naples. . . . It has actually been raining here, after three cloudy days, tho' Herodotus says it never rained at Thebes except to presage Cambyses' conquest. The natives say the English have brought a change in their weather. . . .

To his sister Miss M. Bryce

Keneh.

Jan. 25th, 1888.

At Luxor I occupied myself in re-seeing all the chief sights. One needs to see these things often to get the due and full impression of their grandeur. Especially is this true of Karnak, the hugest mass of building in the world, at which Pharaohs and Ptolemies laboured for nigh three thousand years from Osirtasen III (B.C. 2500 or so) till the Roman times. Imagine a church begun seven hundred years before Julius Cæsar and still being added to by our present sovereign, and you have an idea of

[251]

the lengths of time during which things went on in Egypt. The great central hall with twelve rows of columns as high as those of Cologne Cathedral deserves to rank with St. Sophia and the cathedral of Seville as one of the greatest efforts of human genius in construction.

The sculptures interest me less than they ought, because they are so monotonous, nearly always repeating the same subjects. Those on the outside of the temple walls represent the wars and triumphs of kings, mostly of the XVIIIth and XIXth dynasties (B.C. 1700–1200). The king is always in his war chariot, shooting down his foes, who are mostly peoples of Syria and S. Asia Minor, Arabians, Libyans, and Ethiopians, including negroes, the features of these races being carefully distinguished. Then he besieges their towns, drives off strings of captives with their arms tied, presents them to the gods and slays them before them — a horrid picture of remote man which helps to reconcile one to the miseries of our own time. One of the last of these scenes of slaughter is the representation of King Shishah's victory over Rehoboam.

Yesterday, my last day at Luxor, was devoted to a mountain excursion up a peak twelve miles off. We rode four miles across the cultivated plain, seven miles more across the barren stony desert: left our camels and donkeys in a wild Wady, its bottom of sand and its walls of craggy rocks, walked three miles more, and then climbed a pretty difficult cliff and arrète to the summit. It was only some 1,800 feet high, and, of course, not dangerous, as you may gather from my having acted as guide to three other men. But the view was marvellous, over endless stretches of silent desert, grim grey or brown or red, glowing with light, and bounded by ranges of nameless mountains, rising one beyond another in the far distance towards the Red Sea and Sudan. Some seemed a hundred and fifty miles away, and full six thousand feet high. On the other side there was Egypt, that is, there was the narrow Nile plain with its intense deep green passing into blue, winding like a snake through the parched desert, the great river gleaming in the midst. With the glass one could discern the stupendous ruined pile of Karnak, and fancy the times when the great city stood on both banks of the Nile in the midst of the plain, and her people fled to their savage solitudes at the approach of the Assyrian army which sacked it in the eighth century B.C. There is a striking passage about this capture in the book of Nahum, where Thebes is called No Anion, the city of the great god Anion Ra. It is a new feeling altogether to be in a desert such as this, like, and yet unlike, the desert of Iceland and the desert of Nevada. We got back after dark, the sun turning the mountains as he set into huge jewels, flashing rose light, and the moon carrying us across the fields to Luxor.

Jan. 29th, 1888.

The steamer is almost at Cairo on her return and as the post goes tomorrow, I may add a word or two. Nothing remarkable on the voyage down, less pleasant for me, because I have had only half a cabin; but the beauty of the sky and landscapes strikes me almost more every successive day. . . . Such tints reflected in the broad smooth bosom of this great river, which is more of a Person than any other stream, even than the Rhine, because it is the Maker, Preserver, occasionally also the Destroyer of Egypt.

There has been nothing to see on the way down except the Abydas temples, with unusually delicate sculptures and unusually importunate children: a huge mass of mounds strewn with bones marks the site of the ancient city of This, the legendary first capital of Egypt, and, therefore, the first city in the whole world. It is now represented by a mud village and a small Coptic monastery. To know how low Christianity can sink one must see the service in a Coptic church. There is nothing in either except the words of the prayers, if one knows Coptic, which few do, for it has been a dead language for seven centuries, and the mark of the Cross in front of the shrines to remind one that it is Christian at all, it might as well be Mussulman or pagan; and in fact the only moral benefit Christianity seems to confer on the Copts is that it forbids polygamy. They are, however, rather

[253]

more wily and keen witted than the Mohammedans, whether this is due to their faith or to their being of more pure Egyptian blood, I know not. Strange is the contrast between the modern Egyptian who seems an exceptionally dull, plodding, uninventive person, and the ancient Egyptian of five thousand years ago. Has the blood changed, or have twenty-six centuries of subjection washed the intellectual force out of the people?

In India, which Bryce visited in the autumn of 1888, there was less upon which to feed the historical imagination. While Egypt is eloquent of a solemn and distant past, in India, so deficient in the commemorative instinct, so barren in towering characters and literary accomplishment, the past fades into insignificance beside the urgent claims of the present and the future. Bryce's Indian letters, while full of vivid descriptive pieces reflect the historian's disappointment at the difficulty of associating the visible aspects of the Indian scene with the records and traditions of the past. He is driven, despite himself, to think of politics. In Egypt he could lose himself in antiquity: but "India is of the Present" and travelling in India he could not, with the best will in the world get politics out of his head.

The more so since India had been awakened from her political slumbers by the liberal administration of Lord Ripon, who had promoted local government on Western lines, and introduced a measure (the Criminal Procedure Code Amendment Bill) for giving to all district magistrates and Sessions judges, irrespective of race and colour, the right of trying European British subjects. This legislative proposal, popularly known as the Ilbert Bill from the fact that it was drafted and introduced by Sir Court-

nay Ilbert, Bryce's old friend, roused an unexpected
flame of the fiercest racial controversy. That Indians
should sit in judgement on Europeans was represented as
an intolerable indignity put upon the white race, and as a
serious menace to British rule. Bryce, landing in India
four years after Lord Ripon had laid down his office,
found the air still reverberating with the detonations of
this formidable controversy. Indian Nationalism was
awake and claimant, and the prudent official of the older
school was telling his European visitor that the Liberal
Viceroy had moved too fast and too far.

To his Mother

Off Mt. Sinai,
Gulf of Suez.
Oct. 26th, 1888.

. . . The Canal marked the beginning of the new part of the
journey to me, as I had never before been South of Ismailia, and
the departure from the world of Greek civilization and the
Roman Empire. I have, oddly enough, formed the habit of
always asking whether one is inside or outside of the Roman
Empire. One doesn't think of asking this when voyaging to
America, because one starts from Britain, which was so little
Romanized, and because the ancients knew of nothing at all
beyond the Atlantic. But in passing from the world of Greek
letters and Roman arms and laws in the Mediterranean into
those undiscovered and mysterious regions in which they placed
all sorts of wonders, natural and human, from the time of Homer
and Herodotus down to those of Procop, one feels the transition
directly. It is broken for a time by the sight of the sacred heights
of Sinai, rising in barren majesty about thirty miles off when one
has steamed five hours down from Suez. Whether the Jebel
Muss (peak of Moses) be visible — it is the highest — seems
uncertain, but Serbal and Jebel Katrsiv, the mountain of St.

[255]

Katherine where her convent stands, certainly is visible, bare savage masses 6000–7000 feet high, lying some fifteen miles inland in a shrubless desert. Suez is striking to look at, a little tight pressed town with one minaret in a sandy waste, with the brilliant contrast of the green sea, the red yellow sand, the white, grey mountain faces behind, and the dazzling blue overhead. But it must be inexpressibly dreary to live in — better a desert island amid the wash of waves. All afternoon we see both sides of the comparatively narrow Gulf of Suez, limestone hills along the coast, and loftier peaks inland, whose bold sharp sky line shows they must be of crystalline rocks.

. . . . . .

Oct. 30th.

At last we are out of the Red Sea, and tho' it is still very hot, the breeze is fresher in the wide Indian Ocean. North of us lies the barren coast of Hadramaut, sands on the shore, and behind red and brown ranges of scorched and shrubless mountains, one of the most desolate and unprofitable regions in the whole world, unexplored, and which no one cares to own, with a few savage tribes wandering here and there in it. An odd feeling to be part of a highly civilized group moving past a region of irreclaimable barbarism.

At Naini Tal he obtains his first view of the snows.

The Himalayas so far are not so like the Alps, nor indeed very like any other mountain chain I know, — perhaps most like the Caucasus as seen from the South. Tho' you see but a little bit at once, they make an indefinable impression of vastness. These outer hills where I am are already 8000 feet high; the eye ranges over an endless succession of deep wooded valley and high ridges, till at last in the extreme distance it touches the mass where snow patches shew that the peaks rise above. The weather, which had been clear for some days, thickened the very night of my arrival, so I fear I shall not see the snow peaks after all, a sad disappointment, but the world is full of such. For the rest, the place is extremely pretty, a lake a mile long formed like that of Alleghe by landslips, is enclosed by high steep hills, covered with oaks and rhododendron trees and flowering shrubs, among which the cottage villas of the Europeans stand, often picturesque, each with its tennis ground cut out of the slope of the hill, and its wide verandah running all round the house. Some of the hills have bold rocky points; their barren slopes are of a reddish brown which gives warmth to the landscape. Narrow footpaths wind in and out of the thickets all along the sides and tops of the ridges, giving picturesque glimpses of the huge plain, with its stony river beds on the one side and the succession of ranges towards the Snows on the other. The air is now cool, indeed requires warm clothes, and the rooms are fired, but in summer it is so hot that all the men ride ponies along the paths, and most of the women are carried about in so-called "palkies."

My host, a very nice fellow, with many just reflections on the Ilbert bill and other matters, is also a botanist, so I have been learning a good deal as to the Himalayan flora. He has once or twice been up among the snows of the main range, which, however, it takes ten days' marching to reach from here. Everything is on a gigantic scale; you could put all the Alps between Luzern and Lugano into the space between here and Nunga Devi. Thus these mountains will never be so available for the purposes of climbing and scenery as the Alps are.

Altho' India is an old country one doesn't feel as in Italy, absorbed in the past to the exclusion of present and future, on the contrary, the future is almost as much a matter of curious speculation as in the United States. The country has changed fast under English influences, and must change still further, perhaps even more quickly. There are political movements on foot among the natives for representative government; there are social and religious changes of all kinds; the use of English is increasing; the railways are opening up remote regions and mixing the population. Everybody's mind is uneasy, filled with anticipations of what may come; and at present the great difficulty of finding money to carry on the government makes the officials uncomfortable. Hitherto I have chiefly seen officials and heard their views, which are mostly what are called Conservative; in Calcutta I hope to hear the native case.

To his sister Miss M. Bryce

Calcutta.
Nov. 17th, 1888.

Bidding farewell to my Lucknow friends, I went by night train — one takes nearly all journeys by night — to Benares, and spent next day seeing that famous city, where I was placed in charge of the Secretary of the Rajah — a curious sort of educated Hindoo, but apparently still a believer in his own religion. . . . Benares is the metropolis of Hindoo worship — and especially of the most revolting form of Hindoo worship, that of Siva or Mahadeo and his wives, Parvati and Dhurga. Our childish horror of heathen rites and superstitions rushed back on me in a flood when I saw the hideous idols and loathsome surroundings of these temples — there are thousands of them in Benares, all small, nearly all on the same plan, and all built within the last two or three centuries. The city is picturesque in its streets, but what impressed me most was the view over it from the tall minaret of the mosque erected by that fanatical Mohammedan, the Emperor Aurungzib. From the top of this shrine of one of the two conquering faiths, one sees the countless shrines of the conquered Hindoos spread out below; one descries four miles out in the country the ruins of the Buddhist tope and monastic foundation at Saniath the sole relic of a religion vanished from India, while the latest conquerors are represented by the splendid railway bridge which they have thrown across the river just below the city, injuring the view, but presenting their power in a striking and characteristic form.

However, of all the sights of Benares, the river front is the most rich in variety and beauty. Indeed, I doubt if there is in the world any city frontage to a river or sea so picturesque. The Grand Canal at Venice is hardly more so; Constantinople,

Oporto, Pesth, Florence, Tiflis, less so. It struck me so much that I changed my plan, and spent a night at Benares to see it in the early morning, when crowds of pious Hindoos come down to bathe and wash their clothes in the sacred stream. The wonderful variety of buildings, the mixture of trees, and this buzzing crowd bathing, praying and talking, some sitting on wooden platforms out over the water, make up an extraordinary sight.

To his Mother

In the Hooghly River.
Nov. 30th, 1888.
(Madras, Dec. 5th.)

After four rather over-filled days in Calcutta, I am on ship-board again, welcoming the prospect of three perfectly lazy days, which I use to write to you. It is no effort to do so, but a rest to one's own mind filled with impressions and reflections to pour out some of them, so far as definite, to you. I have been nearly four weeks in India, and seen a great deal of its surface, a good deal of its governing class, and a little of the educated natives.

The Civil Service slightly disappoints one. There is a high average of ability among the service men in the upper posts, — 'tis these chiefly I have seen — but a good deal of uniformity, and a want of striking, even of marked individualities. They are intelligent, very hard working, with apparently a high sense of public duty and a desire to promote the welfare of the people of India. But they seem rather wanting in imagination and sympathy, less inspired by the extraordinary and unprecedented phenomena of the country than might have been expected, with little intellectual initiative; too conventionally English in their ways of life and thoughts to rise to the position. Since the un-happy so-called Ilbert Bill there has been a marked change in the attitude of Europeans to natives, especially in Bengal, and the natives complain bitterly that the civilians as well as the military and the planters, treat them with arrogance and

[259]

make them feel their social inferiority as well as political sub-ordination.

They are more out of the stream of the world's thought and movement than one was prepared to find. Europe seems very far away. Society is monotonous; it is in some places more military than civil, in some more civil than military; it has no-where the variety and sense of intellectual activity which one feels in England. . . .

The ablest and most interesting person is the Viceroy. He very civilly telegraphed to me (when he knew I was leaving today) from his journey, that I should dine with him last night, and I did so, and had a very long and interesting talk with him, ranging over the whole field. The advanced natives are vexed with him for not having kept up Lord Ripon's pace, but he does not seem to me to have done badly for them; whereas that worthy man so forced the pace as to provoke bitterness and throw things back. Lady Dufferin was very pleasant; she has done much good by her efforts for Indian women. . . .

It is far harder to have just notions regarding the natives. In Calcutta they were prepared to make quite a fuss about me; a musical party was given in my honour — a newspaper with report thereof is sent herewith, and inside it a copy of the programme — they issued an elegant card inviting guests to meet the "Professor" (!) M. P. There were some Europeans and Armenians as well as natives, but little fusion, the middle wall of partition stands between. The music was strange and interesting, especially a Persian love ditty, said to be of Hafiz, chanted with wild contortions of face to a monotonous air and queer instruments. . . .

Next day I met by invitation about twenty leading natives and had a long talk with them on public affairs. They com-plained of the indifference of England to India, and wanted to know what they could do. One could only answer that they must try to supply information, exact facts and just views, to the English, of course even this will effect little in the sense they desire. They dwelt on the expense of the government, and the

little influence they had, and two or three spoke very bitterly
on the hauteur with which Anglo-Indians treat them; this is the
real difficulty. I urged them strongly to have nothing to do
with English parties; not to go to Liberals any more than to
Tories in England; nor suffer Indian questions to get sucked
into the party vortex; they did not relish this. There was
plenty of talent among them, and an excellent gift of expression;
but, of course, it was impossible for either side to speak frankly
to the other; they couldn't tell me what they thought of us, nor
I what profound weaknesses we discover in them. Lord Dufferin
said to me that he could not find among them all a single man
with initiative, with the sort of character and courage which
gives strength for practical statesmanship. This has been so for
generations. However, they were friendly and complimentary,
and we parted with many cordial expressions. These Bengal
people are, especially the Hindoos, quicker, more apt and willing
to learn, and altogether more plausible than the men of Upper
India, much like the Greeks under the Roman Empire; but
Upper India holds them cowards and the English hate their
upsettingness. A fine old Jesuit whom I met said the English
had made a great mistake in providing so much cheap university
education; that there is thus created a huge, restless, discontented class, superficially brilliant, anxious for Government
work, because there is none else for it, but wanting in the higher
moral qualities. We are making atheists, too, for when they
drop Hinduism they don't become Christians. The two young
Oxford missionaries whom I saw, very fine fellows who live
like ascetics, High Churchmen, of course, spoke better of the
natives, and deplored the attitude of Anglo-Indians; they liked
Hindus better than Mohammedans, but admitted that conversion was difficult with both. However, it seems Christians
increase much faster than the population, and they are hopeful
of the future. At present the most accessible are the aboriginal
tribes, these might all, they said, be converted as soon as we had
the men. They did not think that religion had any great effect
upon moral conduct.

James Bryce

Besides the viceroy I dined with and saw several other leading officials, all very civil, and have a fair impression of Calcutta, which consists of three distinct cities — native, commercial, European residential. It is quite modern, with no sights except the Botanic and Zoologic Gardens and Museum. The best point is the vast open space called the Meidan, where people ride and drive, the latter after dark. Society didn't seem to me a bit interesting, but probably less frivolous than English fashionables. It is, of course, less purely military and civil than up country, for there are barristers and merchants not a few. The houses are large, cool, airy, each in a large plot of ground, often with lawn tennis. Multitudes of servants, just like slaves in ancient Rome. One would soon get lazy and demoralized. I wonder our men retain so much energy. To be arrogant and overbearing is natural. Habits of expense soon grow; already I have become reckless of rupees, one can't live cheaply, tho' many things are cheap, one ceases to try.

Exotic as we are — more so than formerly because people in the services and commerce run oftener to Europe — our dominion seems fairly based. One doesn't see why, if frontier wars can be averted with Russia and France, we should not reign for another century. But long before then internal conditions will have greatly changed. Altho' Caste and Hinduism seem slightly shaken so far, they are being undermined, and may come down with a run before fifty years.

To his sister, Miss K. Bryce

> In the Neilgherries,
> Coonor.
> Dec. 8th, 1888.

Wednesday afternoon, Dec. 5th, I left Madras, rather glad to escape the hottest and dampest atmosphere since the Red Sea. Before leaving I had to deliver an address to the students of the Christian College, an admirable institution founded by Dr. Miller, a genial, vigorous Scotsman from Aberdeen University, and largely officered by Aberdonians. At the close the students, mostly Hindus (*i.e.* heathens) garlanded and bouqueted me after the usual fashion. There are fifteen hundred in the institution, which is purely educational, but out of which some conversions flow, not very many, except among the very lowest castes. The Brahmin who is more intelligent and cultivated, and much more disposed to learning than the other Hindus, is proud of his lineage and rank and hard to bring over to Christianity.

Madras is a very odd place. It covers twenty-seven square miles, and is really three or four towns, one of them a mercantile place, with a small port and business houses, loosely connected by roads along which are bungalows (villas) standing each in its own big plot of ground, called a "compound." The distances are, therefore, enormous. Everybody must keep horses and vehicles. You seem always in the country, and ask where the town is. If Jonah had been sent to Madras he could easily have gone a day's journey into it and found himself far from the centre. The heat was sufficient to make me perspire all night long, but the residents didn't notice it—they call this "the cold weather."

On Dec. 5th he left Madras for the hills.

You can imagine nothing more lovely than the view down and along the hill face. The foliage even so high is deliciously rich, and the flowers even at this season, splendid in colour. I have just been across to Ootacamund, the summer residence of the Government, and capital of the Neilgherries, riding part of the way, and walking the rest over the top of Dodabhet, the highest of the group. . . . On the higher slopes the flora of the Swiss and Scotch mountains began to appear, with genera which we have gathered. There is a rhododendron tree with splendid crimson flowers; there are potentillas and little bright leguminous plants and forget-me-nots, and pretty ferns, these, however, seldom British. Unluckily, the clouds all round cut off the view of the Mysore plain, but the rolling hill masses all round reminded me more of Europe than aught else in India has done. These hills are inhabited by four or five curious primitive races,

[263]

some of them not Hindus in religion, and still speaking their own languages. Quite a number of Europeans have settled as tea and coffee planters and cultivators of cinchona or quinine, but the shrewd Scotch have preferred Assam and Sikkim, where tea thrives better than here. . . .

Thirukaliondram (?)
(S. of Madras)
Dec. 12th.

Since leaving the Neilgherries on the 8th, I have traversed long distances and seen much. First I went to Trichinopoly, was courteously received by the Collector there, and shown the famous and very sacred temple at Sri Rangam and the singular Rock, a mass of gneiss rising four hundred feet out of the plain, crowned not as you would expect with castles, for in this part of India there are few hill forts, but with temples. The view over the delta of the Cauvery river to the surrounding mountain ranges is most striking. Hence to Madura, where I saw a still more splendid temple and palace, erected by king Timmulla Nayah, the last great native potentate in these parts. Most of it is as late as Cromwell's time, but architecture here changes little from age to age, and it is a vast and splendid work, so entirely unlike Greek or Roman temples and Christian Churches that one hardly knows how to compare it with anything in the Western World. There are many similarities to the temples of ancient Egypt, but I think quite accidental, no connection can be shewn or is probable. As for the heathenism of these parts, it is simply revolting, and I should be tempted were I thirty years younger, to turn missionary and join in trying to rescue these people from their degrading superstitions. It is disheartening to find the English generally, and especially the civilians, sneering at mission work, and pooh-poohing native converts. Probably the latter are often a poor lot, so were many of St. Paul's — They come from the lowest castes or outcasts, and can't be expected to become saints, but their children are often much better. These civilians are said to be often no Christians themselves, but even intelligent agnostics might be expected to desire some better religion for the masses. The Salvation Army are in evidence — "War Cry, sir?" with an English head under a Hindu turban, thrust into the carriage window. He turned out to be from Hanley in Staffordshire, had been eight months out here, learning Tamil slowly. "I have made two converts, one a Brahmin, one a Roman Catholic." I congratulated him on the Brahmin, — that is like bagging a tiger — but felt inclined to beg him not to mind the R.C.s, while there were so many worshippers of Siva and Kali about.

To his sister Miss M. Bryce

Dec. 15th, 1888.
The Residency,
Hyderabad,
Deccan.

. . . I wish I had time to describe Southern India, which delighted me far more than Northern, always, of course, excepting the Himalaya. The rains were just ending, half the country was under water, and in the rest the tanks were full, the air was cool, the great artificial ponds they call tanks had the effect of romantic lakes — all was verdure, and these strange Hindu temples carried one into realms of architecture wholly unlike anything known to the Western world. Beautiful, however, I cannot call them, and scarcely grand — tho' perhaps grandiose: they are too grotesque. Then the Dravidian races of the South with their half-baked civilization and chronicles never rising to history — are a new kind of phenomenon to me, which illustrates something in the ancient world, be it by contrast, be it by likeness.

I reached Hyderabad on the night of the 13th, and the people who were to have received me having, in spite of my letter, assumed that I was coming by a different train from Bombay and not from Madras, failed to do so, so I was left to find such quarters as I could, and had to sleep on a table in a crowded dark bungalow. Next day they were profuse in apologies, and the Resident entertained me one night and the Surgeon Major the next, while the Minister of Public Instruction mounted me by his side on a tall elephant and took me round the city. It is modern but picturesque, less in the buildings than in the dresses and aspect of the people, who wear more colour and arms than those in British territory. This minister, Seyid Hassein, is the most enlightened and Europeanized Mussulman I ever met, except, perhaps, Seyid Mahmud (who dined with us in Norfolk Square), he is an extremely bright, well-informed person, but alas, drinks.

On Dec. 18th he reached Beejapore.

The city is the most impressive I have seen — a space of many miles enclosed by ancient walls, and filled with ruins, ruins of mosques, tombs, palaces, halls of audience, and justice, all built by the Adil Sháhí dynasty, which ruled the Western Deccan from 1480 to 1680. A more inspiring spectacle of departed greatness and majestic solitude I have never seen; it is such a place as the Hebrew prophets imagined Nineveh or Babylon to become, save that we keep a few of the finest buildings in repair, and beautiful specimens of Muslim art they are. One tomb, with a great dome, has the largest dome-covered area in the whole world and a wonderful whispering gallery at the top. There was a full moon, and the scene at night among the trees and homes of ancient glory, where more than a million of people dwelt, and now the jackal howls, was strangely sad.

To Revd. Stopford Brooke.

The Residency,
Hyderabad,
Deccan.
Dec. 16th, 1888.

. . . India is not like Egypt, where one can busy oneself in the past; I have had to listen to as much politics as in England, and thrice have been solemnly interviewed by large gatherings of

native "leaders of opinion," who have descanted on their grievances and aspirations. Fortunately they do not expect me to
make speeches to them in return, nor even to reveal one's half
formed opinions.

It would have been far more interesting to get people to talk
about religions, for religions are by far the most curious phenomena of India; no country suggests so many theories and views
about religion and the tendencies of the human mind thereanent;
but these matters have little meaning for the English, who are
absorbed in rupees and reports; while among the natives religion
has been well nigh lost in the swamps of superstition. I tried to
find your Brahmo Somaj person in Calcutta, but could not, no
one knew the name you gave me, tho' just before I left I thought
I made out who the person designated must be. That movement
doesn't seem to make much way, nor does Christianity; and
though many Hindus turn Mohammedans, the Hindu population increases faster actually than the Mussulman. Nevertheless, I can't doubt that Christianity will eventually prevail;
it is the best, perhaps the only chance, for the country. But I
wish we had some authority, which, like the Pope and a Council,
could add an article to the Christian faith, for one could add
total abstinence; and that would help Christianity on faster and
remove the chief stumbling block which the conduct of native
Christians causes.

There has been time for me to see comparatively little of
Native Indian art in Architecture and Sculpture; but the
history so far as I can follow it, is full of interest. It begins in
India with the Buddhists, whose earliest remains are about 200
B.C., down till, say, 300 A.D. Their work has great merit, and
often reminds one of contemporary or early mediæval Italy.
Then the odious Hindu mythology regains its power; and there
is an end of beauty, tho' some even of the late things have a kind
of heavy grandeur. But from 1300 to 1680 the Mussulmans
breathe a new spirit into architecture and decoration, and produce much which is only inferior to our best mediæval buildings.
Since 1700 there is hardly anything worth looking at, and our

[267]

Western influence is ruining even metal work and corner work designs. No one now seems to care for these things; and the literature is a pale and washy copy of our own.

I have been round all Southern India and am on my way to the Afghan frontier and the dwelling of Akbar, the only first-rate historical figure one can find in this huge country and long history.

To his Mother

Bombay.

Dec. 23rd, 1888.

. . .

India changes so fast; I understand the liking for the easy, breezy, open air, striped cotton suit and lawn tennis sort of life which people lead, yet think that no one need regret or repine at leaving, for society is thin and meagre compared with England; the number of men of learning, or finish, or initiative and mental freshness, and resourcefulness is small — smaller than one gets in London in a month; one does not make the most of one's life here, unless engaged in a great and responsible work, like that of converting or governing the country. I don't find myself more impressed now than on leaving Calcutta, with the intellectual opulence of the Europeans in India, while the really interesting and superior natives seem to be very few.

The only big public question — so far as any question in India is public — here now is that of the approaching Congress at Allahabad. I have been discoursed incessantly by the friends and enemies during these six weeks; and have come to form a sort of view — but we shall see how they talk at this approaching meeting. I hope English Radicals and Tories will hold their peace about it; for we shall do more harm than good by interfering. Regretfully I am forced to think that Lord Ripon, with good intentions, did much mischief, filling native minds with hopes not yet realizable, and setting the teeth of Europeans on edge. The latter are most to blame; but Ripon's indiscretion also.

[268]

Impressions of Egypt and India

To his Mother

Peshawar,
Jan. 3rd. 1889.

Here is the gate of that famous Khyber Pass which filled your mind in 1843 — the retreat is the first historical event that I can recollect from childhood — here is the end of British dominion, and the beginning of barbarism, here, as at Quetta, one is out of India and in Central Asia. You can hardly realize how much in India one misses that history and that poetry which illumine and help one to enjoy travel in the lands of ancient civilisation, filling them with memories and pouring imaginative light round mountains and rivers as well as cities. The native poetry, such as there is in old Sanskrit, is unknown to us, and perhaps would not much interest us; there is nothing since, neither native nor European; one's imagination is not helped to soar by anything that the great ones have written. Few are the inspiring characters in Indian history; dark and blurred that history itself. But here at the gate of the Khyber one has the memory of famous events from the march of Alexander the Great through it down till the 1879 to add to the grand view of the snows of the Hindu Khush rising all along the northern horizon over the hills of the valley of Peshawar. The most striking and indeed awe-inspiring feature in this view is that one sees mountains there, not eighty miles away, into which it is absolutely impossible to penetrate, so fierce are the inhabitants. No Christian can enter Swat; no Mussulman can enter Kafiristan, nor indeed can we reach them through the network of Mohammedan fanatics which surrounds them. They worship the ancient gods, perhaps of the Vedas, perhaps of the Hindus before the rise of Buddhism, whose relics strew these far North Western valleys from which as a living faith it has long since vanished.

The ascent of the Khyber as far as the fort of Ali Musjid, in the narrowest jaws of the pass, is now physically easy, for we have made a road up which one drives, as I have done to-day (Jan. 4.). But we hold nothing more than the road. The fierce

[269]

Afridis dwell on both sides in the hills, perfectly independent, and tho' we now pay a large number of them under the name of the Khyber Rifles, arming them, too, to guard the pass, they can't resist the temptation of now and then robbing and murdering a traveller, so it is only on Tuesdays and Fridays, when the guard are called out, that caravans or tourists are allowed to pass.

Here I am the guest of the Commissioner, a pleasant elderly man, Col. Ommaney, a friend of Sir F. Pollock's, and find with his two daughters almost the only ladies' society I have enjoyed in India, save for one lady in the Himalaya, a very pretty (married) lady who was quite effusive. They are nice simple girls, and bring me back to ordinary life in an agreeable way. The city is interesting, — it is more like Central Asia than like India, full of wild Pathans, with now and then an Uzbeh from distant Turkistan. One receives an extraordinary impression of our power when, standing here on the artillery platform of Jumrood at the mouth of the Khyber and watching the Union Jack, one thinks that from here to Cape Comorin and the furthest corner of Assam not a dog wags his tail against us among these two hundred and sixty millions of people. Yet we can't govern four millions of Irishmen with the aid of the loyal garrison of one million!

Lahore,
Jan. 6th, 1889.

Back from Peshawar, and staying here with Sir J. Lyall, the Lieut-Governor of the Punjab, a brother of Sir A. Lyall, whom you have heard me speak of, an able man, tho' less remarkable than Alfred. Lahore has some interesting Perso-Hindu work in its Mohammedan buildings, and some picturesque narrow streets, but is otherwise not a very remarkable place, nor is the present generation of Punjab officials so striking as that of Lord Lawrence's time. The Sikhs are quiet, but no one trusts their fidelity in case of a Russian advance. Indeed, things would be uncomfortable in India, requiring a heavy addition to the

European army and to expense if Russia were to take Kabul or
Kandahar; yet we can't make up our minds to defend them.
I feel more than ever here that though we might probably
repel any Russian attack, the difficulty of keeping this vast
Indian population quiet with an intriguing enemy on the
border is so great that Russian enmity ought if possible to be
averted, and all the resources of diplomacy used to create good
relations between the countries. War is too great a risk to be
faced if it can honourably be avoided. There is much secret
disquietude here, both as regards Afghanistan and as regards
this so-called National Congress. The disquiet seems to me
exaggerated, but these experienced men, who are not otherwise
illiberal, must surely know better than I do. It will be a pity
if Mr. Gladstone or any of our other leaders commit themselves
hastily on Indian questions. I am reluctantly being driven to
the conclusion that Lord Ripon did more harm than good, yet
there is something in the Anglo-Indian attitude which one
suspects, as tinged by that excessive pride of race which,
naturally, arises in this country.

To his sister Miss K. Bryce

Old Delhi,
Jan. 10th, 1889.

Hence to Delhi, where I was again received by missionaries,
this time a group of young Cambridge men in connection with
the S. P. G. The modern city is not very interesting, except for
the Fort, the palace, fortress of the Mogul Emperors, Shah
Jehan and Aurungzeb. We have destroyed a great part of their
most beautiful work; and much had been defaced and plundered
before our time by Nadir Shah and the fierce Mahrattas. The
wonder of Delhi is, however, the masses of ancient ruin and in
the fine old cities, and of these the most striking is the famous
mosque called the Kutub with its wonderful tower, partly a
minaret for calling the faithful to prayer in the mosque, partly a
Tower of Victory, to commemorate the conquest of the Hindus
by the Mohammedan conquerors, who finally established them-

[271]

selves here in the thirteenth century. It is curious to think of a
vast history going on here from the time of the Norman Conquest when Mohmud of Ghuzni began the subjugation of
Northern India, down to the time of Akbar — the time of
Elizabeth — when Englishmen first began to find their way to
India, and Europe, first thro' the Portuguese, came into relation
with the countries it was to acquire. Endless strife through
all those centuries, which at last made the Muslims masters
of all India except the far South, and brought one-fifth of the
people into the faith of Islam. So the great buildings of those
times are all Mohammedan in Northern and Central India,
indeed after the Buddhist art of the five centuries after our
Christian era, there is nothing to study till the series of Muslim
Mosques and tombs begins at the end of the thirteenth century.
There is less variety in their work than in that of Europe,
during the same ages, but some of it is no less grand and beautiful . . . these buildings, which open up a new world to me;
and shew these countries in the only side which is of much permanent interest to the world, their art production, because for
literature and thought they have done virtually nothing since
the days of early Sanskrit literary effort, and for religion little,
beyond indicating the human gift for perversion, since the
early age of Buddhism. Mohammedanism never even produced
such philosophy here as among the Sufiis of Persia. However, I
must return to my tower — the Kutub Minar — which is
really worth coming all the way to India to see; it is so
original and combines stately grandeur with rich detail so
happily. It was built just about the time Giotto built his
tower in Florence, a century later than the tower of Pisa, a
century and a half earlier than the tower at Venice; and it is a
nobler work than either. Arriving last night at the travellers'
bungalow in this deserted city it seemed splendid, but twice as
splendid this morning when I am departing back to new Delhi.
I have been moving among the Arabian Nights — places fitted
to make the dullest soul imaginative, such as the deserted
city of Tughlukabad, whose stupendous fortifications look as

if built by giants and not by mortal men, a city raised by a stern old Turkish sultan only to be abandoned by his successor. Now not a soul dwells within its vast circuit. It is the whole impression of this region that fills me, not so much the individually striking bits of antiquity to be enjoyed, but rather scenes of utter desolation and horror, where vultures flap their wings over the graves of the dead, and panthers roar at night from dens amid the wall crowned rocks. For many miles the whole ground is covered with huge tombs of these Pathan and Mogul kings and nobles, vast domes reared on a square or hexagonal basis, built with such strength and solidity that they are nearly all sound, tho' the names of the occupants have been forgotten for ages. Among them lie fragments of palaces and pleasure gardens and mosques, sometimes with pieces of marble or of the pretty blue Persian tiling wherewith they were once adorned, all now alike deserted, save that in a few some old priest collects alms from passing visitors. There is among the few mosques which have escaped ruin some beautiful work, both structural and decorative; and one could gladly spend a week studying the phases thro' which Muslim architecture passed as one does with the ancient churches of Italy.

The Cambridge missionaries are very bright, pleasant, simple mannered men — to me no manners are ever so agreeable as those of the best sort of English University man, with a mixture of easy good fellowship and refinement. They are earnestly hopeful of their work, yet admit that not much result is yet seen, and give a painful picture of the moral degradation of the native population. They have made me give a lecture to their students on the House of Commons in which I drew some amusement from the questions asked by the native youths, there is an odd mixture of cleverness and childish simplicity about them, they are at once old and young; an ancient race with minds sharpened by long centuries, yet wholly at sea among Western ideas, and using our phrases as counters whose value they don't understand.

[273]

James Bryce

There is another side to the old India which Delhi, Agra and to a less extent Lahore, the India of the Mohammedan dynasties, Pathan, Turki and Mogul (so-called) have left us besides this gloomy and terrible one of sombre tombs and cities overthrown. It is that of the light and elegant palace buildings. You can imagine nothing more perfectly bright, graceful, and *genussvoll* — one can hardly say pleasurefull — than are the courts and pavilions and audience halls and bath chambers of the Emperors Jehangi and Shah Jehan. The extraordinary profusion of marble, sometimes plain, some often decorated with coloured stones or even with gems, speaks of a delight in colour and the display of wealth which not even Louis XIV reached in Europe; and the taste, the invention and executive skill of the artists employed here surpasses those of any European craftsmen who have worked for European princes, except perhaps a few of the sixteenth century in Italy. Sometimes this admirable decorative genius stretches itself into graver fields and produces council chambers of majesty as well as beauty, like that in the Fort at Delhi; sometimes it is applied to tombs, and ends in the marvellous Taj Mahal, which I have just returned from seeing by moonlight at Agra (Jan. 15th.) It is a vast building, as high as the Abbey, all of white marble, exquisitely adorned with coloured stones of rare beauty, with inscriptions, and with marble lattice work.

Jan. 15th.

I have just been across to Futehpore Sikri, the city of the great Akbar, the only man in all Indian history on whom one can dwell as a striking individuality, great in the European sense of the word. His mosque and palace seem full of himself, they are unlike the work of any other ruler, with a certain bizarre originality crossing and deepening the interest of the majesty and grace which belong to most of the buildings of the sixteenth and seventeenth centuries. He reminds one in some things of Justinian, though he is much greater, in a few of Julius Caesar, tho' he is less complete and wonderful. But all these people are dark to us compared with modern Europeans, equally removed in time.

Impressions of Egypt and India

I am now on my way through Rajput — and to Bombay, halting at Jeypore Jodhpore, where there is a function by the Maharaja in honour of Lord Reay — Mount Abu, and Ahmedabad. . . .

Rajputana,
Jan. 16th, 1889.

. . . I hope Mr. Gladstone and Liberals generally will hold their peace about Indian questions and the National Congress; these things look very different when one is out here and are not to be solved by European formulæ. The great use of all this to me is to enlarge one's ideas of history, a world so unlike ours, yet more like the average world of the past. One feels like writing something, not in the way of describing India or arguing Indian questions, which I am quite incompetent to do, but of setting out the *impression* of India and its place in history as compared with the West and the notions as to human nature it suggests. All these impressions will fade fast enough when one recrosses the sea — I wish I could have conveyed them duly to all before the salt brine has washed them out. The Hindu Sages had a meaning in forbidding the pious man to cross the great water.

To his Mother

Jodhpore, Rajputana,
Jan. 19th, 1889.

. . . It seems odd and hardly consistent with what we claim for our civilized government; but all the evidence goes to shew that the ordinary man, peasant or townsman is just as well off materially, and probably more happy and contented, in a native State than he is in the dominions of the Empress. Here, at any rate, all was cheerful. The Maharaja is an indolent youth, who spends most of his time in the Zenana among his wives, but he lets British advisers spend as much of his revenues as they like to ask for on a college and a museum. There may be little elementary education, but the people don't miss it. Five miles off is the old palace and fortress city where this dynasty lived

James Bryce

before they built Jeypore, a most picturesque spot among steep hills, with one of those artificial lakes, which India is full of, where I counted six black crocodiles sprawling on the margin in the sun. It is now abandoned to fakirs, so I was shewn all over the chambers where the queens and concubines lived, charming little rooms with lattice apertures delicately carved in marble through which they could see the Raja presiding at his Durbar in solemn reception of nobles, people, and strangers in the court yard below.

Arabian Nights; again one repeats to oneself — this is still in spite of railways and post office, the primitive world.

Aden,
Jan. 30th.

. . . We have a small party on board, and a perfectly smooth sea so far, with deliciously warm air, so that one can lie in the lightest clothing in the soft breeze, and watch hour after hour of night, the majestic march of the constellations across the sky. They never seemed so grand, and here one sees some unknown to the North — Argo and the Southern Cross and the huge Scorpion.

CHAPTER XV

MARRIAGE AND POLITICS

The sympathies of peoples with peoples, the sense of a
common humanity between nations, the aspirations of nation-
alities after freedom and independence are real political forces.

J. R. GREEN.

B RYCE returned from India in February 1889. In
the following July he married Marion, second
daughter of Thomas Ashton of Hyde and Manchester, a well-known figure in Lancashire business, and
one of the leading Liberals of the County. The reader
will remember how Bryce came into contact with Lancashire, how he was drawn to the County Palatine first by
his journeys in connection with the School Commission,
then by his work as a barrister on the Northern Circuit
and finally by his Chair at Owen's College and close
association with the movement for providing higher
education in Manchester. It was natural then that he
should come across Mr. Thomas Ashton, who apart from
his commanding position as the chief partner in a great
merchant's business and in a large cotton-spinning firm
was one of the principal forces in the humanising movements of the Victorian age which brought art, music, and
the higher learning to the great capital of the Cotton
Industry. It does not fall to us here to define the precise
share taken by Thomas Ashton in starting the Art

[277]

Treasures Exhibition in Manchester in 1857 or in securing the Hallé orchestra or in promoting the extension of Owen's College and the foundation of Victoria University. Let it suffice to say that in all these good causes this energetic and cultivated captain of industry was as lavish of thought and labour as he was generous. That he was a freetrader goes without saying. As a youth he had worked in the Anti-Corn Law League and was the friend and disciple of Richard Cobden, who used often to stay with his father.

His wife was the daughter of Samuel Stillman Gair (an American of Scottish descent) and Elizabeth Wainwright (an American of English descent) both of Boston, Mass. Mrs. Ashton, however, was born in Liverpool where her father had settled in 1826 as head of the house of Messrs. Baring Bros. On her mother's side, then, Mrs. Bryce was American and of New England stock.

It was a marriage founded upon a perfect communion of tastes. Mrs. Bryce, vigorous alike in mind and body, shared the opinions, took part in the travels and comprehended the various activities of her husband. Her sound education in the ancient and modern languages, her familiarity with large political perspectives, her capacity for mixing easily in all societies, her devotion and gift of sympathy made her the perfect wife for such a man. The days of solitary travel were now at an end for Bryce. Those days had not been without incident, for like all men who have tasted the salt of life Bryce knew the face of danger. Once he had been nearly drowned swimming in a strong current among the Pyrenees; on another occasion in 1881, travelling down the Mississippi by steam-boat he had gone ashore for a walk while the steamer stopped to take in cargo. Either he missed the time or the boat started earlier than he expected for when he reached the landing stage she was already in mid stream. With an American passenger who was in the same plight Bryce persuaded an old boatman to row out to the steamer which had been signalled to stop. But with the shore well behind them the boat sprung a dangerous leak. Bryce urged on the boatman, baled for his very life and spurred his paralysed fellow passenger to activity by threatening to throw him overboard, unless he joined in the baling. By dint of these vigorous measures the steamer was overtaken just in time to avert disaster.

Nor was it only on the water that he met with situations testing to the nerve and muscle. Bryce was fond of solitary scrambling and those who pursue this pastime among the mountains are out for risks. One incident among many may be recorded. In 1883 Bryce spent a night or two in a hut on the edge of the great crater of Kilauea in Hawaii. During the day he rambled over the surface of the mountain, which was riddled with clefts and fissures and in some few places covered with small low growing shrubs. Suddenly, as he was passing through a patch of stunted vegetation, he found himself dropping into a cleft the opening of which had been entirely obscured by brushwood. Fortunately as he fell he caught hold of the branch of a small shrub that was growing some way down the cleft and by this means arrested his fall. But how long would the shrub bear his weight and how deep was the cleft? The auguries pointed to a fiery death in the bowels of a Polynesian volcano. Then he noticed that the cleft was narrow enough to enable him to get his back against one wall and his feet against the other and by this means he gradually worked himself up to the surface. It was a close thing and a good vindication of that alliance between muscle and mind which served the traveller well on many a passage of his wayfaring life.

Upon these solitary adventures, spiced with an occasional seasoning of danger marriage now imposed a curb. From this time forward Bryce had a companion by his side who was equally with himself fond of nature and quick in observation. A joint tour in the late summer of 1889 among the Dolomites and then through Croatia to Venice, followed in the succeeding year by a voyage through Canada and the United States to the Pacific shore was quite sufficient to establish Mrs. Bryce's credentials as a traveller.

One of Bryce' many constituencies was Armenia. Another was the noble body of pedestrians, who, with no implements more costly than a stout pair of boots and a good strong stick, keep their bodies hard and their minds fresh in the pursuit of one of the simplest and purest pleasures which life has to give. From boyhood upwards Bryce had been a great walker. He had walked as a child in Ireland, he had walked as a boy in Glasgow, and again as a young man at Oxford. When he came to London he joined the company of Sunday tramps, of whom Leslie Stephen was the guide, and there can have been few roads and pathways within a radius of thirty miles from the capital, which were not familiar to him. The preservation of open spaces from the inroads of the landlord and the railway, more particularly of such open spaces as were characterised by any feature of natural beauty or specially frequented by the public, was a matter which he frequently brought to the notice of Parliament on the occasion of railway bills. Above all was he anxious to render the wild and beautiful mountains of his native Scotland accessible to walkers, and to remove the ban which had been placed upon access to the grouse moors and deer forests by the imperious dictates of sport.

Here, however, he encountered the polite but massive opposition of a vested interest and a national passion. The pursuit of the grouse and the deer had now become a solemnity of the utmost importance. For the calendar of fashion, of sport and even of politics there was no day more sacred then the twelfth of August, the date at which grouse shooting began, and after which even the strictest of Parliamentary Whips found it difficult to keep his men together tramping through the airless lobbies of Westminster. To own, or at least to rent a deer forest or a grouse moor, was the coveted symbol of social success, just as a summer or autumn visit to the Highlands was part of the ritual of a well-spent year. The pleasures of sport had thus given a value to many a tract of barren country and had been the means of bringing a good deal of Southern, and even of Transatlantic, wealth into the Highlands of Scotland. Shootings were let for fancy prices to men who had made their money in industry, commerce or finance, and it was to be apprehended that the value of a deer forest would be severely depreciated if the tourist were made free to roam over it at will and to frighten the deer during the stalking season.

James Bryce

Bryce was unable to make progress here. He brought in a Bill in 1888 and returned to the charge in 1892 with a resolution which, though accepted by the Government, did not fructify in legislation. "I cannot help remarking," he observed (March 4, 1892), "that the exclusion of the people from the enjoyment of the mountains of Scotland began just at the time when the love of nature and of the sciences of nature had been most widely and fully developed. The scenery of our country has been filched away from us just when we have begun to desire it more than ever before. It coincided with the greatest change that has ever passed over our people — the growth of huge cities and dense populations in many places outside these cities — and this change has made far greater than before the need for the opportunity of enjoying nature and places where health may be regained by bracing air and exercise and where the jaded mind can rest in silence and in solitude." The speech ended with a burst of true but unparliamentary eloquence such as does not often startle the ear of the British legislature. "Man does not live by bread alone. The Creator speaks to his creatures through his works, and appointed the grandeur and the loveliness of the mountains and glens and the silence of the moorlands lying open under the eye of heaven, to have their fitting influence on the thoughts of men, stirring their nature and touching their imagination, chasing away cares and the dull monotony of everyday life and opening up new and inexhaustible sources of enjoyment and delight. It is on behalf of these enjoyments and those who need them most and in the hope of preserving for the people one of the most precious parts

[282]

of their national inheritance that I ask the House to agree to this Resolution."

As we have seen the Irish question caused Bryce many searchings of heart. Here his native sympathies as an Ulster Protestant were at war with what he believed to be the lessons of political prudence as he had learnt them from the history of the free democratic Communities of the Old World and the New. And the course which he elected to pursue was the more painful to him since it brought him into conflict with his Ulster uncles and most particularly with his Uncle John for whose character and opinions he continued to cherish a very strong regard. On other questions of public policy he had very little difficulty in coming to definite conclusions. He was heartily in favour of the Disestablishment of the Welsh Church and as firmly opposed to the extension of the Parliamentary Franchise to women. His attitude upon the first of these controversial questions was natural for he had been brought up a member of a non-established Church and was inclined partly from this circumstance and partly from his survey of the relations between Church and State which existed in America and on the Continent to attach very little importance to the principle of establishment as a factor in religious life. He had also been impressed during his tour through Wales on the Schools Enquiry Commission, with the vitality of the Welsh Nonconformist Churches and the comparative absence of popular support for the Establishment. "The Welsh," he said, replying to Sir Edward Clarke, the Solicitor-General, in a debate on Welsh Disestablishment, February 23rd, 1892, "are a religious people. Their religion is more constant and devout than that of any other people in these realms. They are a patriotic people and devoted to their national language, their ancient songs, their national traditions. Wales is a poor country. It is much poorer in proportion to its numbers than England; and yet in both these respects, as regards her national character and her hold upon the poor, the Church of England in Wales has been a most conspicuous failure. All the national life of the Established Church, all the religious fervour has gone out into the Nonconformist bodies. I do not say all the people have gone, but I say that the passion, the fervour, the ardour of religion, the attachment to the Welsh language, to Welsh history, and to Welsh nationality have gone to the Nonconformists; and the masses have drifted away from the Established Church leaving it the Church of the rich and not of the poor, of the few and not of the many. Why? Because the Church is established; because it has the organisation of the Established Church."

Here Bryce was the advocate of a change steadily contested by the Conservative interest in the country but ultimately carried on the eve of the Great War and without any such disastrous consequences for the cause of religion as the friends of the Establishment professed to discover.[1] On the question of Votes for Women he was from the first, and continued to be, on the conservative side. "I should say," he argued, when a bill was brought forward

[1] Bryce was of opinion that the Welsh Bishops and clergy should continue to form part of Convocation after Disestablishment and (more hesitatingly) that the Welsh Church itself should in the first instance organise itself on its own basis in its own way. *Bryce to Dr. Randall Davidson*, April 29th, 1892.

to enfranchise women (April 27th, 1892), "that in every class of the community women know less about politics than men do. . . . There are other countries more democratic than ourselves. Why do they not try it? There is Switzerland. Why does she not try it? Why does not democratic France try it? Our colonies are democratic in the highest sense. Why do they not try it? In any of the forty-four States of America, where there is almost unlimited facility for trying experiments, why has not somebody been trying them? Wyoming alone had introduced the franchise, a state of only nine thousand inhabitants. Washington, on the other hand, a larger state, after a four years' trial, has rejected it." After summarizing the familiar arguments against the change, that women were not a separate class, that their interests were already sufficiently safeguarded, that only a small minority of women desired the vote, that the entrance of women into politics would cause a revolution in the relation of the two sexes, certainly momentous and probably disastrous, he concluded with a proposition which shows how far the British Liberalism of the nineties was apart from the doctrinaire radicalism of the French Revolution. "We are asked," he said, "to make this change on abstract theory. There is nothing more pernicious in politics than abstract doctrine."

In August 1892 Mr. Gladstone, then eighty-three years of age, formed his fourth and last administration. Twelve years of active Parliamentary work had given Bryce a clear claim to promotion and he was brought into the Cabinet as Chancellor of the Duchy of Lancaster, a

sinecure appointment which leaves its holder available
for a great deal of miscellaneous Cabinet work and is
therefore by no means always the bed of roses which it
appears to be.[1]

The great question overshadowing all others in importance which confronted the new Government, was the
framing and passage of a measure for giving Home Rule to
Ireland. The bill, as is usual in such cases, was forged in
a Cabinet committee and of this committee Bryce was a
member. Nobody, indeed, was better qualified by reason
of his wide knowledge of constitutional law and practice
in the British Empire and throughout the world, to make
a serious contribution to the task of devising a new constitution for Ireland, but unfortunately, the case of Ireland
does not admit of being settled by constitutional analogies,
and the bill which emerged from the Committee, and
finally after a long and stormy passage, received a third
reading in the House of Commons, failed to secure the
assent of the Lords or to awake enthusiasm in the country.

In the tough Parliamentary struggle in Committee of
the whole House Bryce took a substantial part, coming
to the support of the Prime Minister and the Irish Secretary (John Morley) in a number of vigorous and well-
informed speeches, in the course of which German, American, and Colonial analogies were freely quoted. It must
be admitted, however, that the dialectical honours rest
with the opponents of the Bill, who had an easy task in
showing up its many difficulties and imperfections. The

[1] Bryce was offered the choice of the Duchy and the Office of Works. "I
am inclined to hope," wrote Mr. Gladstone, "that you will choose the Works."
Aug. 15, 1892. He chose the Duchy.

JAMES BRYCE, REGIUS PROFESSOR OF CIVIL LAW AND MEMBER FOR
SOUTH ABERDEEN

real case for the Home Rulers lay not in the adequacy of their experiment, but in the contention that the Irish had not been reconciled to the Union and that therefore some other way must be found. Their policy was founded upon an act of faith, easier to justify on a wide historical retrospect than upon the known facts of Irish history. "Making all possible allowances for human frailty," said Bryce, arguing for the arrangement under which the Irish members were to be retained at Westminster, but without power to vote on matters exclusively British, "we believe that this scheme will succeed, and we believe it because we believe that there are good forces as well as bad forces in human nature, and that, on the whole, the good forces are strongest." Such optimism was characteristic of Bryce's outlook on life. To his Parliamentary opponents it offered an easy mark for ridicule and criticism.

An additional blast of hot party feeling was blown on to the proceedings of this fierce and angry session by an incident arising from Bryce's administration of the affairs of the Duchy. Under the terms of a memorandum of 1870, the Lord Lieutenant of the County of Lancashire was empowered to recommend magistrates to sit on the County Bench. The Chancellor of the Duchy discovered that there were more than a thousand Conservative magistrates in the County and boroughs of Lancashire as against three hundred and one Liberals. He determined to redress the balance, and since the Lord Lieutenant declined to fall in with his views that thirty-nine Liberal magistrates should be placed on the Bench, revoked the memorandum and proceeded to the appointment of a number of Liberals and of some working men. An outcry was at once raised that the Chancellor of the Duchy was tampering with the administration of justice to serve the ends of his political party. A rattling hailstorm of Parliamentary questions was discharged at him. The Tory leader-writers professed themselves to be greatly outraged. What would come to England, if the Judicial Bench were to be regarded as among the spoils of a political triumph? That a Minister of the Crown should appoint a Liberal to the Bench because he was a Liberal was regarded in some quarters as the end of all things.

To these fulminations Bryce replied that there were, unfortunately, certain matters, for instance the game laws, rights of way, election disturbances, licensing questions, on which Tories were likely to take one view and Liberals another, and that a Bench composed of representatives of both parties would, therefore, command more confidence than one composed of Conservatives only. Moreover, he was no stranger to Lancashire. Thanks to his educational journeys, he knew the county better than any other part of England, and was prepared to warrant the credentials of his new magistrates. The little storm raged fiercely for a time and then died down. The Bench is no longer the exclusive perquisite of a party nor is it averred that the administration of justice in Lancashire has suffered by reason of the new social elements which are now represented upon the Commission of the Peace. For the moment, however, Bryce was exposed to the kind of criticism which is specially disagreeable to a high-principled and sensitive man.[1]

[1] Echoes of the criticism reached America and were dealt with by Bryce in a letter to W. L. Garrison of the *Nation*, June, 1892.

One of the functions of the Chancellor of the Duchy is that of ecclesiastical patronage. That a Presbyterian should appoint to Anglican livings may seem to be, and doubtless is, an anomaly, but it is an anomaly robbed of all practical inconvenience by sympathy, knowledge, and good sense. In matters of this kind Bryce was largely guided by the advice of his friend Randall Davidson, at that time Bishop of Rochester and now Archbishop of Canterbury, and some letters survive which illustrate the singular care with which he discharged this part of his official duty. A radical parson of High Church proclivities had been recommended for one of the Duchy livings and was in fact ultimately appointed by Bryce to a Lincolnshire parish where he did excellent work. The Chancellor, however, had doubts which he communicated to the Bishop. (April 27, 1894.)

'I had a talk with Mr. Hill and liked him very much. He belongs to a school of opinion with which I am very familiar, and among whose members I have many friends such as Scott Holland. I should like to see my way to placing him in one of the Duchy livings but my difficulty is that they are in purely rural districts, mostly in the East of England, where the people have been accustomed to services of a Low Church type, and where the farmer is suspicious of new ideas. New ideas are just what one wants to implant in such places, but one must also desire that they should be introduced cautiously, and, as a rule, not till the clergyman has gained the confidence of his parishioners by at least a few months or even years of quiet work. And of course in the interests of social peace as well as of religion one sets great store by the maintenance of an attitude of simple Christian sympathy, free from any suspicion of condescension towards Dissenters, an attitude not at all incompatible with high sacerdotal views such as Holland and Gore hold, though unfortunately not very often found in company with those views. It would not be right to exact anything in the nature of a pledge from a clergyman who was being considered for appointment, either as to his political action or as to the line he would take about changes in ritual: and, indeed, I should probably personally sympathise, from what I know of Mr. Hill, with his desire to quicken political life and inspire a zeal for self-government, as well as to introduce a more becoming and impressive mode of conducting the public worship of God than is often found in these Eastern parishes. But I am bound to think of the prejudices and suspicions and misconceptions that play so large a part in English rural life, and of the need of caution and tenderness in dealing with them. So I should be glad to hear from you, in case you feel able to express an opinion, whether you think I may be free from apprehension on these points — which I have mentioned frankly in the case of Mr. Hill, in whose zeal, uprightness, and devotion to duty I should feel every confidence.'

It would be difficult to find a more admirable summary of the considerations which should weigh with a wise man in such a case.

Before the long struggle over the second Home Rule Bill was engaged, Bryce gave up his Oxford Chair. He was able to look upon the twenty-three years during which he had taught Roman law in the University as characterised by a great development of legal teaching within

the University. The number of Chairs had been increased,
the examination for the B. C. L. had become 'the best
arranged and most practically useful law examination in
England,' the study of Roman law so long neglected had
struck in Oxford "deep and tenacious roots." In all this
development Bryce had played not indeed the chief rôle,
for that belongs to the distinguished body of resident
teachers,[1] but always a conspicuous part. A great lawyer
in the technical sense he may not have been, but it would
be difficult to conceive a more attractive way of presenting
the wider historical relations of the law of Rome than
that which is exemplified in the two solid volumes on
History and Jurisprudence which embody much of his Oxford teaching.[2] Moreover, immersed though he was in parliamentary contentions, Bryce preserved throughout his
life not only a zest for the large historical aspects of legal
science, but a keen interest in the minutiæ of legal scholarship. Thus he took advantage of a visit to Rome in
January 1883 to search the Vatican MSS. of Procopius,
in the hopes of finding the lost life of Justinian by The-
ophilus Abbas, alluded to by Nicolo Alemanni in 1623 in
the first edition of the Anecdota; and then having drawn
this covert blank, moved on to the Barberini library where
he was fortunate enough to come across a manuscript life
of the Emperor, previously unknown, and from internal
indications appearing to be the biography of which he was

[1] It is sufficient to mention the names of A. V. Dicey, W. R. Anson, Thomas
Erskine Holland, Thomas Raleigh, J. B. Moyle. Sir F. Pollock, the Corpus
Professor of Jurisprudence, was like Bryce a non-resident who played a con-
spicuous part in the development of the Oxford Law school.

[2] *Studies in History and Jurisprudence* by James Bryce D. C. L. Clarendon
Press, Oxford 1901.

in search. His discovery, published in the *English Historical Review* in October 1887, with a learned commentary, aroused much interest at the time and was intended to pave the way for a biography of the great Emperor. "When will Bryce's *Life of Justinian* appear?" was a question often asked but never answered. Yet the biography was never lost sight of and in the last months of his life, Bryce was projecting an Easter visit to Rome for the purpose of continuing the researches which had been interrupted years before into the life of the great ruler, who had given his name to the Institutes and the Code.

The relinquishment of his Oxford labours, extending over so long a period and associated with so many happy memories, was not effected without emotion, and in his valedictory lecture (June 10th, 1893) Bryce spoke from a full heart of his debt to the famous University to which he owed so much.

"With the regret of parting I carry away the delightful recollection of these years, and a sense which time will not diminish, of the honour which it has been to be permitted so long to serve this great University, the oldest and most venerated of the dwellings of learning in Britain, dear to us not only because our brightest years were spent among her towers and groves, but still more because in her, as now in maturer life, we scan a somewhat troubled horizon to watch for sign of storm, we see an institution which has stood unshaken while dynasties have fallen and constitutions have been changed, and which still and always, placed above the shock of party conflicts and renewing her youth in fresh activities from age to age, embodies in visible and stately form the unbroken continuity of the intellectual life of our country, and still commands, as fully as ever in the past, the loving devotion of her children."

There was little holiday for Parliament men in 1893, but late in the autumn the Bryces managed to slip away to the Basque country. Their way led from St. Jean de Luz, through the Pass of Roncesvalles, to Pampeluna, Saragossa, Tarragona, Barcelona, and Majorca, a golden sunset after months of angry storm.

The next year Mr. Gladstone retired from public life and in the new administration, formed under Lord Rosebery, Bryce, after again declining the Works, took office as President of the Board of Trade not, however, without some misgivings seeing that he had never even been chairman of a Commercial Company. For Mr. Gladstone's powers Bryce had always professed unstinted admiration; not so for his leadership. "He makes too many mistakes and yields too much to his sudden impulses, to be a leader whom one follows unhesitatingly." [1] But the splendid courage and energy with which the veteran statesman had championed the cause of Ireland, of Bulgaria and of Armenia had naturally made a deep impression upon one to whom all these causes were also very near to the heart, and quite apart from this, many bonds of scholarly interest, which bound these two Oxford men together, were sufficient to evoke a feeling in the younger man of deep and admiring gratitude.

His new chief was an old friend, for Bryce had received his initiation into the mysteries of government as Under-Secretary to Lord Rosebery at the Foreign Office; but the

[1] Letter to Rev. John Bryce, July 3rd, 1886.

Rosebery administration, depending as it did upon a majority, small and uncertain, in the House of Commons, was at the mercy of every gust, and long before the new President of the Board of Trade had time to make a mark in his department, the Liberal party sustained a defeat in the House and a disaster in the Elections. One circumstance only, in connection with Bryce's term of office, need be here recorded. It was at that time the custom for a Minister to be in attendance on the Sovereign during her absences from London. In March 1893, Queen Victoria paid a visit to Florence, taking Bryce with her as Minister in attendance.

It was a delightful holiday and full of instruction. "One day," writes Dr. Randall Davidson, "I spent a full two hours with Bryce in the Spanish Chapel in Santa Maria Novella. Bryce had of course written an account of it in a famous passage in 'The Holy Roman Empire.' In that passage he belittles the possibility of identifying the foreground pictures in the great Fresco with the eminent persons of the time — Cimabue, Arnolfo, Boccaccio, Petrarch, Laura, and others, but [on our present visit] partly I think for fun and partly in earnest he set himself to identify not only those figures but a great many others with the men or women then alive whom they might represent, and, as always, he amazed me by the range of his detailed knowledge about each. As often before I felt with him that he had all his historical matter at his finger ends in a way no other man has, and this fresco gave him a splendid text for pouring out details about the Empire and the Papacy. I told him afterwards that it was one of the best lectures that even he had ever given me. The marvel about him is the vivid boyish enthusiasm with which he throws himself into that kind of thing when he is at it. I know nobody like him in those respects."

"I like Mr. Bryce. He knows so much and is so modest." Such was the verdict of the Sovereign upon her Minister.[1]

The verdict of the Minister was full of gratitude and cordiality. "The Queen," he wrote to Lord Knollys on the occasion of her death, "always showed me such real kindness that I feel a deep personal grief at her departure and can the better understand how irreparable is her loss to those who have been privileged to be nearest to her in relationship and affection."

One of the acts, and in the event not the least fruitful, of the Rosebery administration, was the setting up of a Royal Commission, "to consider what are the best methods of establishing a well-organised system of Secondary Education in England, taking into account existing deficiencies, and having regard to such local sources of revenue from endowment or otherwise as are available or may be made available for the purpose." Of this Commission the President of the Board of Trade was appointed Chairman: and there could have been no better choice, for, having acted as Assistant Commissioner to a similar body twenty-seven years before, Bryce was already familiar with the main outlines and with many of the details of the problem.

The plan of the Commissioners of 1867 had never been fully carried out. It is true that by the Endowed Schools

[1] In 1893 Her Majesty had undertaken to read the *Holy Roman Empire.*

[295]

Act of 1865 a body called the Endowed Schools Commission was established, with power to make schemes for the better government and management of Endowed Schools, and that under this Commission and its successor, the Board of Charity Commissioners for England and Wales, no less than 902 endowments had been reformed: but nothing had been done to create either the local or provincial authorities or the Central Council of Education, which had been recommended by the Taunton Commission. Nor had any power been given to Local Authorities to rate themselves for Secondary Education, nor again had a system for the registration of schools or teachers been established. Save that an instrument had been created for the reform of educational endowments, there were few signs of increased organisation in the sphere of secondary education. The chaos, against which Bryce had raised his voice in 1867, still persisted. The brilliant appeals of Matthew Arnold had fallen on deaf ears, and though money was now made available for technical education, and a notable progress had been achieved in the development of secondary schools for girls, and in the growth of a professional spirit among teachers, the habit of thinking about education as a whole had not yet grown up. Endowments were distributed with capricious irregularity, the teachers in the different types and grades of schools lived in water-tight compartments, and the total supply of secondary education was far below the needs of the country.

Matthew Arnold, whose contributions to educational literature are among the best in the English language, had pleaded for the French plan of centralisation. He desired to see order, system, intelligent uniformity, a body of brilliant educational thought, transmitted through all the educational agencies in the country by the steady pressure of a Government Department which knew and cared for the things of the mind. Neither Bryce nor his colleagues would go as far as this. They were centralisers, but with clearly defined limitations. They believed in individual and local initiative. "The maximum of simplicity with the minimum of disturbance of existing relations" was their watchword. So, while they recommended the establishment of a central department for elementary and secondary education under a Minister responsible to Parliament, they conceived that initiative in public action should be left to local authorities, and that the function of the Minister, who was to be assisted by a small Educational Council of experts, should be to supervise and not to over-ride or supersede local action. The curriculum of secondary schools, for instance, was to be determined locally, and not from Whitehall, and since no local authorities for the administration of secondary education were in existence, the Commission recommended that such an authority should be set up in every county and county borough (town with over 50,000 inhabitants) recruited partly from the County Council, partly by nomination of the Minister, and partly by co-optation, and that it should be empowered to levy a rate not exceeding 2d. in the £, for secondary education generally. That teachers in secondary schools should be trained, and that the task of training them properly devolved on the Universities, that there should be a register for teachers, admission to which should be regulated by the Council of Education, that the profession should be unified and that a carefully graduated system of scholarships should be set up, were also points upon which stress was laid. A paragraph favourable to co-education and clearly influenced by the success of co-educational education in America was doubtless largely inspired by the Chairman.

A story is told by one of the Commissioners, that on the evening before the final draft was approved, he came to Bryce and said, "We have no quotation from Matthew Arnold." The Chairman conceived that a Report on Secondary Education with no allusion to Matthew Arnold would be a solecism. Accordingly, Mr., now Sir Michael, Sadler was sent away to search the sacred texts for a suitable observation. His task was difficult, for the Report of the Commissioners was far too conservative to suit the views of the gifted author of *Thyrsis*, but eventually a safe and innocuous sentiment was discovered and incorporated into the peroration :

"Our energies and our prosperity will be more fruitful and safer, the more we add intelligence to them ; and here, if anywhere, is an occasion for applying the words of the wise man : 'If the iron be blunt and the man do not whet the edge, then must he put forth more strength ; but wisdom is profitable to direct.'"

Of Bryce's own contribution to these inquiries Sir Michael writes as follows :

"As chairman of the Royal Commission on Secondary Education (March 1894–August 1895) Bryce rendered to his country a service of capital importance. He brought to the deliberations of the Commission experience of the work of the

Schools Inquiry Commission (1864–7) which was an earlier landmark in the history of Secondary Education in England. The main findings of the Secondary Education Commission became the foundation upon which the new administrative structure of our Secondary Schools for boys and girls has risen. The report ended with the following words written by Bryce. 'It is not merely in the interests of the material prosperity and intellectual activity of the nation, but no less in that of its happiness and moral strength that the extension and reorganization of Secondary Education seem entitled to a place among the first subjects with which sound legislation ought to deal.' The report was unanimous."

A study of Bryce's speeches as President of the Board of Trade suggests the conclusion that had the Rosebery administration lasted longer, a useful direction would have been afforded to commercial education. In matters educational Bryce was never fanciful. He preferred hard intellectual gymnastics to elegant accomplishments and assured the commercial clerks of London that there was no element in their training more serviceable than mental arithmetic. But more controversial matters claimed him. There were speeches in favour of Irish Home Rule, and for the reform of the House of Lords and in criticism of Imperial Preference. Then the rise of the Independent Labour Party filled him with misgivings and provoked a speech at Darwen in which, while it was conceded that the doctrines of Collectivism deserved to be examined and tested with reference to their applicability to each problem as it arose, a vigorous protest was made against the creation of a political party based on class.[1] At Aberdeen again he spoke warmly in favour of Scottish disestablish-

[1] *Times*, 5 January, 1895.

ment urging that the severance of the Presbyterian Church
from its association with the State would assist religious
life in Scotland and remove the principal obstacle to
Presbyterian reunion.[1]

Perhaps, however, the matter which of all others most
deeply moved him in the years immediately succeeding
the fall of the Rosebery administration was the terrible
series of Armenian massacres, beginning with the butchery
of Sasun in August 1894 and continued by order of the
Sultan in the autumn of 1895 and 1896. In scale and
horror these cruelties had not been surpassed, and the
news of them created a feeling of consternation. When
it was learnt that three thousand Armenians had been
burned to death in the Cathedral at Urfa and that more
than eight thousand had been butchered in Constantinople itself, even professed apologists of the Turk were
constrained to silence. To Bryce it seemed an intolerable abnegation of duty for Britain to look on at these
butcheries with folded arms. Our policy, our jealousy of
Russia had been responsible for handing the Armenians
over to the uncovenanted mercies of the Turk. We were
bound to help. If, after application had been made without result to Russia and France to assist us in the coercion
of Turkey, we were not prepared to apply coercion ourselves then we should invite Russia to restore peace as the
mandatory of Europe. That was his position in January
1896.[2] In the autumn he returned to the charge with a
renewed appeal for strong action.[3]

"I remember no movement like this in Great Britain,

[1] *Times*, December 18th, 1894.　　[2] *Times*, January 22nd, 1896.
[3] *Times*, October 2nd, 1896.

none so general, none so free from party spirit, none so spontaneous. It would have been strange indeed, had there not been a strong display of national feeling. For more than fifty thousand Christians placed long ago under the protection of the Powers of Europe have died by the sword; fifty thousand more have perished by famine as the result of the destruction of their dwellings and their farms; and this has not happened through any accidental outbreak of fanaticism. It has been effected by the deliberate purpose of the ruler of the country as part of a plan long ago formed and ruthlessly carried out for the extermination of the Armenian Christians. And the six Powers, the weakest of which could at any moment have stopped this slaughter — if permitted by the rest to do so — have looked callously on, accentuating their inactivity by feeble remonstrances. Russia has done nothing, though Russia in 1877 went to war with the Turks to punish massacres far less extensive. Britain has done nothing, though Britain in 1878 withdrew the Armenians from the protection promised by Russia and bound the Turks to herself by Treaty to secure their safety.

There are three things that might be done. The best would be to put an end to the Turkish Empire and divide up its territories. The Turk is irreclaimable and the sooner Moslems as well as Christians are delivered from his rule the better. But this is a drastic measure for which the Powers are not prepared because their rival claims would be difficult of adjustment. Another plan would be to introduce a thorough scheme of reforms which should, in particular, place the provinces where the Armenian population is largest under a governor or

[301]

governors not removable by the Sultan and put the whole administration under a Commission appointed by the Powers. This, however, would require a persistent and cordial co-operation among the Powers which seems at present unattainable; and Russia has declared her objection to any measure which should give a separate administration to the Armenian provinces. The third course is to depose the Sultan. The advantages of this course are that it could be accomplished promptly and probably with ease — for he is detested by all the better Moslems — and that it would raise no territorial questions.

Bryce's advice was not taken. The British fleet did not go to Constantinople. Abdul Hamid, "the assassin," lived on to receive the congratulations of the German Emperor and was in the end deposed by a conspiracy of his own subjects. No protection was afforded to the Armenians. Indeed fresh and more terrible massacres were in store for this unfortunate people. To have given political effect to the deep sentiment of righteous indignation which moved Bryce and so many who felt with him on the Armenian question would have raised difficulties, possibly dangers, which British statesmen, Liberal as well as Tory, were unwilling to confront. Lord Rosebery publicly declared himself against any course likely to lead to war, or to the break up of the Concert of Europe, which, however feeble and disjointed, was the one available instrument for the improvement of conditions in the Near East, and deprecated independent action by Great Britain. So nothing effectual was done. The indignation subsided, the woes of the Armenians and the crimes of

the Turks passed from the forefront of the national
consciousness, for a problem more intimately concerning
Great Britain had suddenly arisen under the Southern
Cross and was fast assuming an angry and formidable
shape indicative of possible war.

CHAPTER XVI

SOUTH AFRICA

A Nation is a great while before they can see, and generally
they must feel first before their Sight is quite cleared.

GEORGE SAVILE. 1694.

AFTER the Liberal defeat of 1895 Bryce determined
to spend his autumn holiday in South Africa, a
country whose political fortunes had now become
a matter of keen interest, if not of poignant anxiety to
all British students of politics. Such a voyage had long
been present to his mind as an object to be accomplished.
The country was but little known and yet of extraordinary
fascination. Apart from the beauties of the scenery,
reported by travellers to be very great, the development
of wealth from the diamond and gold mines had been
sensational in scale and rapidity, giving a new complexion
to almost every feature of South African public life and
bringing into salient relief the deep opposition of the new
Africa and the old, of the farms and the mines, of the
Dutch and British elements of the population. Through
the influence of the South African millionaires, for which
English history supplied no parallel since the age of Clive
and Hastings, the reverberation of these clashing interests was already audible in the London press, and
British opinion was beginning to be exercised by such
questions as the grievances of the Uitlanders in Johannesburg, the strife of opposing railway systems or the complex

[304]

problems which arose from the juxtaposition of a Kaffir and a white population.

The Prime Minister of the Cape at this time was Cecil Rhodes, also an Oriel man, and since there are few bonds stronger than the link which unites the members of an Oxford College, already known to Bryce and favourably regarded by him. Nor was Rhodes the only friend upon whose assistance Bryce could count in South Africa, for he had met Dr. Jameson more than once and was fully sensible of the unusual charm of the most engaging and talented of Rhodes' lieutenants. On many grounds the moment seemed suitable for a South African voyage.

The story of the impressions which Bryce gleaned from a strenuous three months in South Africa was subsequently given to the world in a volume which issuing at a time when curiosity as to South African affairs was at its height in England, was very widely read and commented on. Bryce had not gone to South Africa with a view of writing a book, but finding on his return to England that fresh political trouble had broken out, and that events in the Transvaal had fixed the eyes of the whole world upon South Africa, he determined to publish his impressions of the country and its inhabitants. Though with characteristic modesty he only professes to touch upon "the salient features," he contrives in the compass of a single volume to compress an immense body of important information on every aspect of South African life, and though many changes have come over the country since 1895, his book still remains the best general guide and introduction to South African studies.

As with all Bryce's writings on travel, what is princi-

James Bryce

pally to be noticed here is the immense variety of his interests. Everything is touched on, archaeology, history, politics, geology, economics, ethnology. He paints the scenery singling out in his bold graphic way the two kinds of charm, that of colour and that of primeval solitude and silence, which it possesses in high degree; but he also discants upon the vegetation with a width of learning which takes one's breath away. Here, for instance, is a characteristic passage suggested by the introduction into South Africa of the Australian gum tree.

"The changes which man has produced in the aspect of countries by the trees he plants and the crops he sows are a curious subject of enquiry to the geographer and the historian. These changes sometimes take place very rapidly. In the Hawaiian Islands, for instance, discovered by Captain Cook little more than a century ago, many of the shrubs which most abound and give a tone to its landscape have come (and that mostly not by planting but spontaneously) from the shores of Asia and America within the last eighty years. In Egypt most of the trees which fill the eye in the drive from Cairo to the Pyramids were introduced by Mahomet Ali, so that the banks of the Nile as we see them are different not only from those which Herodotus saw, but even from those which Napoleon saw. In North Africa the Central American prickly pear and the Australian gum make the landscape quite different from that of Carthaginian or even of Roman times. So South Africa is changing — changing all the more because many of the immigrant trees thrive better than the indigenous ones and are fit for spots where the latter make but little progress, and in another century the country may wear an aspect quite unlike that which it now presents."

It may be added that travelling through Mashonaland and Basutoland he collected and dried thirty-five specimens of plants, eleven of which were new to botanical science and are now to be found labelled Brycea in the collection at Kew.

Into the business then of understanding and exploring South Africa within the limits of a parliamentary holiday Bryce threw all the resources of his Protean vitality and hunting zest. He and his wife (for Mrs. Bryce, too, was an admirable traveller, capable of entering into his multifarious quests and employments) accomplished prodigies of exertion. They made a journey of 1,200 miles in a mule waggon unarmed and accompanied only by a Dutch driver and a native Cape boy through the lonely country between Mafeking and Fort Salisbury. Undeterred by the reputation of its pestilential shores they navigated the shallow and turbid waters of the Pungwe, partly consoled for the shyness of the crocodiles by the gambols of the river-horses. They climbed Machache (11,000 ft.) in Basutoland and Table Mountain (3,600 ft.) in Cape Colony. They interviewed press men, white and coloured, and native chiefs and mining engineers and missionaries and eminent politicians of every school. No important centre of population or scene of historical or archaeological interest escaped them. They saw Cape Town, Kimberley, Mafeking, Bulawayo with the ruins of Dhloto and Zimbabwe thrown in, Lorenzo Marques, Durban, Maritsburg, Bloemfontein, Lang's Nek, ascended Majuba Hill, visited Pretoria, Johannesburg, Ladybrand, Grahamstown, King Williamstown, the native college of Lovedale in Kaffraria, the Cape of Good Hope and the Naval Station at Simon's Town. Now we have a view of the eager traveller challenging the mining engineers of

Kimberley or Johannesburg on their special science. Now we hear of him descending a mine to study more closely the geological formation of the Rand and the *modus operandi* of the miners. Or again, we catch him at Thaba Bosyo, the famous stronghold of the Basuto Chief Moshesh, taking note of Kaffir legends and, after many enquiries of missionaries and others who knew the natives well, framing a general view of Kaffir religion which is probably as near the cloudy and indistinct reality as a northern mind can reach. And mingled with these varied interrogatives were bursts of pure exuberance of spirit such as the drive in a coach and four over rolling sand dunes to the Cape of Good Hope, where the wind blew so strong across the headland that there was nothing for it but to lie prone and then to scramble down the rough face of the cliff for a plunge into the tossing sea.

Coming and going the travellers stayed with Cecil Rhodes, "the strong and strenuous man," as Bryce afterwards described him, "who, with little encouragement from the Government of his country founded the British South Africa Company and acquired vast territories for the Empire." They also saw much of Dr. Jameson and Mr. Lionel Phillips, and at Johannesburg met a number of the people who later on were connected with the Jameson raid or the Uitlander rising. As to the intended insurrection in Johannesburg there was not a particle of concealment. Everybody talked about it and it was fully expected by the officials at Capetown. In the dry and stimulating atmosphere of the Rand the Uitlanders, smarting under very real grievances and exasperated by the misgovernment of the Kruger régime, were in no mood to listen to reason. They spoke with a large and boastful impudence of hidden arms and concealed "maxims" and gave Bryce to understand that a rebellion would shortly break out under the Republican flag.

Maxim, or machine, guns

Of the Raid not a murmur. The intelligence of this ill-starred adventure reached the Bryces on their return to England and then they remembered that a day's march south of Buluwayo they had met a strong body of Rhodesian Mounted Police riding down the track to the *rendezvous* at Pitsani. Nor was it suspected that the sudden appearance of Dr. Jameson in Johannesburg in mid-November might be connected with a design to wrest the Transvaal from President Kruger and to place it under the Union Jack.

In brief the impression which Bryce derived from a study of the political conditions of South Africa was as follows: He thought that the immigrant population in Johannesburg laboured under real grievances, that the government of President Kruger was in certain respects obscurantist and in other respects postively oppressive, but that there was nothing either in the immediate or prospective situation to justify the conclusion that an armed conflict was inevitable. He found no social antagonism between the Dutch and English races. "The Englishman," he wrote, "will deride the slowness of the Dutchman, the Dutchman may distrust the adroitness or fear the activity of the Englishman but neither dislikes or avoids the other. Neither enjoys, or even pretends to, any social superiority and hence neither objects to marry his son or his daughter to a member of the other race. Moreover, among the Transvaal burghers there was a

[309]

movement of opposition distinguished rather by the quality than the quantity of its members, to President Kruger." It was even said that Oom Paul might not be re-elected to the Presidency. In any case it would seem that with tact, coolness, and patience the acute difficulties of the moment might be surmounted and the fusion of the two white races in South Africa finally achieved. From his conversations with Rhodes on the one hand and the leading Dutch politicians in the Cape and Orange Free State on the other Bryce saw no evidence of that general conspiracy "to drive the Englishmen into the sea," which was afterwards freely attested. He left Africa then with the conviction that while the position of affairs was undoubtedly delicate it was by no means irremediable.

The invasion of the Transvaal by Dr. Jameson in December 1895 enormously aggravated the difficulties, inflaming racial passion all over South Africa, alienating the Cape Dutch and throwing the Free State into the arms of the Transvaal. If President Kruger had been a farsighted statesman he would have seen in the criminal blunder of his opponents a golden opportunity for consolidating his position. He would have been magnanimous to the vanquished and sought to apply remedies to the distemper which had produced the outbreak. But it was too much to expect of the old Dopper that he should straightway forgive so considerable and wounding an injury. He took the step exactly calculated to bring hostilities nearer. He refused concessions and imported arms.

The Kaiser's telegram to President Kruger congratulating him on the defeat of the Raid created a storm of indignation in the English Press and was not calculated to ease our relations with the Boer. The suspicion grew up that the Government of the Transvaal was not acting alone, and that its refusal of all concessions and accommodations was the result of some secret understanding with the German Government. Bryce endeavoured to counsel moderation. The Boer Government had behaved stupidly and the Boers had many faults but there was much in them to admire and we should not be prejudiced against them by the calculated caresses of Germany any more than we ought to be prejudiced against Dr. Jameson by the verses of the Laureate or the cheap Jingoism of the Music Halls.[1] As for Germany she "had no more right to interfere in the Transvaal than she had in Afghanistan."

The war which came in 1899 split the Liberal party from top to bottom, Rosebery, Asquith, Grey, and Haldane supporting the general policy of the Unionist Government while Campbell-Bannerman, Bryce, Morley, and Lloyd George carried a vehement opposition to Chamberlain and his policy on to all the platforms of the country. Bryce did not dispute that the grievances of the Transvaal were real, but he held that they could have been removed by steady and quiet pressure. The evils from which the Uitlanders in Johannesburg were suffering were not intolerable. Property and life were safe in the Transvaal. The Rand was prosperous. The country was the best for working men they could find in the world. "I was in Johannesburg," he said, speaking on the Address (2nd February 1900) "two months before the raid and I must say I never saw a town in which the people seemed to be

---

[1] *Times*, Jan. 22, 1891.

enjoying themselves more completely to their hearts'
content." The evils such as they were would have righted
themselves. Immigration was proceeding, wages were
rising, the proportion of Englishmen to Dutchmen would
have gone on increasing. "I said that the grievances were
bad, but Sir, war is worse. Everything in politics is
comparative and the redress of these grievances affecting
a comparatively small number of persons who had gone
into the country with notice that the grievances existed
was a very small matter compared with the disastrous
war into which we have been drawn." He contended that
the Government's handling of the whole course of the negotiations was marked by a signal lack of prudence. They
should have allowed more time to elapse after the Raid
before pressing their demands. They should not have
concentrated upon a requirement that the Boer Government should enlarge the franchise, since the state of the
franchise was a matter of domestic concern to the Transvaal and could not therefore furnish an appropriate *casus
belli*. They should not have raised the suzerainty question. "I do not," he concluded, "believe that the Government wanted war; my opinion is that they went on
thinking that the Boers would yield. . . . Our com-
plaint against them is that this was a dangerous game to
play."

The substance of the argument which Bryce here
developed in the House of Commons had been already set
out in a preparatory chapter to a second edition of the
Impressions of South Africa and constituted the first
serious and influential criticism which the Government
had to meet. That so competent and well-trained an

observer should have reached such a conclusion was in itself an important fact. But in great political controversies, where resentment as to the past is on either side blended with vague apprehensions for the future, opinion will be divided to the end of time as to the fair distribution of praise and blame. Here some will hold with Bryce, that with a more temperate and patient handling of the situation on the part of the Colonial Secretary and the High Commissioner at Cape Town the war might have been avoided; others will contend that some day or another the question as to whether all South Africa should obey the Vierkleur or enjoy a position of essential freedom under the Union Jack was bound to provoke a quarrel and that in view of the steady arming of the Transvaal the sooner the quarrel came the better. Despite the fact that the actual declaration of war emanated from Pretoria the general opinion of the world was at the time enlisted on the side of the small Republics in their struggle against the mighty Empire.

In the campaign against the Government Bryce was one of the most active of Campbell-Bannerman's lieutenants. He sympathised with the Boer farmers in their passion for independence and felt keenly that a calamitous mistake had been made and a fair prospect clouded, perhaps totally, by an intemperate and ill-judged diplomacy. This was an unpopular heresy in England and subjected its advocate to much obloquy. In his own constituency, however, he retained despite the opposition of the local press the enthusiastic devotion of his supporters. Here he was received with ovations which astonished even so experienced a Scot as Campbell-Bannerman. To a

Scottish audience the combination of courage, sincerity, and sound information is never devoid of appeal.

Hostilities once begun, Bryce held that the war should be fought till victory was obtained. He was never one of those who thought that because the British Government was in the wrong the Boer Government was in the right. His view was that grave errors of temper and judgment had been committed on both sides, but that once the sword was drawn, the conflict should proceed until the Boers accepted defeat. Then the settlement should be as magnanimous as it could be made. "To reconcile the races by employing all the natural and human forces which make for peace and render the prosperity of each the prosperity of both, and so to pave the way for the ultimate fusion of Dutchmen and Englishmen in a common Imperial as well as a common Africander patriotism: this should be the aim of every Government that seeks to base the world-wide greatness of Britain on the deepest and surest foundation."[1]

For this reason he was sharply opposed to the policy of requiring from the Boers unconditional surrender. If the Government, he argued (14th Feb., 1901), in the debate in the Address, will not convert the two Boer Republics into two protected States it should endeavour "to secure to these States something like the freedom enjoyed in Canada and Australia subject to the general supremacy of Great Britain." Above all things Crown Colony Government should be avoided. He cited the classic instance of the unwise course pursued in the Southern States of the American Union after the victory

[1] Impressions of South Africa, 2nd ed. Prefatory Chapter XLIV.

of the Federals in the Civil War as an example of what
should not be. "The best day that dawned for the Southern States was when the military forces of the United
States were withdrawn. It was not the maintenance of
military government but the withdrawal of it that made
these States reconciled." So that when the negotiations in
March 1901 had broken down he pleaded for their renewal.
"Who," he asked, "are the conquered? They are the
people we desire to make good British subjects, whom we
desire to be loyal, against whom we do not desire to keep
an enormous garrison at an enormous expense and to
whom even the Government express themselves as desirous of restoring free government at the earliest possible
moment. If you want to make them loyal and contented
subjects, the more liberal the terms the better it will be
and the sooner that consummation will be realised."[1]

On the conduct of the war Bryce had a good deal to
say to the House and the country which was most un-
acceptable to his hearers. He condemned the proclamation of the General in the Field affecting to treat the Boers
as rebels and a proclamation depriving those who continued resistance after a certain date of belligerent rights.
He denounced the policy of farm burning, the execution
of martial law and the establishment of concentration
camps for the women and children of the enemy population. On all these subjects he felt and spoke very warmly.
The severity, as he was disposed to think, with which the
war was conducted, seemed calculated to prolong rather
than to abridge hostilities. "There was a moment,"
he recalled, "in the War of Independence when the resist-

[1] House of Commons Debates, 28th March, 1901.

ance of the insurgents in America against British arms seemed to have almost disappeared and when there was every prospect that British arms would prevail. At that moment the British general made marauding and devastating incursions into several States, including Virginia. What was the result? The spirit of revolt and antagonism which was apparently almost extinguished burst out afresh, and the devastation of Virginia proved to be the turning point of the war. That was what became of so-called stern policies."

Whether the conduct of war can ever be made acceptable to the conscience of humane and sensitive men may be doubted. War is necessarily cruel and a war which is waged by a wholly insufficient force in an immense desert not against a professional army but against a people in arms presents features of special difficulty. That old men, women, and children should be made to suffer at all was a shock to a generation which had grown up during a long spell of peace to believe that the evils of war could and should be limited to combatants; and there were many, besides avowed "Pro Boers" who were much troubled by the farm-burnings and by the news of the mortality among children in the early months of the Concentration Camps. In the light of the melancholy experience which the world has now gathered of what war may become under modern conditions, the operations in the South African War seem to have been conducted with an extreme of forbearance and clemency and the sole palpable tragedy — the deaths of the children in the concentration camps — to have been due to ignorance and mismanagement rather than to malevolence. But at the time much that was reported from the front seemed to many good men to be harsh, unnecessary, and contrary to sound policy, and when the peace came eventually, the fact that there had been throughout an influential body of Englishmen who had raised their voices against military severities made conciliation easier than it would otherwise have been.

In his private letters of this period Bryce wrote with fierce indignation of the lack of statesmanship which had led Britain into the war and of the Jingo spirit which had temporarily seized hold of the nation. "You can hardly imagine," he writes to Goldwin Smith on April 12, 1901, "the moral and political declension of England at this moment. It will, I hope and trust, soon pass: and it is largely due to the campaign of falsehood and misrepresentation about all South African affairs and events which has been assiduously carried on by a large section of the press. Even among Radicals, even among the Nonconformist leaders, clerical and lay, the old ideals of justice, liberty, humanity, as they were cherished from 1840 to 1880, seem to have become obscured. Scarcely an attempt to realize the passion for independence which animates the people of these Republics; little recognition even of their tenacious courage. Disraeli's influence was bad enough; but one is amazed to find one's self wishing for Disraeli instead of those who now direct the Jingo whirlwind."

It is the habit of passenger ships plying between Cape Town and Southampton to drop anchor in Funchal Harbour. Here amid the flowery hills of Madeira the

Bryces received (Dec. 1895) the startling news of the Anglo-American War scare. The Government of President Cleveland had suddenly chosen to intervene between Britain and Venezuela in an ancient dispute concerning the boundary of British Guiana. Of this hoary quarrel few Englishmen had heard; for fewer still was it a matter of the faintest concern. It was then with amazement that the British public read first a dispatch from Mr. Olney the Secretary of State and then a message from Mr. Cleveland couched in language so stiff and accompanied by such a salvo of warlike sentiment from Congress and the Yellow Press, that had these manifestations proceeded from any other quarter, peace would with difficulty have been preserved. Fortunately, England remained calm and Lord Salisbury kept his head; and since the American intervention, though maladroit and provocative in form was inspired by adherence to two sound principles, arbitration and the Monroe doctrine, a pathway was found to an honourable compromise.[1] The immediate effect of this unfortunate incident upon Bryce's mind may be illustrated by two letters to American friends.

To Mr. Theodore Roosevelt

Jan. 1st. 1896.

The news of this so-called "war-scare" met us at Madeira on our way home, and I have not yet had time to read the dispatches nor what passed in Congress nor what the papers have said. But I confess myself astonished at four things.

1) The apparent existence of ill-will towards Britain in a large part of your population. What in the world is the reason? There is nothing but friendliness on this side.

[1] See *Grover Cleveland* by Robert McElroy, and the *Life of the Marquis of Salisbury* by Lady Gwendoline Cecil.

2) The notion that we want to interfere with American rights or with the balance of power in the New World. Nothing further from people's minds here. Our hands are more than sufficiently full elsewhere.

3) The sympathy with a corrupt military tyranny like that of Venezuela, a government which our Foreign Office has found it not possible to deal with. They are not a civilized government at all.

4) The total want of all ordinary diplomatic courtesy and decorum shown by Cleveland and the State Department — according to what I hear — for I have not read the papers.

All these things amaze me so much that I should be grateful for your remarks on them.

As to the Monroe doctrine, I have never been able to see how it applies at all to such a case as this : If the U. S. are going to assume a protectorate over all Central and South America, and see that these so-called Republics behave like civilized States, that is another matter. Then other countries will know whom they have to deal with. But the U. S. have not done so — and certainly that is not the Monroe doctrine — This by the way, however. The subject is too big a one for a letter.

People here seem to have been taken utterly by surprise. Not one man out of ten in the House of Commons even knew there was such a thing as a Venezuelan question pending.

I suppose the victory of the Republican party at the next election is pretty certain, so far as anything ten months off ever is : and I trust you will get a really superior man as the candidate you will elect.

I should like immensely to come over and talk about 1000 things with you — and as we are likely to be out of office for a long while, trust no obstacle of that kind will arise. And I should like to come while you are over the Police Dept.

But you really must not go to war with us — for then how should we be able to come and go and have our talks ?

James Bryce

To Mr. Villard.

Jan. 4, 1886

On our way home we were met at Madeira by the news of Cleveland's Message and the outburst of anti-British feeling in the U. S. I do not suppose there was ever any real danger of war. But I wish you would explain to me its causes. One can well understand England's being hated in France and other parts of the Continent — though the German hostility seems much in excess of any sufficient ground. But why should we be hated in the U. S.? We don't come into hostile contact. We are not rivals, anywhere. We have the warmest feeling towards the people of the U. S., and have certainly strong material interests in their prosperity. So we are astonished at all this fury, especially over a trumpery question which not one man in ten even in the House of Commons had heard of, and which does not touch any material interests the U. S. have. The idea of "making the Caribbean Sea an English lake" (according to Lodge) is quite a novelty to us. I fear it will be many years before the confidence of the British investor is restored.

When the angry waves subsided Bryce contrived to extract some comfort from the squall. The circumstances of the friction occasioned by the Venzeuela boundary question towards the end of 1895 illustrated the way in which the sentiment of friendliness had revived in Britain. " The President's message and the action of Congress were received in this country with amazement. Few persons had the least idea that any serious disagreement between the two Governments would or could arise over a matter which had attracted no attention here. With the shock of surprise there was a shock of grief that Congress should apparently treat lightly a contingency so lamentable as a collision between the two nations. But there was no

[320]

outbreak of hostile feeling towards the U. S. The general feeling was that there must be a great misconception somewhere, and that, so far as national honour permitted every step ought to be taken to remove the misconception, and set matters right between nations made to be friends. Very shortly afterwards, there occurred on the part of a Great Continental State, what we people deemed a provocation. It was resented with a promptitude and a warmth in excess of its real importance." [1]

[1] The Essential Unity of Britain and America, *Atlantic Monthly*, July, 1898.

CHAPTER XVII

OPPOSITION

Had I a strong voice as it is the weakest alive, yea, could I
lift it up as a trumpet, I would sound a retreat from our
unnatural and irreligious strivings for religion.

ARCHBISHOP LEIGHTON. 1660.

D URING the whole period of the Boer War Bryce
experienced great unpopularity. He spoke frankly
and he spoke frequently and in the sensitive and
anxious state of the public mind, his speeches gave offence.
For the moment there was very little chance for the Liberal
politicians. They were snowed under in the khaki election
of 1900, and though South Aberdeen remained staunch
to its member, it returned him by a majority consider-
ably reduced after a fierce conflict. No task is more ungrateful than that of fighting a powerful majority in the
House of Commons as one of a defeated and divided party.
Some Liberals, like John Morley, locked themselves in
their studies and took only an intermittent part in the
fray. Bryce, however, was not among these. All through
the dark days of Liberalism he stood out as one of the
most active of Campbell Bannerman's lieutenants, and devoted to the task of expounding party principles energies
which his historical friends would have been glad to have
diverted to the service of Clio. "How well I recollect one
evening," wrote Lord Althorp, "about 1903 or 1904 when,

in the early hours of the morning (rather an Irishism but you must be well used to them now), you led us with admirable spirit and you flung across the table the most vigorous replies to our opponents. It was a very exhilarating performance."[1]

Perhaps the most important of these gladiatorial occasions was afforded by the Education Bill of 1902 which was piloted through the House of Commons by Mr. Balfour, assisted by Sir William Anson, the Parliamentary Secretary of the Board of Education. The three main principles of this long and complicated measure were the transference of the local control of education from school boards elected *ad hoc* to county or municipal councils, the grant of assistance to Church schools from the rates, and the provision for the establishment of secondary schools at the public expense. Few measures have aroused hotter feeling than this proposal to endow denominational education and even to put "Rome on the rates." The Nonconformists were up in arms, and the Liberal Party, always strong in the support of the Free Churches, took the field in defence of their outraged susceptibilities and found in the championship of undenominational education a welcome balm for their own internal wounds. A whole session of Parliament was expended on the successive stages of this controversial measure, which was swollen by no less than ten pages in the course of its tormented passage through the House.

The principal assailants were Bryce and Mr. Lloyd George, the first full of force and knowledge, but displaying from time to time, by reason of the depth and sincerity

[1] Lord Althorp to Bryce, 19th January, 1907.

of his convictions, a note of exasperation, which detracted from his persuasiveness; the second, quick, electric, alive with wit and ingenuity, and prompt to dart his arrow at the smallest chink in the opponents' armour. The case for the opposition was that the Church of England was no longer the Church of the Nation, that the school boards were doing well, that the proposed new authority was already overburdened with work, lacked popular impulse and would be manipulated by permanent officials, that the evils of sectarian strife would be introduced into public bodies, that it was undesirable to perpetuate denominational education, but that if rate aid was to be given to Church schools it should be accompanied by an efficient measure of local popular control. The Free Churchman asked indignantly why he should pay rates for a form of religious teaching which he repudiated, to which the Anglican asked in reply why a rate was objected to and a tax acquiesced in.

Bryce himself, though a staunch Presbyterian, was one of those rare beings, an undenominational Christian. The doubts of agnostics and the differences of believers were equally painful to a mind nurtured in elemental pieties and sharply opposed to the propagation of doctrine by government. If a cross-grained fate compelled him to acknowledge that the Jews and the Roman Catholics would continue to the end of the chapter to demand a specific form of religious training for their young, he struggled against the perpetuation of a principle, full, as he thought, of danger, within the more liberal zone of the Protestant Faith. Here he desired to see an all-round acceptance of certain simple truths, evidenced by scripture as the basis of popular religious instruction. Whatever dogmatic distinctions and controversies might be appropriate to the adult mind, these were quite inappropriate to the mentality of childhood. Little children did not understand high doctrine, and it was not desirable that they should. The province of a State School was to teach a common citizenship and a common Christianity. "Nothing worse," he urged on the introduction of the Bill, "could be done to the children than to take them in their tender years and to divide them like the sheep from the goats into different religious communities, teaching them to regard one another with distrust." The gravamen against the bill was that instead of making for a greater spirit of harmony in the nation, it gave support to religious differences. "It is not," he said, moving the rejection, "an Education Bill. It is a voluntary Schools Relief Bill." [1]

So much educational progress has been accomplished under the Act of 1902 that much of the criticism then levelled against it from the Liberal benches seems now to be lacking in perspective. The new educational authorities are undoubtedly more powerful and more adequately equipped with funds than the smaller school boards which they displaced, and whatever may be its demerits in the eyes of the undenominational philosopher, the defenders of the statute may point with some pride to the fact that a great development of State-aided secondary education has been made possible under its provisions. That the dual system in elementary education, perpetuated and indeed fortified by the Act, is in many ways an educational

[1] House of Commons Debates, 5th May, 1902.

misfortune cannot be denied. If agreement could have been obtained as to religious teaching on the lines favoured by Bryce and his friends, the elementary education of the country would now be more efficiently organised. Agreement however was impossible then and is difficult now, and the country pays for the luxury of religious variance by maintaining a number of schools at the public cost which fall below a reasonable standard of efficiency.

All through the summer and autumn of 1902 the battle of the schools raged in Parliament and the country and with such vehemence that when the Bill passed into law there were those who resolved that lawlessness was henceforth a sacred duty. The "passive resisters" led by Dr. Clifford, a fiery and combative divine, declined to contribute to the teaching of denominational religion and at regular intervals suffered a miniature martyrdom in the cause of conscience. Bryce did not proceed to these lengths, but the language which he used about the Bill in the House of Commons might be taken as justifying an attitude of inflexible and continuing protest against the quartering of denominational education on the rates and the dissociation of rate aid from popular control.

To follow Bryce's Parliamentary activities in any detail during the next three years would be to rewrite the political chronicle of the time. In most important debates he took a hand, speaking with uniform ease and abundance on subjects as various as the London Education Bill, our policy in Somaliland, the state of Trade and the position in European Turkey. On the two questions of Tariff Reform and Chinese Labour in the South African Mines, he stoutly upheld the position taken by the Liberal

Party, using his experience of American affairs to illustrate the corrupting influence of a Protective tariff on public life and its injurious effects upon the growth of a commercial navy, and reminding the House of Commons that the United States Courts of California placed the Chinese on a civil equality with United States subjects in regard to the holding of property. On matters fiscal Bryce, like the vast majority of well-educated men in both political parties at that time, was a convinced Free Trader, opposed both to Protection and to the new scheme of Imperial Preference which Joseph Chamberlain was pressing upon his party and the country with apostolic eloquence and conviction. Even if he had not been reared in Glasgow, the home and preceptress of Adam Smith, and had not come, as an undergraduate, under the personal influence of Richard Cobden, Bryce could hardly have been otherwise than a Free Trader. He believed that Free Imports were essential to the prosperity of British shipping and British cotton and that the unity of the Empire was to be otherwise encouraged than by a system of fiscal preferences, which, if substantial, must raise the cost of living to the poor at home, and, if unsubstantial, would cause heart-burnings in the Dominions and Dependencies. One alternative which suggested itself was the systematic development of cotton-growing in the Empire, a project of which he was an early Parliamentary advocate. [1]

It is no disparagement to the members of a Parliamentary Opposition to observe that it is their business to oppose. Whatever line of action the Government may decide on, their duty is to discover, if they can, a better.

[1] House of Commons Debates, 5th April, 1905.

James Bryce

The philosopher may frown, the moralist may sigh, but to men of a certain youthfulness and elasticity of temper there is no better sport in the world than to make ministers uncomfortable. Others take their task weightily and vex their souls over the blunders and crimes of the administration. Bryce belonged to the serious brigade. In the sphere of education, foreign policy and finance, he was heartily convinced of the grave errors of the government. Opposition, however, did not act with him, as it does with men of inferior calibre, as an obsession or an acid. He could throw off the whole Parliamentary business in a moment and plunge into literature or travel with the gusto of a boy. The present writer remembers how one afternoon during the committee stage of the Education Bill, Bryce rushed into the Ilberts' drawing-room at Speaker's Court between two amendments and, after delivering a brilliant disquisition on the ancient monuments of Egypt (garnished with an intimidating supply of names and dates) to a lady who had just returned from Cairo, suddenly foamed over with a cascade of enquiries as to the value of a recent German monograph on the Holy Roman Empire in the Thirteenth Century. There was a buoyancy and flexible elegance about the whole performance which robbed it of any appearance of affectation or pedantry.

A picture of Bryce's activities during this period, which represented him merely as the strenuous Liberal politician absorbed in contriving confusion for a Tory ministry would be quite incomplete. Politics were with him never so exacting as totally to obstruct the grand advance towards a more complete comprehension of the world which was the law of his prehensile and retentive intelligence. Not a year passed without one or sometimes two voyages across the sea. There was an autumn expedition to Mexico, Cuba, and Jamaica via the United States in 1901, and a sixth visit to the United States in 1904 with lectures at Harvard and Columbia Universities and an address at the St. Louis Exhibition. And interspersed with these longer and more distant expeditions were shorter tours in Europe and an Easter visit to Burgundy with Edward Bowen, a pilgrimage to the Historical Congress in Rome, which he addressed in excellent Italian, a tour in Umbria and in Sicily, a summer in the Orkneys and Shetlands, an exploration of Hungary and the Balkan States marked among other incidents by a visit of pious curiosity to the birth-place of Justinian twelve miles from Uskub.

Nor were these years barren of literary production. Apart from the two substantial volumes of *History and Jurisprudence* which embodied much of his Oxford teaching, there appeared in 1901 an Introduction to the English translation of Helmolt's *History of the World*, a vast co-operative German work based upon the principle that natural environment rules the course of human affairs and in the light of that idea recounting the history of mankind continent by continent. Whether a universal history should be so planned is very doubtful. Lord Acton was sceptical and Bryce's wide-ranging Introductory Essay indicates that he could only accept Dr. Helmolt's hypothesis with serious modifications. "It is rare," he observes, "to find any nation now living under the physical conditions which originally moulded its

character or the character of some of its component
elements. And hence it follows that when we study the
qualities, aptitudes, and institutions of a nation in connection with the land which it inhabits, we must always
have regard not only to the features of that land, but also
to those of the land which was its earlier dwelling-place."
The classical instance is, of course, furnished by the
migration of the English to North America and of the
Spanish and Portuguese to South America. Plainly the
history of the United States or of Brazil and Peru cannot
be written with regard solely or even chiefly to the conditions of American physical nature. "A History of America
must be a history not only of America but of the Spaniards,
Portuguese, French, and English — one ought in strictness
to add of the negroes also — before they crossed the
Atlantic. The only true Americans, the only Americans
for whom American Nature can be considered answerable,
are the aboriginal Red men whom we, perpetuating the
mistake of Columbus, still call Indians." Other considerations led to the same conclusion, namely that,
however powerful physical environment may have been
as a factor determining the original qualities of the races
into which the human family is divided, its importance
in the later stages of human history is a diminishing
quantity. "When we regard the evolution and development of Man from the side of his relations to space, three
facts stand out — the contraction of the world, the over-
flow of the more advanced races, and the consequent
diffusion all over the world of what is called civilization.
. . . The broad result is everywhere similar. The modern
European type of civilisation is being diffused over the

whole earth, superseding, or essentially modifying, the older local types. But if this be so, it becomes more important for the historian to study the laws which govern the transmission and expansion of culture than the influence of physical environment on the history of man."

In his consideration of the problems raised by this attempt to summarise the whole history of man, Bryce was drawn on to ask himself the question whether the course of history establishes a general law of progress. His conclusion is characteristic not only of his spirit of scientific caution, but of his general conception of the historian's mission. "The doctrine of a general steady law of progress is one to which no historian ought to commit himself. His business is to set forth and explain the facts exactly as they are; and if he writes in the light of a theory, he is pretty certain to be unconsciously seduced into giving undue prominence to those facts which make for it." The matter, however, was not altogether simple, for we must define what we mean by progress. Different people had different tests. Bryce's conclusions were that while there had been a marvellous advance in Man's knowledge of the laws of Nature and in his mastery over Nature, while there had been a great increase in the number of mankind and on the whole in the physical vigour of the average man, and while there had been, as a further consequence, an immense increase in the material comfort and well-being of the bulk of mankind, it was impossible to make any confident assertion as to progress in virtue and happiness. Here every man's view would depend on his own ideal of happiness and of the relative importance to happiness of the ethical and non-ethical elements which entered into the conception, and that until there was more agreement on these points it was vain to attempt to measure the progress which Man had made. "Moreover," he continues, "it is admitted that nearly every gain Man makes is accompanied by some corresponding loss — perhaps a slight loss, yet a loss . . . and in many cases our experience is not yet sufficient to determine the quantum of loss. There is room both for the optimist and the pessimist. The historian has no business to be either."

As an exercise in bold questions and cautious answers, in wide generalisations and minute and various learning, this essay takes high rank among the minor historical pieces of our time. The subjects treated — the causes which have helped to improve the writing of history in the nineteenth century, the meaning, function and requirements of Universal History, the different plans upon which a History of the World might be written, Man's relation to Nature through Time, the origin of racial characteristics, the nature of Progress and so forth — are each and all so vast and the space allotted to these immense themes is necessarily so limited that great novelty is not to be expected. Even, however, in dealing with familiar considerations, Bryce is always fresh, sparkling, precise. The mere sweep of his illustrations, gathered as they are from every quarter of the globe and from ages in the history of mankind the most widely removed, and the equal ease with which he draws upon his stores of natural and historical knowledge, compel admiration. Moreover, from time to time, by asking himself a new question, he hits upon a new thought. Thus, in the course of an admirable passage on the working of racial admixture, he asks himself whether race fusion worked differently in ancient and modern times, and proceeds to answer as follows: —

"There are two noteworthy differences between modern race fusions and those which belong to primitive times. One is that under modern conditions the influence of what may be called the social and political environment is probably very much greater than it was in early times. The American-born son of Irish parents is at forty years of age a very different creature from his cousin on the coast of Mayo. The other is that in modern times differences of colour retard or forbid the fusion of two races." When the question had once been posed, many a competent historian would have hit upon the reply. But how few historical writers do ask themselves new questions! How many excellent writers are content to tread in the quiet footsteps of custom, using the conventional categories of the accepted political science of their time and filling these receptacles with the spoils of their horny-handed toil! Now it was the property of Bryce's mind to excogitate questions. No question was too large and no question was too small for him. His active imagination abounded in interrogatories of every size. Thus his great learning was not of the mechanical accumulating kind but a response to quick, wide-ranging thoughts about man and the Universe. There is then a discovering quality about his historical writings. Even when we proceed along familiar roads, our guide will show unsuspected prospects.

James Bryce

On June 7th, 1902 a large audience assembled in the Sheldonian Theatre at Oxford to hear his Romanes Lecture on the Relations of the Advanced and Backward Races of Mankind, one of those spacious and composite subjects, calling for the resources of the historian, the traveller, the politician, and the anthropologist, in which Bryce's rare versatility was conspicuously displayed. The lecture was neither an oration nor a homily, rather it was a solid treatise in the analytic Aristotelian manner, covering the ground plan of the subject and marking it into segments, distinguishing, for instance, between the four possible results which might ensue from the contact of two races differing in strength, and then illustrating from the history of man each of them in turn. What are the causes which favour or check intermarriage between races brought into contact? What are the different ways in which contact may arise without fusion? What are the specific evils and difficulties which tend to be produced by such a situation? How can they best be alleviated and what is the duty and policy of a dominant race unable to fuse with a backward race with which it is brought into necessary contact? All these questions Bryce handles with a sure and expeditious touch, never outstepping the limits of his evidence and indicating with a true scientific spirit the areas in which uncertainty still prevails. "The subject of race mixture," he observes, "is one of extreme interest to which, as far as I know, comparatively few data for positive conclusions exist. It deserves to be fully investigated by men of science. The difficulties are obvious because the concomitant and disturbing conditions are so numerous."

[334]

It is a pity that Bryce could not have pursued a theme to which he had devoted so much thought, but in the Romanes Lecture he has laid the ground-plan of a great book which, now that all the backward races in the world have at last been placed in more or less complete dependence on the more advanced, can be, and deserves to be, written. As Bryce points out, the subject is not only ripe for scientific investigation, but susceptible of suggesting conclusions as to the future course of humanity.

Another work belonging to this period is of an altogether different character.

In 1903 Bryce issued his *Studies in Contemporary Biography*, a series of twenty minature biographies of men, all of whom, with the single exception of Disraeli, were known to him personally, and many of whom were close personal friends. More than perhaps any other volume which came from his industrious pen, this illustrates the personal character of the author, his capacity for warm and varied friendships, his remarkable gift for appreciating and delineating subtleties of character and for detecting the essential qualities of friends and acquaintances, his large charity and his power of combining in a single picture both the superficial and the profound aspects of the human beings who were known to him either directly, through social communion, or by the indirect channels of public fame. It shows also that had he so wished, he could have succeeded in a wholly diverse line of literary composition.

In this delightful gallery of portraits there figure one Jew, two Roman Catholics, three Anglican Divines, two lawyers, two philosophers, a novelist, an American

[335]

publicist, a schoolmaster, three historians, an orientalist, and five statesmen. There is no woman and, since Americans are not regarded in Britain as foreigners, there is no foreigner. The longest, the most elaborate and in many ways the most remarkable of the portraits is that of Lord Beaconsfield, whom Bryce did not know and of whom, despite the fact that the Jewish Prime Minister was by temperament and policy as far removed from his biographer as can be imagined, he has nevertheless presented an image of delicate fidelity and justice. Nor did personal affection blind him to the defects and limitations of his friends. Freeman's curious miscellany of violent prejudices and strange limitations are exhibited without reserve, as the foil setting off the genuine gold of a strong truth-loving humane nature. Of Lord Acton, another historian, bound to him by many ties of confidential intercourse, Bryce has written a paragraph, which displays perhaps better than any other passage in his writings, the empire which the Muse of History continued throughout all his manifold activities to exert over his heart and mind.

"Twenty years ago, late at night, in his library at Cannes, he expounded to me his view of how such a history of Liberty (Lord Acton had in 1882 drawn out a comprehensive scheme for such a history) might be written and in what wise it might be made the central thread of all history. He spoke for six or seven minutes only; but he spoke like a man inspired, seeming as if, from some mountain summit high in air, he saw beneath him the far-winding path of human progress from dim Cimmerian shores of prehistoric shadow into the fuller yet broken and fitful light of modern time. The eloquence was splendid, but greater than the eloquence was the penetrating vision which discerned through all events and in all ages the play of those moral forces, now creating, now destroying, always transmuting, which had moulded and remoulded institutions and had given to the human spirit its ceaselessly-changing forms of energy. It was as if the whole landscape of history had been suddenly lit up by a burst of sunlight. I have never heard from any other lips any discourse like this, nor from his did I ever hear the like again."

One other feature in this volume may be touched on as illustrating a trait in the author's character. Bryce was full of the minor loyalties. It counted with him that a man should have come from Ulster or Glasgow, that he should have been a scholar of Trinity or a Fellow of Oriel. Thus he wrote a sketch of Lord Chancellor Cairns, not only out of respect for his great judicial powers, but also because Cairns was one of the most distinguished representatives of the Scoto-Irish race to which he himself belonged, and if the question be asked how it came about that Bryce, the Liberal Presbyterian, was attracted to write of Cardinal Manning the Ultramontane, the answer must be that they were both Fellows of Oxford Colleges and that when Bryce was first in residence in Oriel, Manning would, from time to time, on the occasion of his visits to Oxford, descend upon his rooms for a talk. These pleasant preferences and partialities, albeit tempered by the cooling fluid of experience, Bryce preserved with that constancy which the corporate tradition in British educational life does so much to promote.[1]

[1] It may be worth recording that he was offered and declined the task of writing the official lives of W. E. Gladstone, Sir William Harcourt, and John Bright.

CHAPTER XVIII

CHIEF SECRETARY FOR IRELAND

I have personally been a Home-ruler ever since reading
Lecky's account of Ireland in the eighteenth century.

T. ROOSEVELT.

I N the summer and autumn of 1905 there were signs
in the sky of impending political change. Ten years
had now passed (for the khaki election of 1900 may
for this purpose be disregarded) since there had been any
genuine consultation of the Electorate on issues of domestic moment, and now a question was raised, which, from its
size and novelty, was calculated to bring about a new
alignment of forces. In 1903 Joseph Chamberlain had
gone out of the Conservative Government in order to be
free to preach the Gospel of Protection and Preference,
and from that time forward Tariff Reform overshadowed
all other issues. For two more years Mr. Balfour hung
on to office, contriving by prodigies of dialectical skill to
keep together a party which was uncertain of its course
and divided on the main issue of the day. Then in
December he resigned, and the King sent for Sir Henry
Campbell-Bannerman, who formed a Government and
instantly went to the country for authority to govern.

The General Election of that winter resulted in a prodigious and unprecedented Liberal victory. Never had a
British Prime Minister met Parliament with so large a

majority behind him. The Liberals stood for Free Trade. It was on that rock that their power was principally founded, but the feeling of the workers that the introduction of Chinese Labour to operate the South African mines was a sinister precedent, capable of application nearer home, was in many cases a powerful contributing cause of the Liberal success at the Polls. The Home Rule question was not expressly raised. No pledge was given, but Bryce, speaking to the electors of South Aberdeen, dilated on the necessity of simplifying and reorganising the administrative system of Ireland and of associating the people of the country more closely with the management of their affairs.

As a reward for his long spell of vigorous work in opposition and his faithful allegiance to Campbell-Bannerman during the dark days of the South African War, Bryce's friends had good ground for expecting that he would receive high cabinet office. The best places, however, went to the Liberal Imperialists and since Morley claimed India as a right, Bryce, suffering the fate of men who are too proud to ask, was compelled, at the age of sixty eight, to content himself with the most invidious and thankless task in the Government, the Irish Secretaryship.

To the Sultan who expressed to the British Ambassador his anxiety at Bryce's inclusion in the Cabinet, Sir Nicholas O'Connor wittily replied, "Your Majesty may rest at ease. Mr. Bryce has an Armenia on his hands in Ireland."

The situation was made the more difficult for the Irish Secretary by reason of the fact that on the only plane of political action likely to content the Irish Parliamentary Party, the Liberal leaders had estopped themselves from a decisive advance. Home Rule was barred. The recent elections had been fought on other issues and, while some measure of Irish devolution was contemplated, the Liberal party was in no humour to jeopardise its prospects of carrying useful reforms at home by embarking once more upon a matter so disputed and so disputable as an Irish Home Rule Bill. To Bryce, himself a convinced Home-Ruler, this decision implied a postponement of the one measure likely to be adequate to the needs of Ireland. He saw himself condemned to a policy of palliatives and "second-bests," from which some objects of value might be derived, but certain to fail in securing a settlement of the Irish question.

Under the system which then prevailed, the Secretary for Ireland governed the country. Every department of domestic administration, agriculture, education, industry, commerce, labour, and poor relief, fell within his province. For every disorder he was responsible. In the House of Commons he had to defend his administration from the formidable thrusts of the Irish members, for whom it was a standing source of enjoyment to invent fresh tortures for the minion of British authority. No minister was more constantly under the harrow or more continuously on the move. Now the Irish Secretary was expected to be in Ireland, now his presence was required in the House of Commons or at No. 10, Downing Street, or in the slatternly little building looking like the office of a bankrupt solicitor, known as the Irish Office, which overlooked Birdcage Walk. Even in a most peaceful year, the Irish Secretary lay on an uneasy bed.

For a Liberal Chief Secretary nothing could well be

more disagreeable than the social atmosphere of Dublin. He was impartially boycotted by Unionists and Nationalists. Conservative landlords, lawyers and ex-officials met him on business, but few came near the Vice-regal or Chief Secretary's Lodge, and the Chief Secretary and his wife were hardly ever invited to break bread in a Conservative house. On the other hand, the Nationalist party boycotted the Castle severely, and though the Nationalist members would see Bryce on business, they absolutely declined to come to the Chief Secretary's Lodge for any social purpose. "It was only," writes Lady Bryce, "as a great concession to years of friendship that John Dillon consented to dine with us privately at the Lodge just before we left for the United States." Bryce was far too deeply absorbed in his administrative task to regret his exclusion from Irish society, but he thought that social ostracism, as practised in Ireland, was foolish and bad for the country.

The Under Secretary at Dublin Castle was at that time a remarkable man, holding a position more influential than that which usually belongs to the Civil servant. Sir Anthony McDonnell had ruled with signal success an Indian province of nearly fifty million inhabitants, and afforded in his person a striking illustration of the great careers which are open to Catholic Irishmen in the service of the Empire. Caring nothing for the catchwords of Irish politics and being at one and the same time a Home-Ruler and an Imperialist, he looked at the problems of Irish government from the angle of an Indian bureaucrat, intolerant of waste, confusion, and overlapping; and since he had given up the prospect of the Governorship of Bombay at the request of Lord Lansdowne in order that he might clear the Augean stable at Dublin Castle, he expected to have a big say in the direction of policy.

There were no delicate half tones about Sir Anthony. His views on every subject were clear-cut and decided, and he was as incapable of cajoling or persuasive speech as he was constitutionally indisposed to conciliate opposition. His drive, his great ability, his selfless devotion to the public service were of little account in creating an atmosphere favourable to his operations. Neither Unionist nor Nationalist thought that his interests were well served while an Under Secretary so detached from party ruled in Dublin Castle. To many a minister Sir Anthony might have been an uncomfortable subordinate. Not so to Bryce. The Irish Secretary and his masterful lieutenant pulled well together and shared common hopes that it might be vouchsafed to their joint efforts to ameliorate the lot of the agricultural poor, to promote University life, and to pass into law an educative measure of devolution. "We do not," Bryce wrote to Goldwin Smith,[1] "contemplate anything at all revolutionary in Ireland. At present my aim chiefly is to better the condition of the people materially and socially and to wean them from disorder. It is a slow task; one can't expect to accomplish much. I am, however, so much impressed by the intolerable defects of the present administrative system in Ireland, which makes its working from day to day inconceivably troublesome and harassing, that I do hope to introduce a measure for reducing these evils."

To the Cabinet discussions which naturally range over

[1] June 11th, 1906.

the whole field of Imperial politics, Bryce was always in a position to make an instructive contribution. Everything interested him. About everything he possessed a ready store of exact information. Speaking of Sir Henry Campbell-Bannerman, Mr. Henry Higgs tells the following tale: "I found him chuckling one day after a Cabinet meeting. He said 'We had a very all-round discussion, the Morocco question, the Near East, the Armenian question, and constant talk about places not marked on the map. But James Bryce was always ready. He knew every place, how to get there, how long it took you to get to the railroad and how to cross the desert by camels and the rest of it. Just as we were rising, Herbert Gladstone told us about a lady who had been arrested in Regent Street on a charge of loitering and soliciting. Bryce cleared his throat and began, 'When I leave the House at night I often walk home by Regent Street.' Here I put my hand on his shoulder and said, 'My dear Bryce, you must allow us to know something about Regent Street.'" [1]

At the end of 1905 Ireland was preternaturally quiet. The Wyndham Land-Purchase Act had for the time appeased agrarian trouble. Ownership was passing, slowly indeed, but without visible sight of impatience, from landlord to tenant, and if there was disappointment that grazing tracts had not been broken up, the ill-humour had not yet exhibited itself in open agitation. Boycotting and intimidation were on the decline. The Irish sky had rarely been so favourable.

The Speech from the Throne foreshadowed changes in the government of Ireland. What these changes might

[1] Spender, *Life of Henry Campbell-Bannerman*, II, 56.

be had not yet been decided on, but the intimation of change was enough to alarm the Irish Unionists, and an amendment to the Address was moved by Colonel Sanderson, which brought Bryce into the field with his maiden effort as Irish Secretary.[1] His case was that everyone who had recently concerned himself with Irish affairs admitted that changes were necessary; George Wyndham, Lord Dudley, Sir Anthony McDonnell, the Irish Reform Association, Sir West Ridgeway, and that it was safer to introduce reforms now when outrages had fallen, when local government was working well, when the agrarian trouble had been largely removed, than in a period of acute political inflammation. The proposal to grant Home Rule to Ireland had been resisted in 1886 largely by reason of Irish crime. That argument could not be used now. And meanwhile many changes were urgently needed, notably in the field of education, which was half a century behind the British standard, changes which could not be effectively carried out unless Ireland were herself heartily associated with the passing and execution of the measures required to bring them into operation. It was a vigorous and sanguine speech, closing with an eloquent peroration, but throwing no light upon the particular plan for the reform of Irish Government, which was likely to commend itself to His Majesty's advisers.

Some minor irritations had been left over from the Conservative administration which the new Chief Secretary attempted to remove. Chief among these was the recent suspension of the additional grants made under the Wyndham administration for the encouragement of the teach-

[1] February 2nd, 1906.

ing of the Irish Language in the National Schools. The Gaelic League, founded by Dr. Douglas Hyde in 1893, had made rapid progress in its design for the revival of the old Irish language and for the study of Gaelic literature and antiquities, but since the whole movement wore a strong political colour, it was frowned on by Trinity College, and failed to appeal to Mr. Long, the Conservative Secretary who preceded Bryce. Nationalist enthusiasm, however, was warmly enlisted in the Gaelic cause, and though in 1891 the number of people speaking the Irish language alone was little over twenty-six thousand, there were in 1906 a hundred thousand students of Erse and two thousand five hundred fifty-one Primary Schools teaching the language. Taking encouragement from the examples of Hungary and Bohemia, Irish nationalists contended that the recovery of the old language and the old literature and the living use of Gaelic modes of thought and speech were necessary steps to political emancipation.

Bryce had told the House of Commons in 1900 [1] that he did not see much prospect of success in the attempt to make the ancient Celtic language the vehicle for a modern literature. That Irish should be taught with English in the Schools was however desirable, but it should be taught not as a vernacular, but as a literary language. "I have," he said, "the warmest sense of the splendour, the brilliance and the imaginative power of the ancient Irish literature, an imaginative quality quite unique and with a wild charm of the Western sea that is quite its own. . . . Many years ago I happened to spend a summer vacation

[1] *House of Commons Debates*, 20th July, 1900.

in Ireland, when I obtained lessons in Irish — lessons which, to my regret, I have now forgotten — from the son of an Irish peasant who had developed a remarkable talent for philology. . . . The instance of that man makes me believe that if we were to give the Irish-speaking population a chance of studying Irish as a literary language, we might have a much larger number of persons studying Irish history and literature." This argument, it will be observed, was chiefly directed towards the establishment of bilingual instruction in the Irish-speaking districts of the West (a concession made in 1904), not to the spread of compulsory teaching in Irish all over the island. Bryce was, however, generally in favour of the development of Gaelic studies, provided that they were not allowed to interfere with the necessary subjects of elementary instruction. He made then a welcome concession to the Gaelic League. From the 1st July, 1906, a small remuneration was allotted to the teachers in the National Schools for each Irish-learning child.

Throughout Bryce's rule in Ireland the position of Sir Horace Plunkett was the occasion of some friction between the Irish Secretary and the Irish Parliamentary Party at Westminster. Sir Horace, a great and single-minded Irish patriot, the creator of Irish agricultural co-operation, but obnoxious by reason of the breadth of his sympathies to the extremists of the Orange and Green factions, had, as Vice-President of the Department of Agriculture and Technical Instruction in Mr. Balfour's Government, rendered distinguished services to the economic development of Ireland. Bryce, who knew and admired Sir Horace, was naturally desirous of retaining his services, though he had lost his Parliamentary seat in 1900. But the majority of the Nationalist members thought that Sir Horace should have resigned when Mr. Balfour's government came to an end, and put pressure on the Chief Secretary to secure his ejection. There was, however, a great feeling for Sir Horace and his Department in Great Britain, and, though the co-operative movement, which was due to his initiative, had antagonised local traders, there was as favourable an opinion of him in Ireland as an independent man could expect. He was then retained in office while a Commission investigated the working of his Department.

In his first speech on Irish affairs as Chief Secretary, Bryce had alluded to the serious deficiencies in Irish education. To these he recurred in a more extended Parliamentary statement on March 22nd. What were these deficiencies? They were underpaid teachers, inferior buildings, the absence of compulsory school attendance, the great number of very small poor schools, the lack of local interest in education, the absence of any correlation between the elementary and secondary schools. For the reformation of these evils the Chief Secretary threw out a series of suggestions, the establishment of a single education department for Ireland, the union under one system of elementary, secondary, and technical education, the introduction of stricter methods for securing school attendance, the improvement of the buildings, the amalgamation of small schools, an increase in teachers' salaries, proposals not worked out in detail, but serving as an indication of the directions which reform should take.

Whether, had his tenure of office been prolonged, Bryce would have been able to make any substantial advance along this difficult causeway, may be seriously doubted. The real obstacle to educational improvements in Ireland was then, and still remains, the iron determination of the Roman Church to retain its undivided control of the schools. In England the National Schools are supported both from the taxes and the rates. In Ireland the whole cost of the salaries and two-thirds of the cost of building and improvements were financed from the taxes alone. In England the localities are compelled to interest themselves in education and the central authority has power to require the erection of new schools and to hasten their completion: in Ireland there was no such compulsion or encouragement. Compared thus with England, Irish national education was only half-supported and half-endowed. It was like a creature living on a single lung. But the malady is hard to cure, for to any proposal for an education rate, carrying with it, of necessity, popular local control, the priest opposes an inflexible and lethal resistance.

An even greater flaw in the government of Ireland was the defective provision for higher education. Trinity College, founded in the reign of Queen Elizabeth, and served in the course of a distinguished history by many men of real eminence in science, letters and public life, was fully adequate to the needs of the Protestant Episcopalian minority. The Catholic population, however, numbering three and a half millions, was less well provided for. There were indeed the "godless" Queen's Colleges of Belfast, of Cork, and of Galway, founded by

Sir Robert Peel in 1845 and subsequently incorporated together with University College, Dublin (a well-conducted institution managed by the Jesuits), in an examining institution known first as the Queen's and later as the Royal University. But the support given to these institutions by the Catholic community was faint and lukewarm. In all three Queen's Colleges put together there were not two hundred Catholic students. The College at Cork was little more than a school of medicine. The College at Galway contained about a hundred students only, and the Royal University, being nothing more than an examining Board, had no power to breathe life into these forlorn and toneless institutions.

Large-minded statesmen, belonging to different parties, had seen that the only solution of the University problem in Ireland was the erection of a genuine Catholic University, accessible to Protestants and subject to the ordinary Test Acts, but controlled by Catholics, offering a prevailingly Catholic atmosphere and commanding the confidence of the Catholic population. That was the view of Lecky, of John Morley, of Mr. Balfour. However undesirable such a university might be in theory, it was at least better than no university at all. It would provide a liberal education for the sons of the Catholic gentry, a higher form of training for intending teachers in Catholic schools, and would give to the Catholic mind of Ireland a larger and more generous span of intellectual interest and experience.

To the realisation of such an ideal there were great obstacles in the strength of Protestant prejudice. The endowment of a Catholic University out of public funds

seemed to many to be a step back into Cimmerian dark-
ness, a subsidy to the forces of superstition, a measure of
superfluous help to a clergy already powerful and dis-
affected. Yet this is what Lord Robertson's Commission (1901–3), appointed under a Conservative Government, recommended. The report of that Commission
proposed to convert the Royal University into a teaching
body and to subsidize from public funds the Jesuit College in Dublin. When Bryce came into office nothing had
yet been done as the result of the Robertson enquiry.
Moreover the enquiry was not exhaustive. Trinity College, fearing revolutionary proposals, had succeeded in
obtaining exemption from the scope of the Commission's
investigations, and until Trinity College had been looked
into, it was impossible in Bryce's view to form a just impression of the needs of Ireland in the matter of university education. The Chief Secretary therefore set up a
Commission of nine, presided over by Sir Edward Fry,
a retired judge of great eminence, and containing among
its members such distinguished Irishmen as Mr. Douglas
Hyde and Chief Baron Palles, to report on Trinity College and the Dublin University. The new commissioners
were agreed in recommending far-reaching but necessary
changes in the constitution of Trinity College and the
erection of a college acceptable to Roman Catholics in
Dublin. They differed in their views as to the proper
organisation of University education in Ireland as a whole.
A minority of three, despairing of any genuine co-operation between Roman Catholics and Protestants in an
Irish University, reported in favour of two universities,
one consisting of Trinity College and the other to be the

existing Royal University, of which the proposed College, acceptable to Roman Catholics, was to be an additional member. But the majority took a bolder view. Shutting their eyes to the unpleasant contrarieties of Irish feeling and opinion, they recommended the inclusion of all the Irish Colleges, including Trinity College, in a single national University. Such a University would, indeed, of necessity be federal, and federalism is a note of weakness, but since in any case some federation of the scattered Queen's Colleges could not be avoided, this was no fatal objection. The signatories of the majority report were opposed both to the establishment of two teaching Universities in Dublin and to the federation of the rest of Ireland against Trinity College. They believed that it would be possible to preserve under this scheme the essentials of College autonomy and College atmosphere. But one signatory, Professor Henry Jackson, while agreeing that the plan of a single national university was the best, could not recommend that it should be immediately put into operation in view of the opposition which it would inevitably arouse.

Almost the last appearance of Bryce as Chief Secretary was arranged that he might deal with the University Report. Here was a document pointing to the establishment of a single University for all Ireland, which should comprise Catholic, Anglican, and Presbyterian colleges. To the opponents of denominational education in English elementary schools such a solution of the thorny problem of Higher Education in Ireland not unnaturally commended itself. There were to be no religious tests. The University was to provide teaching in non-controversial subjects, the colleges in subjects into which religious controversies entered. In all controversial subjects there were to be alternative graduation classes. Any class in any subject was to be open to any student. The teaching was to be supervised by the Colleges, the enlarged University to be governed by a Senate partly nominated by the Crown and partly elected by University teachers and the whole body of graduates. The weaker colleges, like Galway, were to be affiliated. No payment from public funds was to be made for theological teaching, but it should be open to any College, out of its own resources, to establish any Theological Faculty it chose. "This," he concluded, "is our policy. Our belief is that our policy is likely to receive the support of the Liberal Party in Parliament because it conforms to the principles they hold to — education free from sectarianism — and to their desire to do everything in their power compatible with these principles to meet the wishes of the Irish people. . . . I personally believe it is the only scheme politically possible under the conditions; and I can hold out no hope that any other will be proposed by the present government." This was precipitate. The Report of the Commission had neither been considered by the Cabinet nor yet had it been long enough before the academic public in Ireland to make so swift a decision upon a topic of enormous complexity entirely reasonable. Bryce, however, was naturally impatient to clinch the work on which he had set his heart and to welcome recommendations which accorded with his own enlightened (but undenominational) views as to what Ireland should desire in the matter of University education and for which he had secured the support of the Roman Catholic hierarchy and the General Assembly of the Presbyterian Church. His rapidity of action did not escape adverse comment. Mr. Balfour was prompted to observe that he had "nailed his flag to another man's mast and then sailed for America." And Mr. Birrell, his successor, having to explain to the House of Commons that he had quite a different plan for University education in Ireland, suggested that in painting his picture Bryce had "omitted to leave a few clouds on the horizon."

If Bryce was unable to leave a mark upon Irish education, he signalised his brief term of office by introducing and passing into law the first really big measure for remedying the disgracefully low standard of rural housing in Ireland. Irish land legislation, culminating in the Wyndham Act, had dealt mainly with landlords and tenant farmers; but Ireland was not entirely without agricultural labourers and other rural workers of the labouring class. Some slight provision had already been made for the housing of labourers, but the interests of the tenant farmers had overshadowed those of the humbler folk. To remedy this state of things Bryce carried, amid general acclamation, a useful measure (the Labourers' (Ireland) Act) for providing 25,000 labourers' cottages, furnished with suitable plots of land. The cottages and land were to be owned by the Rural District Councils, who got the land on the Land Purchase terms, and obtained loans for building from the Public Works Commissioners. Assistance to the Councils to the amount of £50,000, in respect of annual charges on loans for land and buildings, was to be given from certain central funds and since the residual charges were higher than were likely to be covered by the rents paid by the labourers, the Act enabled the rates of the providing Councils to be charged up to a shilling in the pound, or more in special cases. There can be no question that this measure, which also cheapened and expedited procedure, did much to help the poor people for whose benefit it was devised.[1]

Like every other Chief Secretary, Bryce visited the West of Ireland to see for himself the poverty of the so-called "congested districts," inspecting innumerable harbours where there were demands for fishing facilities and piers (every little fishing village in Ireland demands a pier) and making stormy voyages to wild and remote islands off the West and South coasts to learn about the life of the people and to better their conditions. For the moment, however, no matter of importance connected with this chronic evil came up for discussion, for the Wyndham Act, passed only three years before, contained special provisions for the benefit of this region and it was not until later that the need for greatly enlarged resettlement operations was pressed upon the Government. One valuable contribution to the economic regeneration of Ireland was, however, suggested to Bryce, perhaps by his travels in Ireland, perhaps by his experience as President of the Board of Trade. He set up an enquiry by Vice-Regal Commission into the Irish Railways.

All through the year the great question of Irish devolution remained in the background. It had been adumbrated in the King's speech, it was ardently championed

[1] *House of Commons Debates*, 26th May and 23rd July, 1906.

by Sir Anthony McDonnell, it was cautiously explored by the new Chief Secretary. Despite two discouraging pronouncements by Redmond, the Irish Parliamentary leader, some progress in the preparation of an Irish Council Bill was made, but it devolved upon Mr. Birrell, Bryce's successor, to introduce the measure, which, after navigating some perilous shoals, foundered on the rock of clerical dictation. Bryce was much chagrined by the failure of a project in which he had discerned substantial hope for an improvement in Irish education. "You will have noticed," he writes to Goldwin Smith, May 31st, 1907, "that the proximate and determinent cause of the rejection of the Irish Council Bill by the recent Irish Convention was the very best provision in it, viz. that which placed Irish elementary and secondary schools under the control of an elective local Irish body. I say 'the best provision,' not that I think such a Council an ideal body for the purpose, but that some such body offers the only practical chance of reforming the present shocking and patent evils of Irish education. They can't be got rid of by Parliamentary action: and the one hope was to get the people themselves to see the evils and deal with them by establishing local control, imposing local rates, and getting the schools out of the hands of clerics, whether Roman or Protestant. It was because the bishops and priests feared this that they gave such vehement, and successful, opposition to the Bill. It was a small measure and full of imperfections. But it might have done some good, if people had tried to work it fairly; and I gathered from the last edition of your book that you thought some limited experiment of this kind might be now tried."

The year, which had been signalised by a welcome absence of serious crime, closed without disturbance. Sinn Fein was in existence, a knot of *litterati* preaching a gospel of Gaelic culture and separatist politics, but offering as yet no serious menace to the Irish Parliamentary Party. Nor for seven hundred years, in the Chief Secretary's opinion, had Ireland been so peaceful. The hour seemed to the Cabinet to be propitious for conceding to a demand which had regularly been pressed for sixteen years from the Nationalist benches, and consistently supported by the Liberal Party, that the Peace Preservation (Ireland) Act, which had been passed by Mr. Gladstone in 1881, should henceforth be dropped. The Act therefore was omitted amid the protests of the Ulstermen from the Expiring Laws Continuing Act, in which it had figured since 1892. In later years this step was widely denounced as the root of serious evils, and when, in the summer of 1914, Protestants and Catholics armed themselves and Ireland trembled on the brink of civil war, the discontinuance of Mr. Gladstone's Act under the Bryce administration was freely cited as a contributing cause of the disorder. The main purpose of the Act of 1881 had been to keep fire-arms out of the hands of Irishmen. Any person having, or suspected of having, a fire-arm or ammunition might be arrested without warrant by any constable, and on the issue of a warrant, any suspected person might have his house searched. It was argued that had the Act been continued neither would Ulster have been able to arm herself against Irish Home Rule, nor the party of Irish secession against the whole connection with Britain.

The case for discontinuance was *prima facie* strong. Mr. Gladstone's Act was confessedly exceptional and temporary. It had originally been introduced for five years only and justified by the exceptional disorders of the times. Now conditions had altered. Ireland was peaceful, almost crimeless, soothed by the medicine of Land Purchase and looking forward to the healing properties of Home Rule. Nevertheless Bryce was opposed to dropping the Act. "As respects the Arms Act," he wrote to Lord Fitzmaurice, November 30th, 1908, "I am now free to tell you, since you are in the Cabinet, that I was not, as you suppose, in favour of dropping that Act. On the contrary, I advised the Cabinet against it. But I had not a single supporter: all were for dropping: and it is no doubt probable that we could not have carried its retention against the Irish, the Labour men, and our own Radicals, except by beating up the Tories to support us. You know how much a Liberal ministry hates to do that. And it is to be remembered that the Tories did not, as a party, oppose the dropping of the Act. There was a short debate, late at night, hardly any Tories present; and the objections came almost wholly, perhaps indeed wholly — though I have not the record by me here — from the Ulster members. Neither Arthur Balfour nor any other Leader on the Opposition side, except possibly Walter Long, who was acting in those days as a sort of leader of the Irish Tories, was present, and the whole thing passed almost unnoticed. Nevertheless, I thought it would have been better to keep the Act: and when it had been determined to drop it, I resolved to pass an Act in the Session of 1907 to restrict the sale of arms on lines similar to, or stricter than, those of the English Act, which ought to be much stricter than it is."

To the management of Irish affairs, Bryce brought the great gifts of grasp, application, and ubiquity, together with a store of knowledge about the country to which few Chief Secretaries, on first taking office, have attained. "We sometimes," writes Lord Lansdowne, "exchanged ideas when he was at the Irish Office, and I used to be struck with his intimate acquaintance with the country itself as distinguished from the people who dwelt in it. He knew exactly where to expect traces of the vein of copper which runs across the S. W. corner of Ireland, and the rare plants which are supposed to have come there from the Iberian peninsula were all well known to him." In texture, however, he was probably too much the Ulster Scot to ingratiate himself with the population of Southern Ireland and his relations were not always easy with the members of the Irish Parliamentary Party. Mr. T. P. O'Connor tells a story, which seems to show that either Bryce or Sir Anthony failed to appreciate the mercurial temperament of the Irish people, for he says that, in the course of the negotiations upon the Councils Bill, it was actually suggested that the members of an Irish Council should keep their seats while speaking.[1] As well might it be proposed to convert mercury into lead by Act of Parliament! If, however, Bryce was not *persona gratissima* to all members of the Irish Parliamentary Party, it must be remembered, first, that he shares that misfortune with most British statesmen who have essayed the ungrateful task of ruling Ireland from the Chief Secre-

[1] Daily Telegraph, January 23rd, 1923.

tary's Lodge, and second, that as a Home Ruler debarred from introducing a Home Rule Bill he was in a position of exceptional difficulty.

"The Irish members," writes Mr. O'Connor, "expressed their disappointment in no unmeasured language," and it was not limited to the postponement of Home Rule. From a Liberal administration the Nationalists expected a generous harvest of political appointments and were surprised and indignant when they discovered that the Chief Secretary was proof against political pressure. So with the Ulstermen bitter and unfriendly and with the Nationalists charged with disappointment and chagrin, the atmosphere was far from exhilarating. Bryce, however, did not expect too much, and was able to find much interest and a certain real happiness in the service of Ireland. For more than a quarter of a century he had been occupied with the Irish problem, and long after his official connection with her had ceased, the image of Ireland, coming to him laden with the joyous memories of boyhood and the later knowledge of her wrongs unredressed and her aspirations unsatisfied, of her charm, her poverty, her superstition, and her quarrels, revisited his mind and stirred his heart.

A great change, however, was at hand, for in December 1906, after thirteen months only of Irish administration, he was invited by the Prime Minister to succeed Sir Mortimer Durand as British Ambassador to Washington.

In the farewell speeches which he delivered to the Reform Club at Manchester, to his constituents in Aberdeen, and to a brilliant company of Pilgrims in London, assembled under the chairmanship of Lord Roberts, he expressed his regrets at leaving Ireland with his task unaccomplished, his indebtedness to Lord Aberdeen, the Lord Lieutenant, "a personal friend of more than thirty years," and to his chief officials, and expressed his belief that a large extension of Irish self-government was necessary. Other topics which attracted his attention were education, now conspicuously improved, and the position of the Second Chamber, a body lacking in moral weight at present and urgently needing the reinforcement of a representative element. But it was natural that in these valedictory utterances his mind should dwell rather on the task which awaited him on the other side of the Atlantic than upon that which he was laying down, and in commenting on the numerous indications of a better feeling between Britain and the United States, he alluded to a recent speech delivered by Mr. Root, the American Secretary of State, in Canada. In the growth of a friendly sentiment between the great Dominion and the Republic on its Southern border, he found one of the surest auguries for Anglo-American concord.

On February 13th, the Bryces sailed from Liverpool in the Oceanic. As the departing ambassador was about to enter the train, a reporter asked him whether, by the time of his return, the House of Lords would have disappeared. With a hearty laugh and a shake of the head, he replied, "No, I think not: things do not move as quickly as that." But that the question should have been asked was significant. The fierce assault on feudal privilege was fast preparing, and the land was shaking under the tread of embattled hosts marching to the clash of arms.

DATE DUE

30 505 JOSTEN'S